Top Distance Runners of the Century

Motivation, Pain, Success: World-class Athletes Tell

Seppo Luhtala (ed.)

Top Distance Runners of the Century

Motivation, Pain, Success:
World-class Athletes Tell

Meyer & Meyer Sports

Original Title: Vuosituhannen Juoksijat

Translated by Matti Hanus and Chris Turner

British Library Cataloguing in Publication Data
A catalogue record for this book is available from the British Library

Luhtala, Seppo (ed.):
Top Distance Runners of the Century - Motivation, Pain, Success:
World-class Athletes Tell
Oxford: Meyer & Meyer Sport (UK) Ltd., 2002
ISBN 1-84126-069-X

Aachen, Adelaide, Auckland, Budapest, Graz, Johannesburg,
Miami, Olten (CH), Oxford, Singapore, Toronto
Member of the World
Sports Publishers' Association
www.w-s-p-a.org

Printed and bound by Druckerei Vimperk, AG
ISBN 1-84126-069-X
E-Mail: verlag@meyer-meyer-sports.com
www.meyer-meyer-sports.com

Contents

F

G

H

J

K

L

M

Forewords

Sebastian Coe.

Sebastian Coe

I am delighted to be able to write a foreword to a book about the great distance runners of the 20th century. I first met Seppo Luhtala during the 1970s, at the beginning of my own international career. We were introduced by Steve Ovett´s coach Harry Wilson at a championship, and it soon became apparent to me that Seppo was not just another athletics enthusiast enjoying the sport of track and field at the highest level.

His detailed knowledge of the event and the competitors were matched by his unquenchable thirst for wanting to know the motivational forces at work behind any great competitor. This book is the synthesis of all these quests. The individual Odyssey of so many champions for the first time under one cover makes this book unique. Seppo Luhtala has made a significant contribution to our understanding of those chosen few we call Olympians.

Kipchoge Keino

I feel proud and honoured to have been called to work with this wonderful book. Through this collection of thoughts, I want to convey my best wishes to success to you, the distance runners of the future, wherever you may be. You have chosen one of the finest sports, requiring hard effort from you, but also giving you more than you ever thought would be possible.

This book has a lot to say to you. The universal world of distance running is showing the way to you, encouraging your quest to the top. Always remember that together we are much more than each of us can ever be individually.

Lasse Virén

It was fifteen years ago when I first heard about the plans with this book. Gradually it dawned to me what an incredible amount of material there would be piled up inside the covers. For me, the finished work now available is quite a miraculous achievement.

It is for you, young runners, that this immense work has been done. Dozens of world-class distance runners will tell you what it takes to become a champion. They will tell about big victories, but also about the unavoidable counterpart, sad defeats. You will learn about both sides of the coin! This book delves into the sport in a most positive way. All this spirit has been gathered for you; please try to learn from it. There is no sport without dreams. I sincerely hope this book will inspire you to fulfil those of your own.

Peter Snell

Real life stories about champion runners were the inspiration for my athletic career. In particular, Emil Zatopek's book "Marathon Victor" conveyed the powerful message that if we would be as dedicated and train as hard as Emil, we too could stand on the victory podium at he Olympic Games. Clearly, everyone cannot have the honour of such an experience, but as the father of the modern Olympic Games, Pierre de Coubertin observed, "the important thing is to have fought well".

Finland has the richest tradition of distance running of any country in the world. Following this tradition, Seppo Luhtala has embarked on the ambitious task of assembling contributions from 100 top runners worldwide. His goal was to capture the essence of the struggle, the training, the failures and disappointments and the success in the words of the runners themselves. This work may be described as having the same distinction as its runners – the highest possible quality.

Emil Zátopek

"Citius, Altius, Fortius" – these three words cover the whole range of world class sports. Beside the athletes, there are also the journalists, statisticians and book writers in eminent roles in this great drama. I have an enormous respect for all people working towards our common goal. It is their duty and honour to develop our sport and the Olympic movement. This book is brimming with reliable information on various lifestyles as well. My sincere belief is that this work will be a source of inspiration for generations to come.

Haile Gebrselassie

For many years now I have followed closely the making of this book of the world top-class runners. I am sure that it gives plenty of important know-how to any runner and increases mutual understanding and friendship in international running. I, Haile, highly recommend this book.

Without youth, there would be no future for any endeavour in life. As to track and field athletics, it is the top stars and their great performances that the young people are interested in. The past and the present thus certainly have an effect on the future of our sport. Through this book, we now have a splendid occasion to tell the youth about the great tradition of long distance running. In our task, we have been magnificently assisted by top athletes from all over the world. Finally reaching the finish line, we are feeling very proud and happy for our common effort. We dedicate this book to every hard-striving distance runner in the world.

LASSE VIREN FOUNDATION

Message from Lamine Diack, President International Athletic Foundation

The International Athletic Foundation is delighted to be able to support this exceptional collection of interviews and stories from our sport's greatest stars.

The Foundation would like to thank the author, Seppo Luhtala, for his seemingly endless energy and dedication to this project, which provides unique and exclusive insights into the most celebrated distance runners of our time. Mr. Luhtala's lifelong commitment to seeing this book become a reality is a tribute not only to his own determination and will, but also to all those fantastic athletes whose accomplishments are so well featured in these pages.

This publication plays an important part of the Foundation's strategy of promoting and developing a greater understanding of our sport and its champions. We hope the readers will enjoy this special compilation of stories and anecdotes as much as we have.

Lamine Diack
President
International Athletic Foundation
www.athletic-foundation.org

NURMI Paavo

Born 13 June 1897 Turku, died 2 October 1973 Helsinki. Nine times Olympic champion: 10000 metres, individual cross country and team cross country at Antwerp 1920; 1500 metres, 3000 metres team race, individual cross country and team cross country at Paris 1924; 10000 metres at Amsterdam 1928. Even Nurmi´s worst races in the Olympic Games were rewarded with three silver medals: 5000 metres at Antwerp; 5000 metres and steeplechase at Amsterdam. Nurmi broke world records in track races 20 times: one at 1500 metres, one in the mile, two at 2000 metres, three at 3000 metres, one at two miles, one at three miles, two at 5000 metres, one at four miles, one at five miles, one at six miles, two at 10000 metres, one at 15000 metres, one at 10 miles, one at 20000 metres and one in the one hour race.

At the Paris Olympic Games in 1924 , Nurmi won the 5000 metres gold medal just 45 minutes after winning the 1500 metres as well.

In winter 1925 Nurmi had a magnificent tour of 55 races in the United States, in which he broke an innumerable amount of indoor world bests. He won 53 times, did not finish once due to illness, and was once beaten at 880 yards, too short a distance for him. Nurmi was declared professional by the IAAF in 1932 just before the Los Angeles Olympic Games, in which he had been aiming at winning the marathon. At the Finnish Olympic Trials he had won 25 miles road race in 2.22.04 (fastest time in the world ever), defeating by some six minutes Armas Toivonen, who then took the bronze medal in the Olympic race just 36 seconds behind the winner, Juan Zabala of Argentine.

Nurmi had such a total attitude towards his sport that he never trusted any other coach except himself. In the 1920s and 1930s he was one of the famous superstars worldwide with such film luminaries as Charlie Chaplin and Greta Garbo. In European and American Press he was known as the "Phantom Finn".

Paavo Nurmi's meaning for athletics, and sports generally in Finland is head and shoulders above anyone else. More than that, during the decades he has grown to be a mythic giant, an essential part of Finnish identity.

The following authentic interview with Paavo Nurmi was originally printed in the newspaper of his club Turun Urheiluliito in 1971, two years before his death. The interview was conducted and recorded by Kauko Niemelä.

In 1914 Paavo Nurmi joined his home town club Turun Urheiluliitto, the black and yellow colours of which he-even after moving to Helsinki for his studies in the 1920s-then represented during the whole of his active running career for two decades. Nurmi always has been faithful to his club, stressing the essence of club spirit.

At over 70 years of age he still feels proud of Turku and Turun Urheiluliitto, which was proved by the fact that he was willing to break his customary silence when a sportswriter from his old club came knocking at his door. This unusual exception turned out to be a most worthy compilation of various interesting opinions of one of the most legendary personalities of the sport.

No hard training before military service

"If I had been aware of the present training methods, I would have run better, especially in 1920-1926. Finnish runners develop slowly, and I think that is the right thing to do. As to myself, I reached the top gradually and also slowed down gradually. As a youngster I had no idea whatsoever of correct training systems, but that applied to all other runners as well. The only exceptions may have been Hannes and Tatu Kolehmainen, who were well served by training programmes mailed to them from the United States by their brother William. In the early part of my career in the late 1910s I did some racing, but there was not much sense in my training regularly, and I then started progressing quickly. The officers in my regiment were positive about sports, and I was able to train as much as I liked for the 1920 Antwerp Olympic Games."

"Playing with schoolmates I usually had most speed and stamina in running games, so perhaps I had more talent for this event than small boys usually have. Also, it should be remembered that I entered working life early, pushing heavy carts as an errand boy on the hilly streets of Turku, which certainly had something to do with the strengthening of my leg muscles."

"In summertime, we used to swim at Ruissalo Park, where we always went by foot, either running or walking. It was 6 kilometres one way, which meant quite a lot of exercise since we sometimes covered this distance-to and back- twice a day." "I was greatly inspired by the news of Hannes Kolehmainen's Olympic victories in Stockholm 1912. A few days later, I bought my first pair of sneakers at 15 years of age. Two years later I started racing every now and then."

Cross country still is an essential thing

Paavo Nurmi straightforwardly admits having made quite many mistakes in his training before finding the correct systems through trial and error over the years. "Those days it was usual for a distance runner to do lots of walking, but in hindsight it was just waste of time. It has been written many times that I was training hard. Well, I can admit I was spending lots of time with my training, but the insanity was not there. If I had known some of the things I learned much later, I would have been a much better runner in the early 1920s"

"I still firmly believe in the benefit of cross country running. However, cross country courses should be quite difficult to negotiate so that running speed would not be a relevant factor. Running training has two distinct phases. First you have to do cross country in order to develop stamina and general fitness. Then, with the racing season drawing near, it is time to do speed sessions and repetitions on the track in order to hone the racing rhythm."

Speed through endurance

"I think Arthur Lydiard is right when he gives such an importance to endurance type of training. However, you should neglect the factor of leg speed. In my view, the present crop of Finnish distance runners (in early 1971) are too slow and tight-muscled because of the fact that they are not doing enough speed training." "As to myself, in the early years of my career I was terribly slow and scared of the last lap finishing kick. Nevertheless, I decided to do something about it, and after a couple of years I had such a spurt in the end that I was afraid of no one. A competitive runner must get rid of all fear when toeing the starting line. If one doesn't trust one's finishing speed, he cannot feel himself secure at any point of race. In the old days, races were usually finishing straight affairs, whereas nowadays you have to be able to sprint at least for one full lap in the 5000 and 10 000 metres. As I see it, bursts from 300 to 600 metres in training are excellent preparation for situations like this."

No success without basic fitness

"My success at the Paris Olympic Games in 1924 was based on the excellent general fitness I had at the time. As early as six month before the Games I had decided to take part in all the Olympic races between 1500 and 10 000 metres. However, with just days to go before the 10 000 metres race the Finnish team leaders-perhaps worried that I would be taxing myself too much-told me they would like to see me forget about the "ten". I did as they wished, but I still think I would have been fit enough to win that race as well."

"Being fit and well-trained, a runner has no problem with racing hard for several days in a row. On the other hand, if he has to race on consecutive days against his wish in dual matches-as often happens-, it is not a good thing to do. In my view, a runner himself must have the last word in deciding what events he will run."

Money doesn't mean everything

"On this way to the top, a runner must have strong ambition together with iron will. Money does not make a runner; a deep desire from within does. You should have common sense when planning your racing programme, concentrating on what is important for you. It is not racing here, there and everywhere just going through the motions. Generally, you should always aim at maximum racing effort, perhaps excepting international dual matches, which often are tactical affairs. It is essential for an athlete to have such a strong mind that he knows what he wants and what it takes to succeed."

Paavo Nurmi was coaching Finnish distance runners for the Berlin Olympic Games in 1936. His pupils had a phenomenal success, taking seven medals out of the nine available in the 5000 and 10 000 metres plus the 3000 metres steeplechase. After that, he left the coaching scene and only continued as a member of the coaching committee of the Finnish Athletics Federation until World War II. Later, as a successful businessman and a building contractor, he always followed the performances of the Finnish distance runners very closely.

"I am not very optimistic about the future of Finnish running. To me it looks like our present international runners are not a talented bunch of people, although I do not want to be too critical. The main fault of our present generation is lack of speed. I do not like those long track races advocated by Lydiard in the start of track racing season, for instance the 25K race at Tampere, in which even the half-milers were taking part. That kind of ordeal is not good for anyone's legs. You must remember that the racing season is long and tough, so why run oneself to exhaustion in May?"

"Long cross country races after the track season are good, but I think 30K is too long; 20/25K should be enough. It is perfectly fine for joggers, who like to test themselves, to race 30K or even longer, but generally I would recommend more common sense in this respect."

"In winter, the conditions in Finland are not good for ambitious training. It takes too much training regularly and effectively in cold weather, on icy roads. Cross country skiing is fine for basic fitness, even if it is not nearly as good as running. I think it is enormously important for Finnish runners to go and train in warmer climate during the winter months. If I were a coach, I would certainly take all my runners to the south. I say this because of the fact that I did not train much during the coldest months. For example, in 1921-23 when I was living and studying in Helsinki, I did not start training until early April."

Don`t make too much haste

Paavo Nurmi did not start ambitious training until he was well over 20 years old. At his prime in 1924 he was 27, but he went on running and racing for a long time, winning his last Finnish championship title at 1500 metres in 1933, at age 36. Based on his own experience, Nurmi advocated a steady and gradual rise to the top. He used to say, "if you progress fast, you will also disappear fast". In Nurmi`s opinion, the most fruitful years for a Finnish distance runner usually are those from 23 to 27. He also said it is good to start some easy training as early as 16 years of age, but you should avoid track training for a couple of years, doing most of our early work in the forest trails." Paavo Nurmi`s most sincere hope was that some day a younger world-beating middle distance or long distance runner will again emerge from the beautiful paths of his home town Turku.

Paper Collage by Seppo Luhtala

Paper Collage by Seppo Luhtala

ABERA Gezahgne

born 23 Apr 1978 Ethiopia.
One of the most surprising Olympic Champions in Sydney, Abera won the marathon gold medal at age 22 on his sixth try at this event, two years after his debut. In December 1999, he had won the prestigious Fukuoka marathon in Japan with a world class time of 2.07.54. Abera´s victory in Sydney made him the first Ethiopian to win the Olympic men´s marathon since Mamo Wolde in Mexico City in 1968.

"I was not any good in high school"

I started training in April 1998 at the age of 20. It was two months before my first marathon, Abebe Bikila Marathon in Addis Ababa. I thought I could be a good runner. I was not any good in high school, but those days I was not serious about running. I knew if I became serious, I could succeed.

I enjoy training very much, taking only a break of two or three days after a marathon. The most important thing in training is to be consistent. You must train year round to be good. You must also have your race in mind when you are training. Since I began training, I have been lucky to have no serious setbacks.

When you lose a race, you should ask yourself why. Did you train hard enough? Did you make any tactical errors? If so, you must work hard in training and preparation so that those mistakes will not happen again.

Self-confidence means that you know you are ready and that whatever anyone else does in the race, you are the man the others have to beat. Yes, it is possible to acquire self-confidence. Hard training is one way. Also, knowing that you have the ability to win any race.

Message to youth: you don´t have to be a great runner at a young age to succeed in running. Hard work and determination are the things you need much more in that respect. The best thing in running is all the great people I have met through running. It was also great to bring the marathon Gold Medal back to Addis and enjoy all the pride that the people felt to have that medal in Ethiopia again.

AOUITA Said

born 2 Nov 1959 Kenitra, Morocco.
5000m Olympic Champion in Los Angeles 1984 and World Champion in Rome 1987, 3000m World Indoor Champion in 1989. Six-time World Record holder at distances between 1500 and 5000 metres in 1985-89. At 5000m, Aouita was unbeatable from 1979 to 1989 and was the first man to break the 13 mins. barrier at Golden Gala in Rome 1987. Perhaps the most versatile middle distance runner in history, capable of a time of 27.26.11 at 10 000m in his first and only race at the distance in 1986 and an Olympic bronze medal at 800m two years later.

800m 1.43.86, 1000m 2.15.16, 1500m 3.29.46, one mile 3.46.76, 2000m 4.50.81, 3000m 7.29.45, 3000m steeplechase 8.21.92, 2 miles 8.13.45, 5000m 12.58.39, 10 000m 27.26.11.

"Running is the most natural sport there is"

I became a runner in 1975, when I was selected to represent my school in a cross country race. Before that, my main interest had been soccer. My first impressions on cross country were not especially positive; soon, however, I started to enjoy the sport. Two years later, having won the Morocco junior cross country title I took part in the World Cross Country in Glasgow. After leading the race in the early kilometres I tired very badly and did not do well at all. In spite of great disappointment

I did not give up. On the contrary, I resolved to train harder and do better in the future. I enjoy my training to a great extent. Sometimes, when I cannot run for one reason or another, I don´t feel good. I never have any motivational problems. I want to win, to be the best. For me, training and racing are parts of the same thing. Training hard makes me race well. I always concentrate very deeply in what I am doing, but I don´t want to reveal the details of my training. It is essential for an athlete to keep himself healthy. That is why I never overextend myself in training; it is not wise to be completely exhausted after a training session. Whenever you are in good shape and you have a firm belief in your training schedule, you shouldn´t have any problems whatsoever with your self-confidence.

Yes, I have had quite many setbacks during my career, injuries bad enough to keep me off races and interrupt training schedules. Races are very, very important for any athlete striving to become better. When your racing is going well, your self-confidence improves further and soon you will be able to reach even better performances. I have won many big races in Olympic Games and World Championhips, but that is not everything for me in sport. I also like to race and break World Records at so many distances as possible. That is a big challenge for me. Giving up? No, I never have had any bad moments during a race.

Cheating in sports is something that I detest very much. Doping is a dirty subject in sports. I have always achieved everything in a natural way. Running is the most natural sport there is, and that is why it should be done in a natural way. Money? A world class athlete needs money to cover his everyday life and training expenses. He well deserves everything that he receives from the promoters or sponsors as a payment for his hard work.

Publicity is mainly a positive thing, especially from the viewpoint of sponsors. Good publicity also keeps an athlete´s motivation high. However, I have to say I don´t especially enjoy publicity due to the fact that I am unable to walk unrecognized in the streets in Morocco. My message to the youth: you must train hard, you have to believe in what you are doing. You have to stay clear of drugs or any other kind of cheating in your life.

ARIMORI Yuko

born 17 Dec 1966 Okayama.
A two-time Olympic marathon medallist, Arimori won a silver medal in the 1992 Games in Barcelona and a bronze medal in the 1996 Games in Atlanta. She was also 4th in the 1991 World Championships marathon in Tokyo. Her marathon debut was at the 1990 Osaka Ladies´ marathon, in which she recorded a Japanese marathon debut best of **2.32.51**. She followed it up later with **2.28.10**, a national record. A marathon specialist with a personal best of **2.26.39 (1999).**

"Running broadens one´s horizon"

The reason why I became a runner was because I wanted to be a physical education teacher. I did not have any idols in those days, when I was in high school. However, if you insist on naming someone, I would say I was looking up to Akemi Masuda (a 1984 Olympian in the marathon) and Olympic Champion Rosa Mota. Yes, I certainly have had motivational problems every now and then. Running is my job, and just like in any other job, I sometimes have to drag myself out of the door to train. I do not enjoy every type of training. This is because it is so hard. In particular, I don´t like any workouts which are timed sessions.

My advice to young athletes is to set yourself lofty goals and never give up trying to reach them. As to a runner´s coach, his duty is to make his athletes aware of their strength, and then utilize it in training. Whenever you have setbacks, be patient. This is what I have learned from my mother! Then try to think positively about the compulsory

interruption of training. Whenever you are beaten in a race, don´t think it as a defeat. Make it your stepping stone to the next race. Learn from the experience and utilize it when your next race comes. I think it is possible to acquire self-confidence. It is important to act with confidence, which, in turn, brings you even more confidence.

Each athlete approaches publicity in a different way. Sometimes the media help us to perform better. However, intrinsically malicious media do exist as well. Except for those malicious ones, athletes and the media can help each other in a peaceful co-existence. I never watch a videotape of a race in which I felt I did not do my best. The 1991 World Championships marathon was one of those bad races.

Cheating in sports: I think it is a bad thing. Some athletes, however, think otherwise. Also, for some athletes performing well is a means of livelihood, so it is a complicated problem. Anything one gains by cheating in sports is meaningless. Do not misunderstand me - I do not condone cheating. All I am saying is that it is not a simple problem. Prize money and appearance money reflect my worth in the sport. They are also directly connected with my livelihood. Personal message for young runners: always have lofty goals and work towards them. The best thing in running is that I happen to have the talent for it. It is a wonderful feeling. Running also broadens one´s horizons.

BARBOSA Jose Luiz

born 27 May 1961 Tres Lagoas, Brazil.
Unusually long career at world-class half-miling; was posting times around 1.45 or faster for 15 years since 1983. World championship silver medallist 1991, bronze medallist 1987. World indoor champion 1987. Popular pace-maker, always willing to lead no matter what the opposition in the race.

400m 45,9, 800m 1.43.08, 1000m 2.17.36, 1500m 3.37.04.

"Your luck is in your own hands"

I started my career in 1978, but my first great results did not come until 1983, when I ran 800 metres in 1.44. That was the year of my first major competition in the World Championsips in Helsinki. I have always loved sports. Originally, I was playing handball, but the reason I became a runner was that I came from a poor background and did not have a lot of opportunity. Running was a gift that the Lord had given to me. As a kid, I always had in my mind to be someone. Poverty is very hard. No matter if I was going to be a doctor, a lawyer, whatever, I was going to be someone. The Lord gave running to me as my opportunity.

If you want to succeed as a runner, the mental part is very important. To reach world class level, first you should have the discipline to do what you are supposed to. For instance, when I go to the track, I am going to do the session that I have decided to do. If I don´t do the hard work in training, I won´t make it well in the competition, either. You have to believe in yourself. You have to have the desire. Yes, I have had my setbacks, but I was lucky because I never lost a full season. I very seldom had any injuries, because I eat carefully, I rest, I have massage. I do everything to avoid getting injured. This is my job; I do the best things to benefit from it. Setbacks can ruin a whole season.

Being beaten always is very hard to take. Everyone of us likes to win, to be a champ, but when beaten, you should think and find something good about the situation, to be able to perform better next time. As to self-confidence, you have to believe in yourself, in life generally. As a runner, you have to believe in the workouts you are doing. Track and field is an individual sport. Your luck is in your own hands. Even if I have a very good coach, who always hugs me and congratulates me after a good race, it is finally up to me how I am doing. I am responsible for my performance. I think self-confidence comes from training, from talking with my coach, from my performances in the races, and also from staying injury free. All the positive things in your mind add to your confidence.

Also, it is easy to lose self-confidence, because there are always people around telling all kinds of negative things to you. You should not think about other people - what they think about you if you don´t perform well. You should just go to the track and perform. You must think about the workouts you have done, and you should believe in yourself. I think that in track and field you sometimes have to be selfish; not selfish as a person, but you have to have your own world. As I see it, the confidence is built day by day, by doing good workouts, by having good performances. You have to be able to control your training and races. You have to be able to control your human emotions. In the 800 metres, the race never changes - it is always two laps around the track -, what changes is your behaviour as a human being. You have to be able to control yourself to be able to fight in the last 100 metres, which is the most difficult part of the 800 metres race.

"Drugs take away the beauty of the sport"

I think anyone who tries to use drugs, or do anything illegal, is not being fair. I just hate it. Things like that take away the beauty of the sport. Sport is a challenge, and if you cannot run without drugs, then you should really step away from the sport and leave it to people who are doing it with sincerity,

honesty, truthfulness. In my opinion, an athlete who gets caught on drugs. should be banned from the sport forever. Publicity can be good thing in sports. For an athlete from Third World, like Juantorena or Abebe Bikila, who have made something extraordinary, publicity has preserved them in history. But they have had to make something very extraordinary to get there, whereas an athlete from a First World country will find it much easier to be carved into history. I do collect press cuttings. I think it is important to have a record of your job; of your races, your interviews etc. I think it is good to have a record of the media recognizing you; of all the work that you have been doing over the years. I think video is great. Video is so nice because you can judge your races; you can see how you have done. That way, you can get motivation and inspiration. I like to preserve the memories of my races to show them to my children, to my grandchildren... Through video, you are running yourself into history.

I have never noticed people being envious of my achievements. They know I have been working hard in the sport. I don´t think people are envious of what I have done on the track. If they are, that is their problem, not mine! I think money is something that everybody needs. But you have to understand there are two papers that make you feel good in life. One is the diploma they gave you from the university: the other one is the paper that you get when you start working - and that paper is called money. I love what I do. I grew up very poor, and I was starving, but I survived. I had no food, I had no money, but I had faith. Now I am happy to be interviewed here and perhaps be able to help young athletes this way.

My message to the young generation is, first of all, love what you do. Then, believe in achieving your goals. Whatever you do in life, don´t surrender. Believe in what you are doing, and I can assure you that you can achieve anything in life. Also, stay out of drugs, because drugs don´t just destroy you as a human being; they destroy your friends, your family. Every time you think about drugs, think about the Lord, and believe in yourself. Drugs just aren´t the thing to do in life. There are so many things I like in running, but the most enjoyable thing is to be healthy, and to do track and field in a healthy way. That is the most important thing in sport to me. That is the great gift that the Lord gave to me.

BARMASAI Bernard

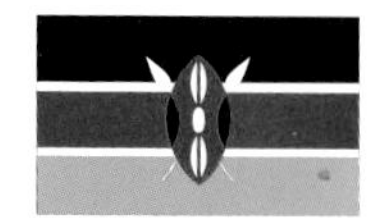

born 6 May 1974 Keiyo, Kenya.
Former miler, Barmasai broke the 3000m steeplechase World Record by more than three seconds in 1997 in Cologne, beating Moses Kiptanui in the process. World Championships bronze in 1997 (fell), 5th in 1999, 4th Olympic Games 2000. Also broke the 8-minutes barrier in Monaco in 1999.
1500m 3.38.48, 3000m 7.36.40, 10K road 28.08, 3000m steeplechase 7.55.72.

"I never did any practice to improve my running style"

I started serious racing in 1993. Before that I had been running to school and back from as early as 1981 (at age 7). In school competition, I took part in the 1500 and 5000 metres, and also won a lot in the district championships. I was also playing football and volleyball. I soon realized I was much better in distance running that in any other sport. That is how I became a runner. I was reading newspapers and saw people like Patrick Sang and Moses Tanui had been doing well in the European running circuit. I thought, "perhaps I can do that as well". I wanted to see if I could become a much better runner if I worked at it.

In 1993 I was training in Nyahuru with Tanui, Moses Kiptanui and Tom Nyariki. I was doing cross country and track. That was the year when I began training hard. At first I was coaching myself, but during the last few years I have been coached by Patrick Sang. Yes, I am still enjoying my training even if it is sometimes very strenuous work. "A day without training is like a day without eating." Training is much harder than competing. Sometimes you are training alone, sometimes you are doing it with a group. These are very different things. The only problem I have had so far was with my knee. I had to ease down my training in order to care of it. I did not race at all until I felt good again. My advice when you have an injury is to take a rest, see a doctor and take all the measures to cure the injury. You should have faith in the doctor and listen to him. A long career is more important than the races you are going to miss. Also in this matter, discipline is very important.

Whenever you have been defeated, you should learn something from it. You can go back to your training programme and see what is wrong. Or, perhaps you should change tactics. Never be frustrated by a defeat; always enjoy your running. Self-confidence is very important for an athlete. If you have been training well, you should believe the results will come. I always asked myself, "Why can´t I run a World Record myself?" The answer always was, "Of course I can do that." If everything is okay - training, body, food, family - you have to tell yourself that everything is good, so the only thing you can do is to win. You will have the self-confidence if you are sure that all the necessary things are 100% all right, without any distractions.

When I first came to Europe, I had no idea how good I was, but I soon realized I was able to run as fast as anyone in the world. I really did not think about times, but I thought the World Records by Kiptanui and Wilson Boit Kipketer would be beatable. I was also aiming at various stadium records, like in Zurich. In Cologne I was so, so happy about the World Record because I had no idea before the race that it would happen.

Moses Kiptanui has been running so long on the very top that he certainly is a great example for the others of us, his Kenyan teammates. My message for young athletes: it is very important to have discipline in all the aspects of training. By that I mean hard training combined with easy training, enough rest and proper food. As to my running style, which many people have been admiring, I can say it is a born thing. It is natural. I never worked for it. I have been asked this countless times, but the truth is that I have never done any specific practice to improve my style.

BARRIOS Arturo

born 12 Dec 1963 Mexico City.
Ran World Records in the 10 000m (27.08.23 in 1989), 20 000m 56.54.03 and one hour race (21 101m, both in 1991). Also ran the fastest ever 10K on roads up to that time in 1986 (27.41). Barrios´s success started an enormous wave of inspiration for distance running in Mexico, showing the way to several other world class runners in his home country. Barrios today is a citizen of the United States.
1500m 3.37.61, 2000m 5.03,4, 3000m 7.35.71, 3000m steeplechase 8.46,9, 5000m 13.07.79, 10 000m 27.08.23, 20 000m 56.54.03, one hour 21 101m, half marathon 1.00.42, marathon 2.08.28 (1994).

"You must have a burning desire to succeed"

I started running in order to get myself into good shape. I was doing runs of 20-25 kilometres without any competitive goals whatsoever. There were no track races available in my area anyway. I continued doing long runs because they were great fun. At age 16 or 17, I started training a bit harder to get into my school running team. At the time, however, I was not considering running as a career; my main goals were doing well at school and getting a degree from the university. Of course I get a deep enjoyment from running. If you don´t, then it is better stop and do something else. To succeed in running or any other field in life you need lots of discipline. You don´t get anywhere without patience. For me, it is a natural thing to enjoy my training. Well, perhaps not if it is raining or the wind is blowing, but I know that I have to do my training even then.

I haven´t had many injuries or other setbacks. I have had occasional pain in feet and knees; nothing major. During the last ten years, I have been injured just a couple of times. Training wise, my last six or seven years have gone really well. My longest pause has been about two weeks, which really doesn´t mean anything. Self-confidence means that an athlete believes in himself; he knows what he is doing, and knows what he is capable at. Training for distance running is very hard, as well as the races, but you will succeed when you believe in your coach and your training system. Self-confidence is something very personal. It is very difficult to define; it is something that comes from inside the person. An athlete must have a burning desire to succeed in sports as well as in life generally. When starting my career, I had three dreams: (1) to get into the Olympic team, (2) to win a medal in the Olympic Games, and (3) to run a World Record. I have achieved the last one of these. When I have run a World Record, it has not been a surprise for me because I had been training so well. However, you need to be lucky as well to run a World Record. Everything must hit the right note. There cannot be any problems in your training, and you must be in 100% shape both mentally and physically. Weather, however, is something that you cannot control. If it is windy or too warm, then you will have no chance. I was lucky with conditions in Berlin in 1989.

"There are individuals who kill the sport"

I am very, very sad about the fact that things like drugs and blood-doping have been used in my sport. Individuals like these kill the sport. Sponsors and ordinary people soon think that everyone in sports is on drugs. Money may mean different things to different athletes. You must be in a financially secure position to be able train and compete. I think it is great to be able to do what you enjoy, and get paid for it. Publicity is an essential thing in sports - in fact one of the most important ones. In my life there is not much publicity, because I live in the United States, where no one recognizes me. Yes, I do read the papers, although I don´t take the trouble of trying to find them from anywhere. I also keep some clippings, but only from my World Record races or some other major things. Videotapes are good for learning. For instance, when I have fallen in a race, video gives me the chance to see why and how it happened. This way, I know how to stay away from trouble in the future. My advice to a young athlete is, believe in yourself. Never give up. Train hard, with discipline. However, don´t forget that succeeding in school work is more important for you at this time than succeeding in running. During my running years, I have been able to meet people, to see different countries, different cities, and that I have learned new languages. For me, all that is the best thing in running.

BAUMANN Dieter

born 9 February 1965 Blaustein, Germany.
The only European long distance track runner in the 1990s to have reached Kenyan class. 5000m Olympic Champion 1992, Olympic silver medallist 1988, European Champion 1994, 10000m European silver medallist 1998. The first European to break 13 minutes in the 5000m. Coached by wife Isabell Baumann (née Hozang), a junior international runner for Austria in the early 1980s. **800m 1:48.40, 1500m 3:33.51, mile 3:51.12, 3000m 7:30.50, 5000m 12:54.70, 10 000m 27:21.53.** Because of a committed doping offence was declared by IAAF ineligible until 21 January 2002.

As to the mileage, training camps etc., my plans always focus towards the next big international championships. A detailed plan is done just for two or three weeks ahead. Usually I have been able to follow my plans except in case of illness or injury. The main workouts like long runs and track sessions are carried out as accurately as possible. Easy runs may differ in length. With the programme being planned I try to follow it as closely as possible, for one or two weeks ahead at a time. To a large extent, I enjoy my training. I never have any motivational problems. I want to see what is ahead in the future. I am hoping to be able to look admiringly at my career when it is finally over. As a young runner one thinks that the age of 35 is far ahead, but in reality the years are passing by very fast. However, there is no reason why you couldn´t succeed even at 35 years of age. When Carlos Lopes won the Olympic Marathon in Los Angeles in 1984, he was 37 years old. I don´t feel my training being too strenuous. Even if I am not a cross country specialist I do 90% of my training away from the track. I never have a feeling that I have done a very hard session. Actually I feel it stimulating to run fast.

"Altitude training is a basic thing"

At the beginning of my career I had a coach; then I had another one whose main task was to take care of all the practical things in running. After that I trained without a coach for three years. Later, for the most part of my international career I have been coached by my wife Isabell, with whom I make a very good team. When I was not even 20 I was running around 60-70 km a week. Those days I had just one fast session in a week. Now I am averaging about 120 km a week with two fast sessions; never more than that. I am usually doing 12 sessions a week, which means twice a day at the most. In my weekly training, I concentrate on doing a long run of 1 hour 30 minutes plus two fast tempo runs at the anaerobic threshold. This means, for instance, 8 x 1000m in 2.50 with a recovery of two minutes between the runs.

The quality of my training is always relatively high, which is why I can race even in winter without any special preparation. Nowadays, high altitude training is one of the basic things in all endurance events. It is one of the key factors for an athlete who wants to run on international top level. On the other hand, the lowland runners cannot get to the mountains often enough; thus we must be able to use our own training facilities as well as we can. The Kenyan runners have their own problems. John Ngugi, for instance, suffered from malaria after the Seoul Olympics, and for the same reason was unable to defend his title in Barcelona.

My main advice in case of injury: stop running immediately!

Even if I am surprisingly beaten in a race, it is not a catastrophe for me. I try to analyse why my opponents were better. Generally I believe that losing in a race is the best way towards a victory. Life goes on. You have no need to worry too much. Next time it may be just the other way round if your training goes well. I always try to find out the strong and weak points of my rivals in order to beat them. Before and after a race, I respect them as great athletes. I have a very good relationship with all my main rivals. Self-confidence is the most decisive factor for an athlete.

A big race is won by the mentally strongest competitor. Physically all the runners usually are the same - very good. Self-confidence can be acquired through good training and low-key competitions at the beginning of the season. To win a big race, an athlete has to be convinced that he/she can do it, but it takes a good bit of luck as well. Mental toughness is part of an athlete´s born talent. I believe it is easier for a young athlete to consciously develop this ability. In my mind, it is much more difficult for an older athlete to get rid of mental inferiority. I have never felt that Africans are unbeatable. I know I am as good as they are when I can train without injuries. One gets the best out of oneself at the right moment by good planning and a specific mental process. Of course, training can be detailed only to certain extent. In 1992 I was able to run my best during the period of perhaps two weeks before and two weeks after the Olympic Games. Thus I tried to choose meetings that could improve my performance in the Olympics. That is why I was racing in Seville, Stockholm and Hengelo. After those meetings I went to a six-week high altitude training camp in Flagstaff, Arizona. Yobes Ondieki was there at the same time, and he was able to run much faster than me on the training track. I never have felt an urge to give up in a race. I prepare mentally for competition and never think about losing. Rather, I try to figure out how I might be able to reach the best possible result. The aftermath of a race is not very important for me. If I am beaten in a top class race, of course I am disappointed, but I can also accept the fact that I am racing against equally strong athletes.

Honesty is a main principle in my life, and that is what I expect of everybody in every situation. I cannot forgive any form of cheating in sports. As to publicity, there are two sides in a coin. I need to justify my contracts, but on the other hand publicity sometimes has a negative effect on my training. I try to control my publicity as much as I can. I like the atmosphere of a full stadium. What I don´t like is being confronted by complete strangers in the street. I try to read most of the articles written about me. It is a kind of self-defence to know what has been said in the papers, but I don´t let unpleasant writings bother me for too long. Yes, I preserve some of the cuttings. In general I am interested in politics and in everything that is happening in the world. I am not a prolific "video-viewer" but when I have a chance to watch, I don´t mind if it is a good or a bad race of mine.

I do not really feel connected to a race of mine which I am watching afterwards in TV or videotape. Rather, I see myself as an outsider like any people interested in the sport. My own memories of a race usually are connected with different kinds of things: how everyone was so nervous before the race; how I, for instance, was fully concentrating on Yobes Ondieki not running away from me in Berlin Grand Prix in the way he did in the 1991 World Championships - and so on. I don´t remember anything of that race except for the finish. Yes, I am well aware of the fact that many people are envious of me. Mostly I try to ignore them, and in a sense this envy even stimulates me to aim higher. In the early part of my career, money never was a factor for many years. The improvement of my performances and the new possibilities in international track and field have enabled me to make a living out of my hobby. I earn money doing what I enjoy doing very much. However, in every situation in my sport, the activity itself with the performances and being in good physical shape, always have the priority over money. My message to young runners? For my part, I want to say that I wouldn´t change a thing if it were possible to go back and start all over again. As a young boy I tried running and discovered I had a talent. Then I started working on it and developed into what I am today. This is what I would recommend everybody to do, no matter what his/her field. For me, the best thing in running is the feeling when I am in great shape. I get that feeling from running very fast, working hard and yet feeling like a bird on wings. This can happen as well in a workout as in a race. It is wonderful to be able to run for one and a half hours in the forest with changing speeds without feeling tired!

BILE Abdi

born 28 Dec 1962 Las Anod, Somalia.
First Somalian World Champion in any sport, having won the 1500m world title in Rome in 1987. A big (185 cm, 75 kg) and enigmatic runner of many comebacks, returned to good form and took bronze medal in the 1993 World Championships. Sixth in the Olympic final in Atlanta 1996 at age 33. Full name: Abdi (own name) Bile (father´s name) Abdi (grandfather´s name). Lost 20 family members in the Somalian civil war.
800m 1.43.60, 1000m 2.14.50, 1500m 3.30.55, one mile 3.49.40, 2000m 4.59.77, 3000m 7.42.18.

"I trust in what my body says to me"

It is always difficult to plan one´s training programme perfectly. Due to many injuries, I never have had a season during which everything has clicked. Because of persistent injury problems, my career has been one long and winding mountain road. I have been fighting with setbacks for the whole of my career. I have had more injuries than any other runner I have known. Due to these problems I have missed many important meetings. I find it very frustrating not being able to train. In a situation like this, many a runner has given up. My attitude, however, is to fight over the obstacles. We know that some athletes have made a miraculous comeback after most difficult injury problems. Whatever I am doing - walking, running, sitting -, I always know how my body is feeling. I know what is best for myself. I trust in what my body says to me. Every athlete should have a firm belief in what he is doing. Some, however, are prone to imitate other athletes´ training methods. Someone might be able to do what I do in training, but it might not be good at all for

him. Whenever a young runner is racing with world-class athletes, he is certain to finish last. However, if he is mature enough to understand the level of his training, age and experience compared to those of his rivals, then even the last place doesn´t destroy his self-confidence. In my view, self-confidence is something that you can improve all the time, if you have a realistic view on life.
I, for instance, came from a small country like Somalia, and I had no experience whatsoever of racing with the big names. Before the African Championship, as a newcomer, I was terrified of being lapped in the 1500 metres. After finishing eighth, just 50 metres behind the winner, I was very happy and thinking "that was fine, I was running O.K."

"To evaluate the meaning of mental strength is more like a science"

Mental strength is something that is very difficult to analyse. At birth, every person has certain abilities. He may have 10% of one ability and perhaps 90% of another one, but he is able to develop all of them. There are really no limits on what a person can learn in his or her lifetime. An athlete may be beaten in a race because he hasn´t been training hard enough, or because of the fact that his body was not working as it should. So many things can happen. A defeat in a minor race is soon forgotten, whereas a poor performance in the Olympic Games will ruin your whole season. I consider all my rivals as my friends. I like all of them. There is no sense to be in sports unless you are enjoying the many friendships and feeling yourself happy racing with the best runners in the world. What is aggressiveness? People show their aggressiveness in many ways. Some of them jabbering away the whole day, and they are considered tough guys. In a running race, that kind of aggressiveness is of no use. I wouldn´t win even one race without being aggressive. That means a runner has to be aggressive even if he is not talking big or behaving strangely in some other way. The young generation has forgotten what it takes to succeed in life. People have become soft and lazy. Today we have first-class running tracks and all the assistance to help you, yet some people are complaining about bad tracks or bad shoes. For people like them, it is impossible to train when it is raining. When I was young, we didn´t have much of conditions to train, and yet we were reaching to the top. Running is a sport that requires a lot from you. The best thing in running is that it is excellent for self-discipline. A hard-training athlete knows that you have to be ready to fight in life to succeed. One day, I was talking with Steve Scott. I asked him how he would react in case he would have to stop running. Steve´s answer was, "I don´t think that would worry me, because I have learned so much self-discipline. Nothing can stop me!"

BITOK Paul

born 26 Jun 1970, Emdin, Kenya.
Not a record runner, but a clever tactician.Twice 5000m Olympic silver medallist behind Dieter Baumann in 1992 and behind Venuste Niyongabo in 1996. Two silvers also at World 3000m indoors (1997 and 1999). In 1997 at Turku, Finland, Bitok won the Paavo Nurmi Double by running 1500m in 3.36.87 (then pb) and 5000m in 13.26.25 with 80 mins. recovery.
1500m 3.35.82, one mile 3.59,6, 2000m 4.54.36, 3000m 7.28.41, 2 miles 8.19.55, 5000m 13.04.48, 10 000m 28.51,6.

"I saw aeroplanes in the sky"

I started running at age 14 after having seen some other guys in my area running, and it looked so enjoyable to me. So I followed them. I had no goals at that time. I never thought I would be running outside Kenya. Then I read in a newspaper that some of the best runners were racing abroad. I also saw aeroplanes in the sky, and that is when I realized I could also go to foreign countries. Idols? No, I never had any... Yes, there was one. Paul Kipkoech, 10 000m World Champion in Rome in 1987. I wanted to be as good as he was.

I had a coach for a few years in 1989-93, but after that I have been coaching myself. I don´t believe I could get anything from a coach. I have enough knowledge on training. One must find the way to train that suits oneself. I haven´t made any big mistakes since leaving the

Army. I had some problems there. It is some 100 miles from Nairobi to Eldoret, and sometimes I had to make that by foot! It was very strict. I am happy to be free from the Armed Forces. Every human being is sometimes ill. I have had attacks of malaria. Flu. Mosquitos. Bad water... Whenever that happens, you have to find a doctor as soon as possible. Self-confidence is a feeling that comes from inside your brain and body. You cannot be confident without having trained hard. Winning is good for self-confidence, but you have to remember you don´t win if you haven´t been training.

The most important thing in training is that you take it seriously. From Monday to Friday, training must be the main thing in your life. Saturday and Sunday, you can take it easier, perhaps going for a little jog. You have to follow very closely everything that is happening in your body. The same applies during a race. I don´t mind publicity. It is good to be a well-known person, like Paavo Nurmi, who won the 1500 and 5000 in the Olympics the same day. Money is O.K. for an athlete, but it means more to me to be well-known than rich. When I started running, I did not think about money at all. Doping? No problem for me, because I am not taking any kind of drugs. Sometimes when you are suddenly beaten by a surprising runner, you may think he may have been on something...

Videos are always good when preparing for a big race. Where did I do it right? Where did I make a mistake? It is tough in Kenya. Now (in 1997) we have about eight runners capable of making it to the World Championships 5000m in Athens. Only three will make it. Our trials system is fair. It is the best possible. When you are fourth, you are out. It is as simple as that. You cannot blame anybody. The best thing in running is the enjoyment of racing. If you enjoy racing, you are doing it in relaxed way. I also enjoy my training sessions. I like the feeling of pushing hard.

My advice for young Kenyan runners: concentrate on what you are doing. When you train or race, don´t think about your cattle or land. Think about your running future. Some Kenyan athletes are missing home when they are abroad. Whenever I notice that, I try to talk with them, helping them. It is very difficult for some runners to live abroad, especially when it is winter and very cold. To some Kenyan runners, alcohol is a problem. They may take ten drinks and then drive a car! The Kenyan flag is very important to me. Whenever I see it, I realize I am a Kenyan athlete, and I feel proud of that. I am friends with all Kenyan runners. No problem!

BOIT Mike

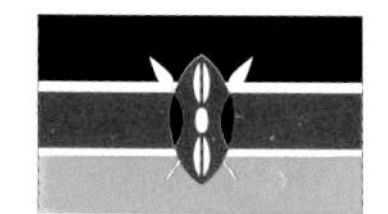

born 1 Jan 1949 (possibly 1948) Eldoret, Kenya. Member of Nandi tribe. One of the greatest and most durable middle distance runners in history who, due to Kenyan boycotts, twice lost his chance to excel in the Olympic Games. Before that, Boit won the Olympic 800m bronze medal in Munich 1972. Commonwealth 800m champion 1978, Boit twice missed the World Record by a few 100ths of a second (1.43.79 in 1975 and 1.43.57 in 1976). After his 20 year running career Boit made Doctor´s degree in sports physiology in the United States. **800m 1.43.57, 1000m 2.15,3, 1500m 3.33.67, one mile 3.49.45, 3000m 7.50.82, 5000m 13.35.70.**

"Athletes were given a glass of milk twice a day"

I started serious training in high school when I was introduced to interval training. That was in 1966 at St. Patrick´s Iten High School when I was a second year student. That was at about age 17. I started running just to represent my class and because there was a peer pressure to support my class. I did my best and won the event. I was therefore selected to represent my school. With the encouragement of other students I did my best, and that is how it all started. I tried the sprints first but it happened that I did not have the explosive muscles, but I was more successful at the 400 and 800 metres. I was not too good in the cross country, so I concentrated on the events in which I did better. In the 800 metres I was the best.

At primary school my father wanted me to be a cyclist. He was not too keen on running, although he took me to watch the Rift Valley athletics championships at Kapsabet Stadium when I was 12 years old. There was a capacity crowd and every event was extremely exciting. I remember Kiptalam Keter who was a famous 800m runner from Nandi at the time. He ran at the front from the start to the finish. In spite of that my father initially did not encourage me to take up running seriously. He liked cycling himself. He always discouraged me from running too fast down the hill especially where it was littered with small stones. He was apprehensive that I could hurt myself in case I tripped as I was tall and thin. He also discouraged me from playing soccer for fear that someone could kick and hurt me, so he advised me to play sick whenever teachers tried to push me to play soccer. As to my idols, they were athletes like Kiptalam Keter, 400m runner Paul Boit and long distance runner Kanuti Sum, who all came from Nandi district. The competition at the district was of very high standard, and most of the athletes who won a Nandi district title later became Kenyan national champions.

At school we all trained by running about three miles every afternoon for three weeks before the school championships. Later, when I became successful in running, I started winning prizes such as farm tools, kitchen utensils and occasionally a blanket. My father was happy and started to encourage me, but my mother had sort of mixed feelings. While she appreciated the prizes I won, at the same time she wanted me to concentrate more on my academic work. She also suspected that too much running probably was not good for my health. Some of my close friends were happy with my success in running, but some tried to discourage me probably because they were jealous. I thought I would end my running career after primary school so as to concentrate on my education, but at St. Patrick´s athletics was taken more seriously and athletes had extra privileges. For example, if you did not have the money for school fees, the head teacher did not send athletes back home - but if you weren´t an athlete, he did. Also athletes were given a glass of milk twice a day, a privilege other students did not get. I therefore had to wait until after high school to terminate my running! The one time I seriously considered leaving the sport was when I was dropped from the Kenyan 4x880 yards relay team that broke the World Record in London in 1970. In the 800 metres rankings I was in the top four, but I was dropped in favour of an athlete who was basically a 4x400 metres runner on grounds that he had more experience.

"It is normal to feel the tension"

I always believed that I was better than any of my rivals as we lined up before the start of the race. When I could not convince myself of that, I always ended up running poorly. Most Nandi youths never are over-excited about any competition, because there is less pressure to succeed from parents. However, in a major competition it is normal to feel the tension to arouse the adrenalin for extra effort, especially in World Championhips and Olympics. Tension prior to a major competition can manifest itself in many ways. For example, one may experience a loss of appetite on the day of competition. Under such circumstances the athlete must force himself or herself to eat properly provided it is not too close to the racing time. Having lunch at noon or 1pm in preparation for a race at between say 3 and 4 o´clock is quite in order. Such tension often disappears an hour or half an hour before competition, and the athlete may experience some appetite, but it would be too late to eat anything at that time.

As to losing a race, one is afraid of being defeated especially when you know you have not prepared well, but that kind of nervousness diminishes when an athlete is well prepared and has the confidence to challenge anyone. So being afraid or not afraid is in essence relative to the state of fitness level of an individual. Most athletes prefer to pull out of a race for fear of losing when they are not fit. My first success was in 1964, when running for primary schools at Nandi district championships I placed 3rd in the 800 metres. As to international competition, my first one was in 1971 at Abidjan, Ivory Coast, where I won the 1500 metres. My first competition in Europe was in 1972 Munich Olympics where I ran the 800 (3rd) and 1500 (4th). The Olympic success gave me the confidence to continue with the running career and the opportunity to pursue university education under an athletic scholarship. I became convinced that I was as good as anyone in the world in the 800 metres, and that changed my attitude which raised my expectation. The only negative thing about my athletic scholarship was that I had to be away from Kenya for many months, but I enjoyed my studies in the University. My training was evolving in the way that it became necessary to increase the mileage in my morning runs to improve my endurance, and I also took speed training more seriously. After my Olympic success, I enrolled on an athletic scholarship at Eastern New Mexico University. It was the division of small universities, and so the competition was not difficult for me, although as an Olympian I was expected to produce records anytime I stepped on the track.

"I was a reluctant athlete"

My biggest disappointment in New Mexico was the desert environment - strong wind, dry, hot and flat country with no hills and with plenty of rattle snakes which meant you had to be on a watch out especially when doing long runs in the morning or evening. I had been raised at an altitude of seven thousand feet where it is generally cool throughout the year, so I could not adjust to New Mexico with snow in the winter and the summer temperatures of 100 degrees F. From 1972 to 1976 I had very few defeats, and most of the time they were close races. When I went to graduate school at Stanford University I had a busy academic programme. As a result, my training suffered, which meant I lost many races. My training also became inconsistent and I suffered many injuries, which was frustrating. I got my first coach at Kenyatta College in 1970, and he was the man who persuaded me to take running seriously. I was a reluctant athlete, and without him I would not have gone to the Olympics in 1972. His name is Alex Stewart, a Scottish teacher who taught at many colleges in Kenya for over 20 years. When I went abroad it meant that I was under a university coach. He was Bill Silverberg, who had been a former steeplechase runner in the U.S. international team. In my view, the most important thing for a coach is to know the athlete personally, so as to know the strength and the weakness of the athlete in order to be in a better position to maximize his talent. What is the most difficult thing is to prepare the appropriate programme to maximize the potential of an athlete with minimal risks for injuries.

"You cannot always be right"

I would advice to plan two years ahead in general, but specifically it is good to plan for one season so that you can determine when you want to be at your best and how to build it. Occasionally one may not be able to follow the plan exactly, but it is wrong to be too much off the target unless the plan was poor, in which case it obviously must be adjusted. A good programme is one that is flexible. You cannot always be right because other variables often come into play, and they must be accommodated. Yes, I have made mistakes in my training. A bad error is to do speed training before you have warmed up properly. The risk of injury is too high. I have made that mistake once, and it was a setback. I think it is the most important thing in training to know how to avoid injuries - by not using old pair of shoes, by avoiding speed training without proper warm-up and stretching, by obeying the coach, and by learning to accept defeat and take it as a lesson.

I had problems with an Achilles tendon injury which interrupted my training every year now and then since 1977 until I officially retired in 1985. I still have the problem even when I have rested without serious training for more than 10 years. There is little I learned from this problem... I only learned to endure the pain and resisted surgical operation on the tendon unlike some world class athletes mainly because I was approaching retirement. I hoped that with less serious training I would achieve natural recovery, but as I said this has not been the case. I think I got the problem by using the spikes too often in my training. I would recommend that young runners use spikes very rarely, only when training for speed, but any endurance training should be done with good training shoes which are light and have a firm sole. Heavy shoes with soft sole can cause excess strain on the knees, and one must avoid getting a knee injury. It is also important to note that when you have a knee injury you must not run on soft ground like grass or sawdust, or a beach. For some reason people tend to run on soft grounds and wear shoes with soft sole when having knee problems.

"With 100 metres to go I wanted to give up"

Before any race, you must convince yourself that you are the best of the lot. You should concentrate on how you are going to win the race and try to imagine where you should be at each part of the race and when you plan to make your final attack. Kenyans in general are not good planners but they are good racers. It is possible to achieve both of these when an athlete is in top codition. In other words, you cannot plan to go flat out when you are not fit, but when you are fit, you can jeopardize your potential by being too conservative. When you ask about self-confidence, in my view you can build it through the kind of training you do, which means you will know that you are capable of running, for instance, every lap at 65 secs. pace in a 5000 metres race based on the kind of training you have been able to do.The mental power is a step above your self-confidence. Given a situation in which two or three athletes have the same fitness level, what determines the champion is the mental power which is the ability to achieve maximum concentration in order to channel all your energy to a specific target. When this sort of inspiration is lacking, the mind is likely to wander around and you might start thinking about how good the others are and how they are gaining on you. In this situation, a wrong signal is relayed to the muscles, and you will slow down. There was just one instance in race when I wanted to give up. In 1981 in Stockholm I was running against Sebastian Coe in the 1500 metres, and we were taken through the 800 metres very fast by the rabbit James Robinson of the United States. Seb must have gone through in 1.50 and I a little over. With 100 metres to go I wanted to give up and looked behind, seeing the rest were 50 metres away, so I had to struggle to the finish line in fourth place behind Seb, Steve Scott and Jose-Luiz Gonzalez in about 3.34. Every athlete must prepare oneself mentally before any race.

The difference is the level of preparation and the mental power of each individual. Part of the preparation is knowing the strength of your opponents so that you can capitalize on their weak areas in order to outperform them. As to doping, those who cheat in sport must live with a guilty conscience, and one can easily develop an attitude that you cannot excel without cheating. In other words, the more you can cheat the more you will rely on cheating, and that way you will lose confidence in yourself.

Good publicity in sport is desirable, but especially for young athletes bad publicity can be very damaging. Every one needs publicity, but we must accept constructive criticism. - With an inexperienced journalist it is unfortunately far easier to write a negative story than a positive one. It is sad that in many countries sports is seen as less important, and the new and relatively inexperienced journalists are given the responsibility of dealing with sports reporting. What I have noticed during the years is that it is normal that when you achieve a certain status, you create friends and enemies. So long as you have more friends than enemies, it should not be a bother. Also, it is a fact that you cannot influence everyone to like what you do. In that case, envy and jealousy are part of human nature, and often there is little we can do about it. However we should not be preoccupied with our perception of how other individuals feel about us, especially when one is in a leadership position.

BONDARENKO Olga

born 2 Jun 1960 Slavgorod, Southern Sibiria (née Krentser).
10 000m Olympic Champion 1988, 3000m European Champion 1986. Two World Records in the 10 000m: 32.30.80 in 1981, 31.13.78 in 1984. Indoor 3000m World Record 8.42,3 in 1986. A runner of slight build (154 cm, 41 kg) and excellent finishing kick. Made a come-back into international racing (mainly on roads) in the late 1990´s.
1500m 4.06,2, one mile 4.27.48, 2000m 5.40.16, 3000m 8.33.99, 5000m 14.55.76, 10 000m 30.57.21, marathon 2.43.24.

"You have to take care of your health"

I usually planned my training schedule for one month ahead at a time. Generally I was able to follow my plans as I had wished. If there were problems, they annoyed me. However, I also tried to be flexible with my schedule. I never had motivational problems; rather, I was enjoying what I was doing. I never felt depressed or worried about the many months of strenuous training looming ahead. What I tried to do was mobilizing and "tuning" myself mentally for the training schedule. There was a deep desire inside me to accomplish the work I had been planning. I was always honest with my training diary, never fooling myself. Also, I always knew why I was doing a specific training session. If I occasionally missed a session for some reason, I did not try to compensate for it later. What was gone, was gone. I have a feeling that, over the years, I did not make any big errors in my training. My advice for young distance runners is to enjoy their sport and work hard so that you will be able to reach higher and higher. There were some injuries and some adversities - also outside athletics - during my career. I have schooled myself to get over all possible difficulties. I try to analyse all matters carefully. You should not be afraid of any setbacks; they

can be conquered. The main thing, however, is that every athlete has to take good care of her health. Whenever I had been beaten in a race - and if there have been some good reasons for it -, I didn´t take it hard. I was able to look at myself and see what went wrong. However, it is not always easy to face the facts. Before a race I always forgot about friendships and feelings like that, but as soon as the competition was over, I was back to normal again.

I believe self-confidence can be acquired only by winning and possessing top athletic skill. The base for big victories come from the will for winning, hard work and the capacity to endure it, and mental training. As I see it, the will to win is a thing with which you are born. Even in my top racing years I sometimes had a feeling of wanting to give up in a race. I think it is possible to prepare oneself mentally for winning a race - or for being beaten, for that matter. I think a proper mental preparation is necessary for a good performance.

After being defeated in a race I felt like working harder to prove that I could win, and my "tuning" to my rivals became more intense. What I don´t like in sports is cheating; if you do that, it is nothing but cheating yourself. For me, publicity was a positive thing. I never tried to avoid it. I usually tried to read everything written about myself, but I did not preserve all the clippings. Yes, I enjoyed watching videotapes on my races because they were of much help in trying to find out the mistakes I had done, and what abilities I was perhaps missing.

Whenever I heard or read negative things about myself, I felt it very badly. I also sometimes saw people being envious about my myself. I found it most annoying, and the fact is that it sometimes caused problems in my life. All I can say about money is that it never was the most important factor in my career. My advice to the young generation is: Don´t be afraid of setbacks or hardships in your life. Remember the proverb, "It is the dogged that do it." I wish young runners great patience and industriousness in achieving top results. For me, the best thing in running is the feeling of winning a race.

BORDIN Gelindo

born 2 Apr 1959 Longare, Vicenza, Italy.
One of the greatest marathon runners in history: Olympic Champion 1988, European Champion 1986 and 1990. World Championships bronze medallist 1987. As a young man, Bordin was badly injured in a traffic accident, but he did not lose his fighting spirit and recovered well enough to become a world-class distance runner.
3000m steeplechase 8.49,2, 5000m 14.06,6, 10 000m 29.00.65, half marathon 1.02.06, marathon 2.08.19.

"Running gives you lots of time to think"

The reason why I became a runner was an unusual one. There was a running race in my home village. Those days I was a soccer goalkeeper, but I decided to have a go, and I noticed I was enjoying the running experience very much. I immediately told my friends I would be leaving football... You know the rest of the story. The most important thing in training for the marathon is learning to know yourself. You have to learn to understand, what kind of workouts are important, and the meaning of recovery. You have to be patient, because that is the only way to have success. You have to know yourself, because there is no one to help you during the race. A marathon runner is his or her own boss in a race. The essential thing in training is to learn all the different training methods and to get to know your body. When you have learned these things, you have to express your skill during the decisive phase of the race.

I believe that every great champion has some difficult moments during his career. There are also moments of hard decisions. You cannot avoid bad performances, especially in the early part of your career. A strong belief in your capabilities and the will to go on are the decisive factors. I have had some unbelievably difficult times. At 20 years of age I became seriously ill, when I got an intestinal bug while training in Mexico. It took a full year for me to recover. Later, I had a bad accident when I was out running; I was hit by a car. It looked like I would never be able to run again, and no one could tell me if I had any chance to get back. I believe these setbacks have been some of the essential things during my career. They have made me mentally stronger, giving me stability and determination which are so much needed in the big races.

My message to young athletes is that in very many cases, the champions have had to climb to the top through defeats and setbacks. You cannot have success without setbacks. You should not worry about being beaten in a race. What you have to do after a bad performance, is to have a positive look into

the future. As to myself, I was not a splendid athlete by all means in the early part of my career. I am deeply convinced of the fact that if an athlete has a high degree of determination, he will become mentally even stronger during the years. With patience, you will eventually succeed.

The basis of all progress is to develop all the various abilities, mentally as well as physically so that an athlete will manage the bad days he eventually will have. This, perhaps, is the most important advice that I can give to a young athlete. He or she must learn to deal with all the problems in life generally. It is only when you are mature enough to be able to deal with the problems in a positive way that you will be able to build your running career.

"You must feel confident in your heart"

Self-confidence is something very essential in sports. In fact it is all basis for a sporting career, and for other aspects in life as well. I have never had problems with self-confidence. I have learned to know my good and bad sides, mentally and physically. I have worked very hard to develop myself, especially as to the technical aspects of running. This work has gradually improved my racing success and, in turn, given me even more self-confidence. I certainly believe that I have become an excellent runner due to the strong belief in the training plan that I have been following. Even in the early years of my career, when I had big problems in my training, I strongly believed I would find the right path, which eventually would take me to big victories.

You must feel confident in your heart, because that is where you have most of your resources to win. I have been very fortunate to be able to travel all around the world, learning to know and understand many kinds of people. For me, the world is just one big family. In the early part of your career, it is important to develop your language skills and build life-long contacts with people. A sporting career may turn out to be a positive or a negative experience. No matter if your goals are big or small, the contacts between people will last a life-time anyway. I have been lucky enough to train and compete in all parts of the world. I feel it is essential to become friends with all kinds of people - no matter what colour or race - in different cities, in different countries. Even if we look different, we still are the same.

I deeply enjoy doing long runs by myself, especially in Finland and Sweden,where there are vast forests and where you can smell the distance running tradition in the air. It is invigorating to run alone, talking with your mind and body, at the same time forgetting the everyday problems. On runs like these, I often think about the future.

I don´t think it is possible in any other sport to be able to enjoy the solitude of life in meadows, forests, far away from cars and houses, just being immersed in your thoughts. When you are running automatically, in a simple way, feeling it as a part of your everyday life, it gives you lots of time to think. I find it important to think about all the various things you have in your life, especially in relation with other people.

BOULAMI Brahim

born 20 Apr 1972 Morocco.
A world class steeplechaser, Boulami has finished 7th in the Olympic finals at Atlanta and Sydney. In 2001, he was running faster than ever. In Zürich he broke the 8 minute barrier and a week later in Brussels he made the World 3000m sc Record 7.55.28.
3000m 7.42.99, 5000m 13.28.06, 3000m SC 8.02.90. - Brother Khalid B. (b. 1969) 1995 and 1997 World silver medallist and 1996 Olympic bronze medallist at 5000m.

"The future is like a cloud through which you cannot see"

I am 28 now (2000). I did not start serious training until five years ago, aged 23, after getting a degree from the university. I had already been running at age 15, but that was for one season only.

My decision to come back into distance running was inspired by my elder brother Khalid, who was a member of the Moroccan national team. He always told me, "you can become a very good runner, but you have to train". So, after finishing my studies, I came back and made up my mind to see what I can do.

Motivation? No problem! Training is not easy, but you

have to love being a runner. There always is some suffering in training, but there is not going around these things if you want to achieve something. I enjoy all kinds of training even if it is sometimes very hard. The most important thing in training is to keep training (smiles)! To keep training all the time... When I was studying, and training only every now and then, my results were not good at all. It is by no means easy to get into the Moroccan national team. After getting into serious training, my very first steeplechase was 8.38, then 8.30, then after coming to Europe I ran 8.24, and so on. I was progressing nicely.

When you are young and you decide to try your talent as a runner, the main thing is to believe in yourself and to keep training even if you don´t know what the future will bring to you. The future is like a cloud through which you cannot see. For me, my brother was an inspiration, without whom I wouldn´t be here. In Morocco we also had Aouita, who was something very special. I think young athletes need to have idols in order to learn something from them.

I have had many injuries. What they have taught me is that you have to be careful and patient when something goes wrong with your body. I believe in God, and I trust him whenever I have problems. Difficulties definitely make you stronger.

You may be beaten in a race even if you are in good condition. Everyone has to face defeats in this sport. You have to believe in yourself, and try to do better next time. Without self-confidence, you cannot be a good runner. You will get the confidence from training. From winning, too!

Running is good for your health. You are lucky if you really love this sport. Running is good for everyone, no matter if you finish last or if you are a world class athlete. There are many other healthy sports as well, but you can run no matter where you come from, a poor or a rich country.

With time, running becomes a part of your life. I know, because if I stop running for a week or two, I do not feel good any more. When running, I feel good and free. Also, it is great to spend maybe 10 years of one´s life competing at the highest level. I think these are the best things in running.

BUCHER André

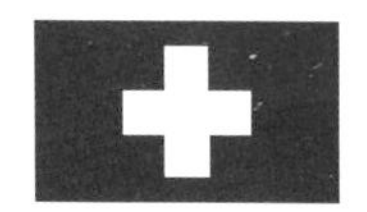

born 10 Oct 1976 Neudorf, Switzerland.
A tall and stylish runner, Bucher began at longer distances and steeplechase before winning silver medal at World Junior 1500 metres in 1994 and then finally finding his true talent at 800 metres: European silver in 1998, Universiade silver in 1999, fifth place in the Sydney Olympic final, World Champion in Edmonton, 2001. Bucher´s personal bests make him perhaps the most versatile athlete among the present middle distance runners:
400m 46.32 (2000), 600m 1.14.72 (1999), 800m 1.42.55 (2001), 1000m 2.15.66 (1999), 1500m 3.38.44 (1996), 3000m 8.16,9 (1998), 5000m 14.06.77 (1998), 10 000m 30.40,5 (1996), 3000m steeplechase 9.09.73 (1995).

"...even if it doesn´t always match perfectly the sports theory"

I started running when I was 10 years old. A friend of mine took me to a street race in a nearby village where I won my first race straight away. A couple of months later, I joined the local athletics club in which I have ever since trained under the same coach. I started serious training at age 15.I never had any idols in running or athletics in general. As to motivational problems, I still love running and the lifestyle connected with it. But surely if you train 365 days a year for many years, you´ve got your bad times, too. I guess this is just normal in any sport or job. Running at first seems to be boring and self-repeating. But if you consider all the different training sessions such as long runs, coordination drills, weights (gym work), speed work, track work - and also the fact that you get to travel around quite a lot for training camps and races, I don´t think that training and running is all that boring. Training is an alternation of easy sessions and hard sessions, which means running is not fun all the time as every athlete needs to work hard. But it is most important for young and older athletes alike that at the end of the day, they enjoy running and training in itself. The most essential thing for a coach is to bring the theoretical knowledge of training and the individual needs of an athlete together. A good coach is the one who knows his athlete and knows what is good for him, even if it sometimes does not perfectly match the sports theory! I have been pretty lucky in not having any serious injuries so far. For any young athlete it is important that he or she is not just doing his training as being told from day to day without thought. One must also listen to one´s body and take its signals seriously. A race is like a game. If you risk something, you might win or you might lose. But if you don´t take any risks, you will lose every time. So a defeat in a race just tells you that there is more work waiting for you to be done. Life goes on...! Before a race, I always keep in my mind how long and hard I trained for this. So, I don´t have to hide behind my rivals. I just try to go out there and do my best. Don´t think of what the others might or might not do. Think only of what you can do! With publicity came a lot of benefits and also a lot of drawbacks. As for me, I don´t like the publicity that much, which is why I try to stay in the background if possible. But I guess it is also part of the business and important in finding sponsors.

As to videotapes of a bad race of mine, it is no problem at all for me to watch them,

Cheating: I guess it is the same all around, no matter whether you talk about politics, economics or sport. The more money there is involved, the bigger the chance that someone tries to gain success by cheating. There will always be athletes who try to win by taking drugs. It is therefore very important to have an anti-drug agency to fight those who are unable to compete or race within the rules. I didn´start running because of money. It it had been the money, I should have tried soccer, golf, tennis... (which doesn´t mean that I would have been successful at all, I just wanted to say that money never has been my motivation in athletics!). On the other hand, running became my profession and also my business, which means earning money with my running is important to a certain point if I wish to keep living the life of a professional runner. Running is a passion and if you do it in the right way without cheating, you will have many great moments and memories in athletics with your family and friends. The best thing about running is to be out in the nature, to train and to target at your goals, aims and dreams.

CACHO Fermin

born 16 Feb 1969 Agreda, Soria, Spain.
A great 1500 metres runner: Olympic Champion on home soil in Barcelona 1992 (last lap 50,4), Olympic silver medallist 1996, European champion 1994 and bronze medallist 1998, World Championships silver medallist 1993 and 1997, fourth 1999.
800m 1.45.37, 1000m 2.16.13, 1500m 3.28.95 (European record in 1997), one mile 3.49.56, 3000m 7.36.61 (European indoor record 1996). Is planning to move up to the marathon after the Sydney Olympic Games.

"As soon as I don´t enjoy running any more, I will quit"

Whether I enjoy training, depends on what kind of session I´m doing. For me, track training is more enjoyable than logging kilometres on the roads. Running long and slow is boring and monotonous to me. My attitude towards training sessions is that there is always one day less left before the race. I am concentrating on doing the best training session I possibly can. I never think about those sessions in advance. My coach knows me as person, but he also knows my physical abilities. He immediately notices my inability to change rhythm in the final phase of a race. What he usually does in a situation like that is to make some changes to my training schedule. I never ask why he is changing this or that. If I miss a training session for some reason or another, that´s it. I don´t try to compensate for it the next day by running more or harder. Rather, the rest day usually is most useful for recovery. If I feel tired, I don´t force myself to train. I want to tell to young runners that there is nothing more important than regularity and common sense in training. It is not the correct way to think that "tomorrow I will train hard, and then I will do nothing for three days". It is absolutely essential to train regularly, to adapt your body to more strenuous work. This is important for all athletes, not just youngsters. My attitude towards a defeat in a race depends on what I have been aiming at. If I had a good race and yet was beaten fairly and squarely, I will analyse the reasons for what happened. Was it a tactical mistake? Naturally I am also pondering whether I had not been training well enough. How I take a defeat depends on how I was beaten. A complete catastrophe annoys me more than a race in which I was perhaps fourth or fifth. At this level of competition, it is no shame to be beaten. The only thing you can do is to find out the reason why you did not do well. After that, you have to get back into training and start aiming at the next race. You don´t manage in athletics without self-confidence. Before a race, if you think "those other people are better than me", you have already lost it. You must teach yourself to be mentally tough. During the race, the only thought in your head should be, "I will win". I firmly believe that it is possible to prepare mentally for a race. Hopefully you have someone with whom you can talk and whom you trust. If so, that is good, but the best way to cultivate self-confidence is through training.

As I see it, the will to win is born with you. Some people have the ambition, the will to win, to be the best at school, to be the best in the ball games. Of course it can be cultivated, but I still say it is something that is born with you. Of course, I am not running for money; rather, I am running because I like to run. Also, it must be admitted that this way I am earning better than in some "ordinary" job.

The best thing in running is that you can wake up every morning knowing that you are able to do what you enjoy so much. I like the fact that I am training for upcoming races. As soon as I don´t enjoy this lifestyle any more, I will quit. As I see it, the biggest difference between the European and the African runners is in the lifestyle. We, the white people, have become lazy through living such an easy life. In Africa, everyday life requires much more from you.

CLARKE Ron

born 21 February 1937 Melbourne, Australia.
18 world records: two at 2 miles, four at 3000 m, four at 5000 m, two at 6 miles, three at 10 000 m, one at 10 miles, one at 20 000 m, and one in the one-hour run. Improved his own 10 000 m world record by 36,2 secs. to 27:39,4 at Oslo in 1965. No other runner broke 28 mins. before 1971. Three junior world bests in 1956. Carried the torch to the stadium in the opening ceremony of the Melbourne Olympic Games in 1956. Clarke´s only Olympic medal was a 10000 m bronze in 1964; in Mexico City in 1968 his chances were robbed by the 2240 metres altitude. Ron Clarke was the idol of a whole generation of distance runners all over the world in the 1960´s and 1970´s.
880y 1:53,6, 1500m 3:44,1, mile 4:00,2, 2000m 5:08,7, 3000m 7:47,2, 2 miles 8:19,6, 3 miles 12:50,4, 5000m 13:16,6, 6 miles 26:47,0, 10 000m 27:39,4, 10 miles 47:12,8, 20 000m 59:22,8, one hour 20 032 m, 15 miles 1:14:24, 30 000m 1:34:35, marathon 2:20:37.

I started serious training at around 18 years of age. I chose running because I seemed to be quite successful in it as a junior, breaking records at school, state and finally national junior level before having any specific training programmes.

As to the idols, I really didn´t have any those days, although I did highly respect Emil Zatopek and John Landy. Later, having met Emil personally, I liked him very much and counted him as one of my very best friends. At first, I had no specific goals except to run as fast as I could. I mainly ran alone, sometimes also with my brother who was training for football, and at other times with a couple of senior runners who were trying to encourage me such as Neil Robbins (steeplechase international) and Les Perry (Olympic 5000 and 10000 metres runner). It was Neil who took me along to Franz Stampfl, and Franz it was who trained me in my early years.
Even if my family always encouraged me to do any sort of sporting acitivity, at no stage did I have any idea how long I would go on doing it. Running never was as important as my family or business career, and whenever it interfered with these, I stopped running - finally for good in 1970, when I considered it

would affect my family life. I never found training difficult or boring. It was just a nice relief after a day´s work at the office to be able to get out and run freely. As to the racing, I always had the highest respect for my rivals and looked forward to races with them at all times to see how my fitness training and ability would match theirs.

I don´t think I was ever over excited before races, but I found racing similar to academic examinations in which I was testing my preparation against the examiners´ questions. The difference was that in a race it was my rivals against whom I was testing myself.

"I would rather have lost well than won badly"

I was never afraid of losing as much as it terrified me into not taking a risk. I feel the essence of competition is taking risks, and I would rather have lost well than won badly. I had success in my junior racing from the very beginning. I started with schoolboy victories at all distances from 100 metres through to cross country events and continued through my early years into junior titles, both for the state and nationally until I was beaten by another outstanding runner called Herb Elliott.

I don´t think I ever planned to, say, run in the Olympics. I had no idea if I was going to be good enough for that but I did like to see how far I could improve, and everything just kept on evolving. The only difficulty I had was an Achilles tendon problem in 1964, which I had to work hard to overcome. In order to prevent any further problems, the doctors gave me a series of

exercises for 30 minutes every evening, which I religiously followed. Certainly no other injuries did occur until towards the end of my career when I had some problems with my groin. My biggest disappointment was the IOC choice of Mexico City as a place for what should have been the peak of my career at the 1968 Olympic Games. As it happened there, it was an unfair competition. I never got disappointed when I only had myself to blame but I thought that decision was made in circumstances over which we had no control, and that really was a disappointment. As far as losses are concerned I think I learned from all my losses and from some of my wins. I think we go through life learning all the time in racing, in family and with business. I don´t really remember too many of the defeats. I always regard defeats as a challenge to improve, an incentive to train harder. Some sort of adrenaline always flowed after getting beaten to overcome it. So, rather the opposite - I was never ever discouraged by a loss.

"In fact I don´t regard a coach as essential at all"

Franz Stampfl was my coach, and it was Franz who advised me from time to time even later in my career. Otherwise I had no other coaches except a close friend whose advice I respected very much; his name was Frank McMahon. In fact I don´t regard a coach as essential at all. I did not feel any changes in training motivation except perhaps for the one or two days after a defeat. I always had self-confidence in that I always believed that you could perform at least as well as you performed before, maybe even little better.

You couldn´t control how good other people were, so if you ran to your best and you were better than the other people you won, or if they had a bad day, you were lucky enough to perhaps win. But you had to do this by running to your best ability, so I just worried about myself and running to that ability by proper preparation and proper mental approach. I suppose I reached international level at the 1962 Commonwealth Games in Perth when I came second to Murray Halberg, beating Bruce Kidd, Kip Keino and Bruce Tulloh among others.

I always liked travelling. My first trip abroad was to compete in New Zealand after those 1962 Games. Then, after breaking my first world record the following year I went racing indoors in America and enjoyed the experience very much. I enjoyed meeting top class runners and talking with them about their approach to athletics. As well I also enjoyed meeting outstanding sportsmen and businessmen in other areas, a world which I would probably not have moved into, had it not been for my running ability. I do not think I had a specific breakthrough in my career except perhaps the 10 000 metres world record in 1963 when no one expected me to break it. However, in that race I think I improved more than two minutes over my previous 10 000 metres times. Certainly I was never a perfect athlete as I had a business career and family to look after which took 9-10 hours of my day, which meant I sometimes skipped training although I tried not to. I know that I could have improved much more had the financial incentives been sufficient to give the ability to be able to train more regularly.

"I never planned my training for a very long time ahead"

I never planned my training very much except that I set a pattern rather than a day to day, or month by month, timetable. I don´t agree with strenuous training at all. I think that each day should be hard enough to make certain it has an effect but also easy enough to make sure you can train well the following day. So, I really never had any single very tough training sessions. I kept that type of all-at-it effort for the races. When recording my training, I always was honest to myself. For instance, I never ever logged in as mileage my morning jog if I had one.

I found that two or three days a week before going to the office I had time to run 4 or 5 miles easily, but that was never ever put into any calculation of mileage. One training session per day is all I believe anybody really needs, and when runners split their training sessions and mileages I think they are the worst of it. I probably did some mistakes in my training but the results came out, so I think had I had the chance to do it again I would have paid more attention to my nutrition. The best advice I can give to young athletes is to be consistent, not to be impatient to get results too quickly because a proper foundation is needed. Injuries are mainly gained from training too hard too soon, so do not expect to perform well in a race without the proper background in training.

As to the setbacks, I think the only ones during my career were those in 1964. I don´t think I was ever surprisingly beaten in a race except by Naftali Temu in 1966 when I underestimated his ability. Obviously after every race whether I won or lost I analysed what I did correctly or uncorrectly and saw how I hoped to be able to improve. For me, bad performances were challenges. I really cannot believe anybody not performing badly in that they don´t run to their ability. Even in the race against Temu in the 1966 Commonwealth Games I think I ran as well as I could. I just underestimated my rival and therefore adopted wrong tactics. If a runner is inconsistent, then it must be something with either his nerves before a race - the reason for which he has to work out for himself - or his training programme being not hard enough, or too hard.

"I think self-confidence is a matter of having trained well"

As I see it, self-confidence is a matter of having trained well, having prepared correctly. If you are correctly prepared for a race, you are self-confident. If you do not prepare properly, then you may have some doubts about yourself. To sum it up, the requirements of a great victory are being mentally aggressive, and physically prepared. I think a lot of nonsense is being talked about winning and losing, and the mental power for it.

Most people are very tough competitors, but the problem with most of them is that they don´t train consistently enough to support their mental competitiveness. Winning is easy for somebody that has the talent. The main factor I find missing in a number of athletes is aggression in developing their talent for the win. They seem to be more frightened of losing and therefore have very negative approach in their races. As to dropping out of a race, I didn´t ever want to do it, but I once did give up. Unfortunately it was on the last lap of the 1964 Olympic 5000 metres, in which, had I kept battling it out I think I would have got second or third. However, I was overrun with a lap to go, a number of people jumped me and I was disappointed I wasn´t well clear of the field and I didn´t persist. It was my most shameful moment in athletics.

Again I think you prepare yourself for winning and losing by preparing yourself to be aggressive in the race and having the proper physical preparation. About cheating: I despise cheats in any sport including those who would seek a false advantage by taking artificial aids of some sort.

Personal message to young runners: Train consistently and sensibly so that you can compete to the best of your ability with confidence and aggression - then you will gain interest and satisfaction from your endeavours whether you win or lose.

The best in running: For me it was the international nature of the sport which allowed me to widen my human knowledge so much by coming into contact with such a broad strata of people geographically, socially, financially and politically - and life is all about experiences.

COE Sebastian

born 29 September 1956 London, England.
The only man to win 1500m Olympic Gold twice, in Moscow 1980 and Los Angeles 1984. 800m Olympic silver medallist in Moscow and Los Angeles. 800m European Champion 1986, silver 1982, bronze 1978. Eight world records at 800m, 1000m, 1500m and one mile 1979-1981, of which that of the 800m stood for 16 years and that of the 1000m still remained unbroken at the end of 1998. Coached by father, Peter Coe. The Golden Era of Steve Ovett, Sebastian Coe and Steve Cram still is one of the most illustrious chapters in the history of British athletics and middle-distance running. After his running career, Coe became a member of the British parliament.
400m 46.87 (relay 45,5), 800m 1:41.73, 1000m 2:12.18, 1500m 3:29.77, mile 3:47.33, 2000m 4:58.84, 3000m 7:55.24, 5000m 14:06,2.

I was born to be a runner. I started running because I have always enjoyed the physical sensation of movement. I have been told by my mother that even as a child I would prefer to run alongside the pushcart than sitting in it. I always preferred running to cycling. I found it physically easier and would think even at the age of 8 or 9 it was nothing to run 2 or 3 miles into town and back again. I have to be honest in that at the age of 12 to 14 running was not my first love. Those days it was soccer. I used to play regularly for school and for my area. But I rather fancy that I was never going to become another Pele or Johan Cruyff. I probably made the right decision when concentrating on athletics. I don´t think I ever had any idols, but there have been people in my career that have impressed me with their athletic ability. One of my favourite runners in terms of style and racing quality was Emiel Puttemans of Belgium, who was running extremely well when I was coming through into the sport in 1972-73. In terms of Olympians, for me there is only one hero and that has to be Lasse Viren. Many people have criticized Viren for only competing well at the Olympic Games and not being concerned what happens between them. Well I have a certain sympathy and understanding for that attitude because I did not do very much in the 2 or 3 years since 1981 through to 1984, but I then came back to win an Olympic title again. I think often athletes run too hard and race too often, losing sight of the fact that there is only one major championship. It is not going to be easy in the next few years to concentrate in the Olympics or other championships because there are so many competitions that athletes are being drawn towards.

"Long term planning"

In 1971-72 my coach (father) set down an 8 year plan for me through the 1980 Olympics. So that´s long term planning. The most important thing in training, without no doubt at all, is consistency. It is not how much mileage you can run in a week. It is not how many training sessions you can cram into a three week period if you´re going to be injured for another three weeks. The important thing is planning one´s training so that it is consistent work, and not just over one season or over one winter, but consistent over 10, 12, 15, 20 years. This is because in athletics nothing good happens overnight. It is like planting trees, in which everything takes time to develop slowly.

Coaching young runners

I don´t think that you should be thinking in terms of quantity or mileage at a young age. If somebody is serious about running, it is the job of the coach to make sure that he is running within the framework of safety both physiologically and biomechanically, and certainly mentally, because it is not good for athletes at the age of 13 to 14 to specialise so much that in one event that nothing else is given any consideration. I actually think that to discuss mileage totals at the age of 13 or 14, or even 15, is very counterproductive. What you should be doing with an athlete at that stage is trying to make some sensible assessment in where that athlete´s best event may be. That may be extremely difficult, but at that stage you should have a reasonable inkling into whether or not the athlete is going to be an endurance based runner, or is he going to be a sprinter by his shape and by his size and muscle bulk and that sort of things.

At the age of 16 to 18 the training becomes more serious, because if you think your athlete is going to be good enough, you are plotting a path for him for a transition between being a junior and a senior. Senior athletics in United Kingdom starts at the age of 18, so before that you are trying to maintain his development, hopefully working to preset plans and targets, but you also have to consider that at the age from 16 to 18 the athlete is changing physically all the time. You have still to be very careful about the quantity and quality, about the right kind of recovery, the proper spacing of races etc. You must also be aware of the fact that the biggest drop-out in athletics statistically occurs between the ages of 16 and 18. Thus very few good junior athletes go on to become good senior athletes. On the other hand, it is often the athletes that haven´t sparkled particulary as juniors that come through to make good senior athletes. They may have had perhaps less pressure, less training, less quantity work that has saved them to senior ranks. I don´t have any advice for young athletes who find something else to do. If you generally feel that there is something more important at that stage in your life than athletics, then I have to be honest about it - you shouldn´t be in athletics. My advice to any coach having a problem getting an athlete to train on a regular and sensible basis - and when his athlete replies, "well there are other things" - I would say to the coach it would be much better for him to spend his time with somebody that he didn´t have to worry with internal motivation.

That sounds quite brutal, but my message to that kind of athlete is actually try and find something else that he gets more pleasure from - and if you actually get more pleasure from playing a musical instrument, for example, and you don´t like being on a running track in regular training, then don´t bother because you are actually wasting your time, and in fairness, you are wasting your coach´s time as well.

"Never, ever lose sight of speed!"

My training always has the same pattern whether I am racing or not. In the mixture of all round body conditioning it is important during the winter months never, ever lose sight of speed, even if it means at the end of a training run just having a hard sprint for 80, 90, 100 metres. I never lose sight of the fact that in the summer I have to run quickly even if the distance is important as well as a background and good aerobic fitness, but the name of my game is to be able to run 1:41-1:42 in 800 and 3:29 in 1500 metres. My planning depends much on what the season holds. If for instance I am entering an Olympic year like Moscow, Los Angeles or Seoul, where I am having to run many races back to back, then my major concern is that I am strong enough to be able to do that, and that calls upon slightly different type of work during the winter months. This year (1989) I am only concerned about running quickly and perhaps having two weeks between races. So I am not that concerned about running much more mileage, and I can concentrate a little bit more on the speed earlier in the season knowing that by August or September I may go to Zürich, race just once and have 5 days before I perhaps race in Brussels. Yes, it bothers me if I cannot follow my plan, because any athlete knows there is nothing worse than knowing you are going into the season underprepared. It is frustrating that for reasons away from your control you are unable to get the right quality and consistency of training before competing. That is probably the worst feeling an athlete can have.

However, I feel flexible in my training in a way that I do a certain workload within a two-week period, but if for instance this morning I was due to run simply 100 metres repetitions on the track, and it is raining, cold and windy, then I would substitute that training session for something that I might be able to do slightly better in those conditions. But as long as I can get the planned work done within the next day or so, that is fine. Sometimes, however, there are training sessions that you just have to do, irrespective of the conditions.
I don´t believe that you can run mileage to the exclusion of speed or in fact just do speedwork to the exclusion of some kind of mileage. At no stage of my season was I ever just running mileage without at least doing something that

was a little quicker, either uphill or even doing speed drills in the gymnasium or weight training that was geared to improving leg speed. I don´t actually like the idea of saying to an athlete, "right, well, it is now October, and until January you are going to do nothing but mileage, and then between January and April you are not going to do anything but hills, and then from April onwards nothing but track work".

I don´t believe that is the way to maintain speed and endurance throughout the season any more than it is possible to go a full year without doing weight training or gymnasium work. Before Stuttgart 1986 I had one of my best weight training sessions only 6 or 7 days before the European Championships started. Now, according to the textbooks that is wrong, but it worked for me, so I actually think that you must mix up all the systems that you are attempting to work on throughout the year even during the heavy part of the track season. I was still regularly going out and running for an hour, sometimes one hour and a quarter, and most mornings would start off with a distance run of some sort.

"I couldn´t tell you what my mileage has been"

Mileage doesn´t worry me. I don´t even add up my mileage, except sometimes in winter. When I get into the summer, that is unimportant. I basically run twice a week purely for aerobic conditioning, perhaps one and a half hours each. The rest of the week is steady running to warm up and warm down or at the end of the day to help clear lactates and acids that build up from hard track running. Mileage for me is not an important or obsessional target to be counted at the end of each week. It has only been important in terms

of quality of what I have done. I can remember all my track sessions and my times, but certainly for the last six weeks I couldn´t tell you what my mileage has been. A middle distance runner must never stay away from speed. After doing just long mileage, it is frightening to wake up in April and notice that the track season is starting in one or two months.

"You can always get good ideas"

You have got to be very careful about the way stories get retold from coach to coach. Sometimes when a training session of an athlete has been told 10-12 times between different coaches, times become altered, recoveries become altered, the distances become altered. I think it is sensible for any coach or athlete to be aware what others are doing, because you always can get good ideas. I mean there are good ideas and we have all listened and spoken to people who have run different types of schedules at different times of year. You may not have agreed with them, you may have thought they are not relevant to what you are doing, but it is always sensible to know the current thinking. There are some coaches who are giving a great deal of thoughts to the development of their event whether it is 800, 1500 or even 100 metres. But you have to be very careful about writing down schedules; that is why I am never really comfortable about writing or talking much about schedules in books, because what suited me may be very destructive to someone else.

The secret of my finishing kick: I had natural speed, and I started my career as a sprinter long ago. Moreover, I have been taught to run like a sprinter. You learn to change gears through training. In several training sessions during the summer, I do accelerations from the points marked down on the track. Or, my coach suddenly signals me to accelerate in the midst of a repetition without advance warning until another signal allows me slow down again. Weight training of a middle distance runner: Weight training has to be done in three phases. The first thing to remember about weight training is, don´t ask an athlete to lift weights if he or she isn´t strong enough to actually handle them. At the beginning of the season, presuming that you take four or five weeks off at the end of the year from September to October, I would start my weight training phase by doing three weeks in the gymnasium just simply getting into shape again, to be able to lift to handle the weights properly, because there is a technical aspect of weight training as well, which is very important. It is not just about lifting huge weights - it is actually lifting weights in the most economic way and also biomechanically the safest way, so that no athlete should just go simply in a weight training room and think that it is just a matter of brute force. Weight training is so much easier if you actually have good technique, and also very much safer.

From October/November through until January I was doing heavy weights, long repetitions. From January to May I was reducing the number of repetitions, but increasing the weight, making the lifts much more explosive. From April/May onwards I would cut my weight training program to perhaps one good session a week plus one light session a week. That would mean back to one heavy weight session, in which I would do squats so that instead of 20-30 reps with 200 pounds I would do 1, 2 or even 3 pyramid sessions, where I would perhaps get up to 300-320 pounds and the equivalent with arms, then equivalent with lower back and stomach. From that point on I would do just one maintenance session from about May or June right through the season, still remembering the fact that a hard weight training session should never be done within 7 or 8 days of a major competition.

"If you enjoy all your training, then perhaps you are not training hard enough"

No, I do not enjoy all my training. I enjoy being on the track and also running with a group on the track sometimes, as I do the solitude of training. Sometimes it is pleasurable to be able to go out on a lovely day and run down by the river here. But when someone says he wakes up every morning enjoying all his training, I think he is perhaps not training hard enough! When you think about your hard training ahead, I think you have to look at it in terms of a game, of an intellectual and physical pursuit. That is a challenge. The target is there, you are here, and you have got to get there. You have to avoid obstacles like injuries, you have to pick the right races, and you have got to peak at the right stage for the races whether they are for selection or whatever. That is all the way to to peak, you know. It is a steady improvement, it is an intellectual game. There are training sessions that I do that are significantly harder than track racing. Sometimes you need to bring to a hard training session kind of mental concentration, more taxing than you do in a race. I have never felt as bad in a race as I have after some training sessions. That is how you train hard, but you can´t train hard every day. You may only have one of these sessions every 8, 9, 10 days, but in order to fully achieve these targets you often need to go into a training session in the same mental stage as you do for a top class race.

The essential thing in training is continuity. It is more important than any single training session. If you miss a training session because you are injured, then obviously you cannot suddenly replace it later, because if you are injured, you are off for a few days, and then you have to start gently, making sure that the injury does not occur again. If you miss a training session for any other reason, then you seriously have to ask yourself why you missed it. You can´t just suddenly say, "well, I can´t do that, I can´t be bothered with that today, but I will do two of these sessions tomorrow to make up for it". But it doesn´t work like that. You don´t miss training for any reason. It must be something very, very important. These reasons have to be somewhere in the region of life and death. Towards the end of my career, I did not recover from hard training as quickly as before. It is more difficult to recover for a 33 year-old than for a 23 year-old. You also have to be careful when mixing different types of training. Of course I did not neglect the importance of recovery even in my younger days, for I well knew the importance of rest. To be able to benefit from training sessions, you have to be able to recover. I don´t think I have made any bad errors in my training. But nobody is perfect, and in hindsight, on occasions I might have done something slightly differently. I think that my record in major championships speaks for itself, because whether it was bronze or silver, or if I have been lucky enough to win a gold medal, I have never since 1977 come away from a major championship without a medal. I was never stuck in the heats, so in my case we are only talking of the difference between 1st, 2nd and 3rd in major race, which is not a lot. Speaking on setbacks, if you use them as a motivation, that can be very useful. I think back to 1983 when I lost the whole of that summer, missing taking part in the World Championships. To have sit out watching such a meeting on television, feeling ill and not very well at all at the time was frustrating. But to know you are only still a year away from the Olympics was a big motivator. The most difficult period in any athlete´s life is knowing what to do when you are injured or unable to run. That is without any doubt the most difficult time any athlete or coach will face. It is then that a coach can give his athlete support in terms of medical backup. It is the time when the coach-athlete relationship is most successful.

Having said that, it took me some time to appreciate that a victory achieved after a real setback is sometimes much more enjoyable than when everything has been going well. It is a real mental, physical and intellectual challenge to come back from a setback and then win something.

"There is a big physical difference between young athletes"

There is nothing in training that is going to replace natural ability in terms of what you can do. You can minimize - or you can attempt to minimize some of the weaknesses and to enhance some of the strengths, but if you are not naturally a good sprinter, you can make some training schedules, you can improve leg action. You can improve muscle quality, you can do all sorts of things in the weight training room, you can do speed drills, but you cannot actually physiologically put in what is not there. So, of course talent is a very important natural ability, actually it is more important than anything else. As to defeats in a race, every athlete is going to have them. Young athletes especially are notoriously up and down in their performances. We have all done that. I would sometimes run brilliantly, then very badly the next week. Young women especially with their biological changes are prone to fluctuating performances

that their coaches must understand. There is a lot going on in a young child´s life. Children often are combining their sport with some academic pursuit, Then of course, when they leave school, they either have the transition where they go to University or they get in to a career. This means a whole series of transitions and difficulties in the lives of young athletes that sometimes reflect in their performances on the track or in the cross country or on the road. This is something that a coach must be aware of, but you must also remember that there is a big physical difference sometimes between young athletes of the same age.

"I don´t think self-confidence is only about winning or losing"

It is wasteful to be too concerned about what your competitors are doing in the build-up of the races or what they are going to do when they are in the race with you. It is far more important to be fully confident about your own abilities. Self-confidence comes with an understanding of what you are doing and the rate of progress that you should be making. Sometimes when that progress is not as fast as you would like, you become discouraged. Sometimes athletes have to be slowed down a little bit because the rate of progress is too fast, and they may be running or competing in the wrong distances. It is crazy to ask a 14 year-old child to think about specialising in 3000 metres, because at that rate he will be a marathon runner by age 18. As I see it, self-confidence tends to come with a general and steady improvement. There is a rationale behind being asked to do certain types of training sessions, and once you have been asked to do those sessions, if the race goes well, then there is a reinforcement of what you are doing. However, I don´t think self-confidence is only about winning or losing. It is about how you work with perhaps a coach or how the attitude of your family is towards what you are doing. There is nothing worse for an athlete than to feel that his family looks at him as some strange creation because at 7 o´clock in the morning he chooses to put on a pair of training shoes and run on the pavement. As to self-confidence, I was stepping a big leap forward in about 1976-77 when I started racing against athletes I had only ever watched on television, people like John Walker, Thomas Wessinghage, Eamonn Coghlan etc. Suddenly I was competing against them and more often than not actually winning. That was very pleasing, but it was also indicative of the fact that I had arrived at international level, where I was good enough to be asked to compete against the very best in the world. I have always got along very well with my father. We have never had any big problems. My family fully understood what I was doing. There were no major difficulties with holidays, studies or other things. We did not have three separate units, just one. This fact made life much easier.

The difference between winning and losing often comes from mental strength. There have been some races that I have had no business to win physically, because I have not been in good shape. Yet I have willed myself to win simply because the mind has taken over and has been more dominant than the physical side. On the other hand, there have been races that I have lost when I have been in supreme physical condition, but haven´t had the mental strength on the day to match the physical preparation. This is a job of a good coach. Coaching is not just the physical preparation, it is about the all-around preparation of an athlete. You are really looking for the synthesis of physical and mental strengths to manifest themselves on one specific afternoon perhaps once every four years.

"Cheating is the antithesis of healthy, fair sports"

I think it is possible to cultivate the mental strength of an athlete. I don´t think we should run away from the fact that winning and losing is the only measure in athletics. It is certainly not the only measure in terms of human experience. Because if it was, then you would only have one happy person and 30 000 unhappy persons in the London Marathon. And we know that to be untrue.

If you are an athlete, or a coach with a group of athletes, and your only measure of assessing their performance in a race is whether they won or lost, then neither the athlete or coach is ever going to learn enough to be able to go very much farther in the sport. Athletes sometimes need to be helped in terms of understanding how to change negative thoughts into positive thoughts and generally more confident and comfortable with themselves about what they are doing. As to cheating, there is no place for that kind of things at any level in sport, whether it is at club level or at international sport. The words "cheating" and "sports" do in no way actually go together. They are antithesis. Cheating is the antithesis of healthy, fair sports. Publicity: you neither need it, nor you need it. It is a balance again. You have to be aware that my sport is popular in this country and all over the world because the media has given lots of coverage and introduced athletics to people that 15 years ago thought the only sport was soccer. As athletes, it is our responsibility to ensure that the sport is as popular or more popular when leave the sport than when we got involved with it.

Yes, I have kept some press cuttings. So have my parents, but in fairness there have been so many of them that it has been impossible to keep them all. I have never run for money, but I would be less honest to say that it hasn´t been a very nice by-product of what I have been able to do on the world stage for several years. And it is nice to secure some sort of financial security from your own talents in a way that a surgeon or musician or whoever is able to do. I certainly know that my racing program has never been built around how much I could earn on the track. It has always been built around what is the best route to get me through a major championship. My message for the youth is that every athlete has a responsibility, whether they like it or not, to nurture the well-being of the sport. If they see something that is wrong or morally unacceptable, it is their obligation to make it public and make their views heard.... Not to sit back and say, well O.K., I am not going to do that, it doesn´t affect me, therefore I want to forget about it. This is a sport that we all have a part in, whether we are fun runners or competitive Olympians.

The best thing in running? There are many things I love about running. I love competition and some forms of training. I enjoy the social side, of being a member of this country´s best athletic club. I enjoy the friendships that I have developed through athletics all around the world whether it is with Mike Boit or Kip Keino in Kenya or athletes in the United States... The coaches and the people involved in the sport, but also people whom I have met through my travels that have nothing to do with athletics at all.

Cova Alberto

born 1 Dec 1958 Inverico, Como, Italy.
One of the most successful 10 000 metres runners ever: Olympic Champion 1984, World Champion 1983, European Champion 1982. A big-meet racer, well known for his lightning-fast last-lap acceleration.
800m 1.53,2, 1500m 3.40,6, 3000m 7.46.40, 3000m steeplechase 8.37,2, 5000m 13.10.06, 10 000m 27.37.59.

"Through running, I have been able to express myself"

I competed six times in the World cross country championships: 1980, 1981, 1982, 1983, 1984 and 1986. Yet I never prepared for those races in the best possible way. For me, the World cross country always was just a very good training run for the summer season. Of course, even in cross country races I was trying as hard as I could in spite of the fact that I was not feeling in top condition. Times have changed. In the early 1980´s the best 10 000 metres runners - Kunze, Schildhauer, Vainio, myself - had a good finishing kick. Those days, Carlos Lopes was the only one able to take it out hard for the whole of the race. In Athens, Helsinki and

Los Angeles the medals were fought until the very end by several runners. It is not so any more. There are people like Antibo, the Kenyans etc., who want to make it clear long before the last lap. Different athletes have different abilities. 10 000 metres races have become faster and more monotonous than before. I think it is difficult to compare runners from different eras. It is easy for me to understand the athletes from my own decade, because I was racing with them. I feel good about having been in the great races myself and now being able to watch them as a spectator. It is most essential for young runners to learn training in the correct way and to learn to know oneself.

After choosing his/her event and deciding to start serious training, an athlete must have a firm belief in his/her talent and ability. It is a fact that you can be a top athlete for just a certain part of your lifetime. That is why you should take it seriously and do all your best to find your limits. Running at the world class level has been a fantastic time for me.

For me, the best thing in running is that I have been able to be in this sport and measure myself against the best in the world. Through running, I have been able to express myself. Many times I found a solution to a problem which had been bothering me while I was having a nice and easy run in the forest, by myself, with the crisp air fondling my face. It is great to be able to listen to one´s body. Running teaches you to know your body and soul. Self-confidence is something absolutely essential for an athlete, especially in an individual sport like distance running. Without deep self-confidence, without inner strength, without connection to your own mind, it is most difficult to become a top athlete in this kind of extremely strenuous sport.

In my case, when I started to lose the connection between the mind and the body, I soon started to have motivational problems. I even went to a doctor to see what was wrong. After realizing I had no will any more to do what I had been enjoying so much during the years, I decided to retire from running. I don´t think it is a good thing to do something that you are not enjoying. I had lost my motivation due to the fact that my results were not improving any more. There was a danger that running might have become a burden to me. I stopped running practically overnight, very soon after realizing the enjoyment had gone. I was told I retired too abruptly, but I do not agree. I think I made a right decision in the right moment, and decided to start another chapter in my life.

CRAM Steve

born 14 Oct 1960 Gateshead, England.
1500 metres World Champion 1983, European Champion 1982 and 1986, Olympic silver medallist 1984. Ran three World Records in 1985 (1500 and 2000 metres, one mile). Member of 4x800m World Record relay team in 1982. Ran a 4-minute mile at age 17. Cram´s times still are absolutely world class a decade after his retirement from racing.
400m 49,1, 600m 1.16.79, 800m 1.42.88, 1000m 2.12.88, 1500m 3.29.67, one mile 3.46.32, 2000m 4.51.39, 3000m 7.43,1, 5000m 13.48,0.

"...doing it with total commitment"

In winter I generally plan about 8-10 weeks ahead, but in summer I work in 3-4 week cycles. Race plans sometimes change during the track season, and therefore training plans have to change accordingly. I like to think I am reasonably flexible as to my schedules. I think it is important to be able to react within your training programme to changes in form, injuries or racing plans. I never have any motivational problems. Obviously I don´t enjoy every training session, but generally speaking - yes! I try not to look too far ahead, but rather concentrate on what I am doing presently. The prospect of a particularly hard session is something to look forward to. I do not keep a training diary. If I did, I cannot see the point in cheating yourself by writing down something that you haven´t actually done. Yes, I always know why I am doing a particular training session. To miss a session occasionally is no great problem and you cannot make up for it in later sessions anyway. I have often made various errors in my training.

Usually they have concerned training with an injury when I should have rested or done something less strenuous. My advice to young runners: patience is a virtue. Training takes a long time to manifest itself in race performances. An athlete also needs to be able to develop their training over a long period of time.

"Look upon setbacks positively"

I have had many setbacks in my career, predominantly injuries. I have learned that any athlete training hard is bound to get injured at some stage! However, when you are injured, do not think of it as a major setback. Look upon it positively, i.e. the rest will help rejuvenate you physically and mentally. As to unexpected defeats, I take them quite badly. I like to think I am capable of honest analysis, but I try not to dwell too long on the negative aspects of any performance. Facing the truth however is the only way of making sure it doesn´t happen again.

Immediately prior to a race it is important to be detached from your main rivals. You must view them as hostile to your own ambitions in the race. There is plenty of time for friendliness afterwards. Be respectful of people you defeat and they will return the feeling when they turn the tables on you. Unnecessary aggression towards a competitor can cloud your judgement and affect your performance.

"Application to the job"

Confidence in your own ability is of paramount importance. If you don´t believe you can win, nobody else will! Good performances in training help you to gain confidence. Analysis of your competitors´ weaknesses coupled with your own strengths helps to create a feeling of superiority. To be able to win something big you have to have great self-belief. Motivation. Application to the job. That means doing the right thing at the right time and doing it with total commitment! You must want to win. Badly! I tend to think you are born with a natural competitive adge, however it is possible to refine and cultivate it as an athlete develops. For instance, a promising 13-14 year old may not be as strong or as well trained as his rivals and therefore not expected to win. However as he develops physically, his will to win becomes more important, and once he is on equal terms physically, his competitiveness will become the deciding factor. I have never dropped out of a race because I am running badly. It is a bad habit which will only get worse!

However I have certainly felt like pulling out before some events when I have been unsure about my state of preparation. Usually your physical state of fitness will determine your prospects of winning or losing. On other occasions, though, your mental state will determine the result.

Mental rehearsal is an important technique in preparing for a race, an essential factor if you are to perform to an optimum level. No athlete can win every race. Therefore defeat has to be taken philosophically. You don´t have to like it, but any feelings of regret, inadequacy or aggression have to be channelled into future victories. A cheat in sport is a cheat in life. Even if you are never caught, how can you sleep soundly at night when all your achievements are a lie. No, I don´t need publicity, however it is pointless wasting energy always trying to avoid it. I view it as a necessary consequence of success.

I think it is mainly negative because most people only take notice of bad publicity. I very rarely watch videos of my races, good or bad. However the occasional glimpse on TV etc. of a particularly bad race usually causes some discomfort.

Whatever there is being written about me in the papers - good or bad - nearly all of it is untrue, but I don´t take it hard. Yes, I have noticed some people being envious, but that is a natural human emotion. It doesn´t bother me; I get anvious of others at times. It has never caused any real problems. Money is a difficult factor to incorporate into the formula. We all require it, and receiving it for something I enjoy is a very fortunate situation to be in. However once it becomes a motivational factor, then I believe any chances of continued long term success are seriously curtailed.

Any young runner´s reasons for competing must be pure and simple. Winning, enjoyment, fitness, friendship, participation. Anyone setting out to use it as a career is foolish. Through hard work and dedication a career is indeed possible, but athletics has a lot more to offer than that. At the end of the day you get out of it what you are prepared to put into it. Strive to become the best you can, but do it with enjoyment and patience. The best thing in running for me, apart from a general feeling of fitness and freedom, is the exhilaration of unexpected victory!

El QUERROUJ
Hicham

born 14 Sep 1974 Berkane, Morocco.
Successor of Noureddine Morceli as the Middle Distance King and the fastest 1500m runner ever, El Guerrouj ran a World Record of 3.26.00 in Rome in July 1998. World Champion 1997 and 1999, World silver medallist 1995, World indoor champion 1995, 1997 and 2001 (3000m). Fell in the 1996 Olympic final with 400m to go, surprisingly beaten to 2nd place by Noah Ngeny in the 2000 Olympic final. Junior World Championship 5000m bronze medallist 1992, member of winning Moroccan World Road Relay Championship team 1994.
800m 1.47.18, 1000m 2.16.85, 1500m 3.26.00 (World Record 1998), one mile 3.43.13 (World Record 1999), 2000m 4.44.79 (World Record 1999), 3000m 7.23.09, 5000m 13.46.79. Indoor World Record holder at 1500m (3.31.18) and one mile (3.48.45).

"By running, I am able to express myself without talking"

I am quite flexible in my training. The only motivational problems arise when I am not in good shape. Thanks to the encouragement from my friends and relatives, I have been able to get over difficult moments.

Sometimes I find it hard to start another strenuous training period of several months. However, when you are able to see where you are aiming at, and start training with purpose, it all suddenly feels much easier. Every athlete has to make sacrifices. I and my coach are not planning anything haphazardly; we always have deep discussions on various matters. Thanks to him, I always know why I am doing this or that training session. I find it very, very important that an athlete has a high respect for his coach. Sometimes I may miss a training session. Whenever that happens, we move the training schedule forward to get everything in. As a junior, I had a muscle injury that took a long time to recover from. No athlete can avoid injuries completely. Young athletes must take good care of their injuries. If they don´t, they may never get rid of these problems. So far I haven´t had surprising defeats, but I don´t think they will worry me whenever they may happen. You must never forget that there is only one winner, but thousands of also-rans in the sport. The best way to get over a defeat is to learn to deal with success as well. My self-confidence comes from the people I am living with. They are there to help and encourage you, to evaluate your performances, to tell you how you might become even better.Cheating in sports? I don´t know what it means. This question should be asked to those people who are suspected of cheating. There cannot be top-class sport without publicity. There is no doubt that publicity is a positive thing.

I always like to watch my races in video

The meaning of money? Is there any person who can truthfully say that money is not important? My message for the youth: I think I am still a member of the young generation myself, but there are even younger people than me, who will be even faster! For me, the best thing in running is that it gives me a chance to express myself without talking.

ELLIOTT Herb

born 15 Feb 1938 Subiaco, Perth, Australia.
Destroyed his opposition in the 1500m Olympic final in Rome 1960, winning the gold medal by 20 metres in a World Record time of 3.35,6. Two other World Records: 1500m 3.36,0, one mile 3.54,5 (both in 1958). Lost just one race in the 1500m or one mile during his career (at 14 years of age). Coached by legendary Percy Cerutty, whose training methods - including the famous sand hills at Portsea - are etched into running mythology.
440 yards 50,8, 880 yards 1.47,3, 1000m 2.19,1, 1500m 3.35,6, one mile 3.54,5, 3000m 8.09,5, 5000m 14.09,9.

"Training is for racing"

I did not enjoy my training as it was almost always painful. However, there was a sense of satisfaction and achievement at the end of a training session. There were many occasions where I didn´t feel like training, but I always did, and was never prepared to compromise on that matter. Many months of strenuous training ahead used to excite me, but the single very hard training session of today would often fill me with dread. However, I always did it. I never did miss a training session.

My advice for young athletes: it must be realized that training is training for racing. You should therefore practice in training what you wish to achieve in the race. In the case of a 1500 metres runner, this means the intensity and the ability to continue to run harder and faster when your body is tiring. These are the things that you have to practice in training, as well as visualising the competitor trying to pass at the time when you are tiredest and fighting them off. I had one or two minor setbacks in my career.

They were very frustrating, but I don´t have any particular advice about this. As to defeats, I don´t have any sensible advice about getting over them, either, since I never was beaten in an important race. For me, every training session was a mental preparation for winning. All the work for winning a race was really done in training. The race was just the inevitable goal for all the work done. I had very mixed feelings about publicity. There were parts of it which I enjoyed and there were parts of it which were irritating. I had a habit of never reading anything about myself during the racing season, as such comment was distracting.

ERENG Paul

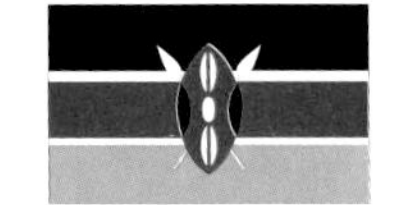

born 22 Feb 1967 Trans-Nzoia, Kitala, Kenya. Member of Turkana tribe.
A former 400 metres runner, Ereng made a sensational breakthrough in the 800 m during the 1988 season, winning the Olympic gold medal in Soul. World indoor champion 1989 (world record 1:44.84) and 1991. Ereng´s last 200m lap at the 1989 World indoors certainly as one of the most amazing sights in the history of 800m running.
400m 45,6, 800m 1:43.16, 1000m 2:17.37.

At school we had various kinds of competitions, in which we were rewarded with points. We played soccer, volleyball, took part in running races. At 14, I ran 400 metres in 59,3 seconds. I was very happy with my performance. A friend got me into a cross country race as well, but I was feeling so tired I had to slow down to a walk. Nevertheless, I was encouraged to go on with some training, and the following year I improved my 400 metres time to 56 seconds.

In Kenya, after you have turned 16, you are not called a junior any more

At 16 years of age, I ran 52,5. I was a spectator at the Kenyan Championships in 1983, and returned home even more excited about running. In that meeting the Kenyan team for the first IAAF World Championships in Helsinki was selected. I was most impressed by 400 metres runner David Kitur. He also was still at school, yet he was very big and strong. But I also saw many tall and thin runners in that meeting, which made me think: "Hey, I am tall and thin too, perhaps I can do some good racing, too."

The Olympic year of 1984 made me fall in love with athletics and running, becoming a turning point in my career. At 17, I went to Nairobi to see the Kenyan Olympic trials and then watched the Olympics in TV. Women´s 400 metres was won in a time of less than 49 seconds, and Ruth Waithera of Kenya finished 8th in 51.56. For me, it was mind-boggling since my personal best at the time was 50 seconds. Edwin Koech and his 800 metres rivals also seemed supermen to me. Cruz, especially, was fantastic...

So were the 400 metres runners. I was very impressed with the Olympic victory ceremonies. The medalists were standing in attention, listening to the winner´s national anthem. It felt like the victor on the highest podium was speaking to the whole world. It was then that I made up my mind to win in the Olympic Games. Four years later I did it, but not in the 400 metres.

In a way, the Los Angeles Olympics were the beginning of my athletics career. I resolved to represent Kenya in the 400 metres race at the 1988 Olympics. However, when I was studying in the United States, my coach made me an 800 metres runner. At first I thought it was a mistake... In my view, moving to a longer distance would take much more time.

"I was ready for 2:10 in the 1000 metres!"

In the summer of 1988 I was beaten by Nixon Kiprotich in all our races, but I wasn´t worried. I knew the reason for my defeats. In my first race of the European season I ran 1:44 in Sweden on June 24th. Then, during a flight to Lausanne, I got a flu. I was coughing, and I couldn´t breath properly. In my race in Lausanne I was feeling very tired. After that I was racing every three days and wasn´t able to rest enough. I was chronically tired. I said to myself, "After resting for two weeks I will beat these guys even if they don´t believe it now." With the Olympics drawing near, I was doing some speed training in Nairobi. Mike Kosgei was watching me train. He said, "Lots of people will be greatly surprised." Nevertheless, I had some trouble in the trial race in Nairobi.

At an altitude of 1700 metres I went through 400 in 49 seconds, passing 600 in 1:14.74 and 700 metres in 1.27. At that point I was feeling completely spent, but I managed to scrape to the finish line as a winner in 1.45. Later, thinking about the race I realized it was crazy to start so fast. "With a more realistic first lap I can do a very fast time. Running 1:42 will be easy for me."

"Take care of the winner not being an American!"

In Seoul my first round time was 1:46.14, which was unbelievable to me. I felt as if I could have easily gone 4 seconds faster. Having heard my time I thought it must be a mistake. By continuing 200 metres I certainly would have been able to run 1000 metres in 2:10! I felt like I had been just jogging.

I was very happy and believed I would run as easily the next day. However, in my second round race two runners fell over, and I was pushed badly enough to almost be tripped down as well. Cruz left the rest of us far behind. I tried to catch him, then gave up and let him go. My time now was 1:46.38, yet I was feeling tired. I kept telling myself that was not significant at this point.

Then, in the semifinals I faced a very tough opposition. There were great runners, Cruz, Peter Elliott, if I remember right, a Russian who had run well in Oslo, and Niang of Senegal, who had beaten Nixon (Kiprotich) earlier. I still had never beaten Nixon, which many people thought meant I had no chance among the first four in the semifinal. In fact, my personal best was slower than any of these four... I think my time was only about sixth fastest.

Mike told me to run as well as I could. "Nixon has an easy task, but you have to put everything into it. You must have 100% luck to succeed tomorrow!" Well, it happened that the rest in the field were tired. I was looking around in the straight, seeing nobody. I was just coasting in, yet my time was 1.44,5! At last, it was the day of the final. Walking to the stadium, Auoita said to me: "Take care of the winner not being from America or South America. Bring the gold to Africa!" For me it was a mystery why Aouita was

hoping I would win. I guess he had experience and he had seen what I was capable of. Well, I won so easily I thought it was no faster than 1:46...
A year later I realized I was in better shape in 1988, even if I remained unbeaten in all my races in 1989.

"Young people must learn to enjoy sports without pressure"

Young runners must have goals, but they have to take care of not aiming at them too stressfully. You must train hard without pressure. Somehow, even if you are training hard, you have to feel easy, enjoying what you are doing. At the time of travelling to the Olympic Games I had no idea of how fast I must run. Nowadays, every time I am racing, people keep asking me how fast I am going to run tomorrow. I don´t know. Maybe fast, maybe slow. In the Olympics no one asked me anything, and I didn´t know what kind of times I would run. I did 1:43, which is a big improvement from 1:45.

If I had been required to run faster, I would have done so. At the start of the competition I believed someone would run 1.37. I really mean that, because I thought the first lap would be run in 47 seconds and the second one in 50. As to myself, I thought I would be able to run both laps in 50 seconds, which means a time of 1:40. I would have been very happy with that even if I would not have won. I ran the Olympic final without pressure.

That is the way it should be. Your result is what it is, so why to be nervous about it? Thus, my message to young athletes is that they should be in sports without any pressure, just enjoying everything they are doing.

Thinking too scientifically, or aiming too strictly at world record times, for instance, has the drawback that you put limits on yourself. You lock your mind. I don´t like to be too scientific, because if you are, you tend to think too much. The way to attack barriers is to free one´s mind... You have to forget about scientific data and world record numbers. A bad performance is like a bad dream. It will come eventually; it cannot be avoided. We are human beings. If you desperately try to avoid being beaten, this attitude results in harmful pressures. It is much better to stay away from this kind of thinking. There will always be another race. Remember, this is called sports. Racing is a play. You won today, I will win tomorrow. Those who don´t understand this, don´t understand the essence of sports either. There are no supermen nor semigods in sports. We are all human. There is a certain cycle in life. An athlete who wins all the time is not able to enjoy his wins.

Self-confidence is everything. It makes an athlete... People are envious even in Kenya. One reason for envy is money. However, we shouldn´t be envious of each other even if someone succeeds better that his friends, or someone is faster on running tracks than his friends... In a way, there is good envy and bad envy. Bad envy causes destruction. Good envy gives an athlete more motivation to train harder than before.

Nowadays, meaning of money is getting bigger. We don´t survive without money. An athlete must have a coach, the equipment, the resources to be taken care of in case of injury or illness. Money makes things easier. When you are poor, you have to fight about everything. Money is good, because it brings security in your life. Without money you are lost. I tell you an example: I had friend, a high jumper. He had an accident; he died because he couldn´t get a tetanus injection quickly enough due to lack of money.

"...but at the same time something intensely enjoyable and happy"

The best thing in running is the competition, the challenge, through which one gets more self-confidence for everything in life. When you think you will perhaps be able to run a world record some day... It becomes almost a kind of religion. When you believe in something you don´t know exactly, it requires mental balance. Running gives more faith to everything a man or woman is doing. If you are a teacher or otherwise helping other people, by running you will be able to preserve your faith. "I can do this: I know I can help these people away from this misery. Running is full of pain, but at the same time - and most of all - it is something intensely enjoyable and happy. We know that paradise, heaven, cannot be reached without pain.

Through running you can acquire strength, endurance and faith in order to reach your goals. This process of aiming at goals - and eventually reaching them - is the best thing in running.

FOSTER Brendan

born 12 Jan 1948 Hebburn, County Durham, England.
One of the most versatile distance runners in the world in the 1970´s: 5000m European Champion 1974, 10 000m Olympic bronze medallist 1976, 1500m European Championships bronze medallist 1971. Ran World Records at 2 miles in 1973 and 3000m in 1974.
800m 1.51,1, 1500m 3.37,6, one mile 3.55,9, 3000m 7.35,2, 2 miles 8.13,7, 5000m 13.14,6, 10 000m 27.30,3, marathon 2.15.49.

"I felt excited about the future"

I started training seriously at the age of 17 thanks to the fact that I began to enjoy running and racing more than playing soccer. I soon noticed that I was better at running than at anything else.

I had two idols those days: Peter Snell and Harold Lloyd. My first aim was to become the best runner of my club Gateshead Harriers, of which I later became President. I had my mother and father supporting me really well in my sport as well as I had my friends. I don´t think I ever considered packing up my running even if, obviously, on many occasions training was very difficult and boring, but you always overcome this because of the ambitions in the mind.

I did not have any particular views about rivals in my first races since most of the lads were fellow members of my athletic club. In the early days I was not too nervous about the races, but in later years like in the Olympics I obviously was very nervous but always able to control my nerves. My first successes came after about two years of training and racing. The first time I ever ran in the Youth´s National Cross Country I finished 10th and realised I was one of the best in the country in my age group. That was when I decided to get very serious about my running. This race was given some coverage in the papers, and I preserved the press cuttings of it afterwards.

Obviously I was very excited about my success and thought I could be even more successful. With my coach, I began to plan my training and racing programme. I had two and a half years at University when my running did not go very well. For some reason, however, I kept training because at the end I always thought it would be worthwhile but to cope with it I began to do other things as well. The biggest disappointmens in my career were losing some of the races I thought I could win. It was difficult to get over these things. What I learned was to try not to let it happen again.

In 1970 I reached international level, winning a 1500m bronze medal at the Commonwealth Games in my breakthrough race. My initial performance was fairly successful, and I felt excited about the future, but I certainly did not consider myself a "perfect athlete" by then. It took three more years of international competition until in 1973 I finally broke a World Record.It was a big moment for me meeting some of the great international distance runners for the first time and discussing with them: Ron Clarke, Ian Stewart, Gaston Roelants...

As to my training, in my top years we were planning my schedule for six months to one year ahead at a time, but there was a detailed programme only for about six weeks. I was able to follow the plans fairly well. I was concentrating on what I was doing that day, never thinking about the many months of hard work waiting for me. Sometimes I was feeling nervous about a single important and hard training session. Yes, I must admit I sometimes had motivational problems and periods when I did not enjoy my training. I always was unable to avoid errors in my training. What I learned was that if a training session occasionally was missed, there was no use trying to compensate for it later.

"One has to face the facts"

My simple advice for young distance runners is that your training must always be progressive, but you have to do it gradually. Never take too big bites too quickly. I was very lucky in the respect that I rarely had setbacks through illness or injury. As to surprising defeats, I think an honest analysis is the only way you can possibly deal with them. It is not easy but one has to face the facts. The next victory will come unless a serious deep down analysis of the defeat has occurred. Self-examination of racing performance and training schedule is totally essential, even for young runners, when coping with bad performances.

My attitude towards main rivals was always nervous anticipation before the race and friendliness afterwards. Self-confidence obviously mainly comes from

winning, but also convincing yourself and talking to yourself of the manner of your victories and how you will win. To become a great runner, you must have the right mental approach to major events. It is absolutely essential to prepare oneself mentally for winning. Thoughts of losing just should not be entered in your mind until after the event. Never in my career had I an urge of giving up during the race.

My view on self-confidence is that some of it is born and some of it comes collectively through a growing confidence in performance due to increasing success. As to all kind of cheating, I want to say please, keep it out of our sport. I have always managed very well with publicity. For me it is mainly a positive thing even if I don´t read everything that has been written about me, and do not collect press cuttings. What I can say about money is that a major problem exists when the prime motivation for running and racing is a financial one. It is essential that it needs to be performance orientated, rather than financially.

To train hard and consistently, enjoying your racing, and striving to improve one´s personal best times and to win great victories is the best thing about running.

GÄRDERUD Anders

born 28 Aug 1946 Stockholm, Sweden.
A precocious talent, Gärderud had many ups and downs for more than a decade before crowning his long career with an Olympic Gold Medal at 3000 metres steeplechase in Montreal 1976 with a World Record time of 8.08.02, which still remains a Swedish record almost a quarter of a century later. He already had run three steeplechase World Records in 1972 and 1975.
400m (relay leg) 47,8, 800m 1.47,2, 1500m 3.36,7, one mile 3.54,5, 3000m 7.47,8, 3000m steeplechase 8.08.02, 5000m 13.17,6, 10 000m 28.59,2, 1500m steeplechase 4.00,6 (World Junior record in 1965, never broken since).

"I had several conflicts between running and orienteering"

I started serious training at age 19 for the simple reason that I had noticed I had talent for the sport. I could have become a top class orienteerer as well. All my best sporting friends those days were into orienteering. I enjoyed orienteering myself and was successful in it as a junior. Yes, I had some idols, but just local ones. My first training runs were done with friends in my home town Lidingö, near Stockholm. There was a strong tradition of orienteering and distance running in the late 1950´s. I was encouraged by both of my parents, who had been competing in these sports themselves. I had several conflicts between running and orienteering during my career, sometimes to the extent that I seriously considered leaving running. However, I never did so. I have always had a longing for physical exercise, especially out in the nature.

There have been motivational problems. In spite of my early talent, training sometimes was very difficult to me. In my early career I was hoping to bring success for my club. Many times I was feeling over excited before races, nonetheless managing to keep it reasonable. It got worse later when everybody was expecting me to become another Gunder Hägg. I was not always able to control my nerves. It took a long time before I finally got hold of my self-confidence after many years of hard training. I finally became convinced that I was able to live up to peoples´ hopes.

I have always wanted to be successful in whatever I have been doing. In every race there is just one winner, but many honourable losers. However, you can be a winner and a loser at the same time, depending on what you have been aiming at. For me, sports is a question of winning and losing, but in other parts of life I see it in a quite different way. I started competing in orienteering at age 12, winning all my races. I did not start track racing until age 15. My first races are the ones I still have the best memories of. The best runners in Sweden aged 16 made the national finals after qualifying races all over the country. I knew their names from the newspapers, and now suddenly they had faces as well.

I cannot describe the excitement I felt while meeting my new friends and then racing against them. Many of them are still some of my best friends. Some of them became excellent runners and are now coaching the next generation. Some also have children on the way to the national team! I was so happy getting new friends that I decided to go on running so that I would make the various teams. I also realized I had to start training hard because no runner likes to be beaten. I was so happy of my early success that I kept some of the press cuttings. Maybe I was lucky, but I can´t remember any negative experiences from my early years in the sport. No, I had no plans of aiming to the very top at that point of my career. Being the best runner in my age group in Sweden was enough for me. I was happy to make the national team, and that was all. As to my first coach, at first we were learning from each other. Later I had a lot of respect for famous Swedish coach Gösta Olander, who taught us many things about running. From then on, I have listened to the opinions of many successful athletes and coaches. I have also had an education as a sports teacher, which - together with all other experience I had - finally made me the coach of myself.

A coach should be with his athlete as often as possible in training. That is the only way to find out the athlete´s demands. Also, a coach must make an athlete believe in himself so that he will become psychologically strong. The most difficult thing for a coach is to make an athlete understand that he has to work very hard for many years in order to be successful. An athlete must get through those hard years even when he cannot yet see the finish line. For a young athlete, being too successful in early years can be dangerous because later, when he has to deal with problems, he may think that he can be happy with what he has achieved so far, and doesn´t want to fight forward any more.

In that respect, early defeats can be helpful if you are able to work with the problems in a constructive way. You have to learn from the very start that problems are there to be solved and not to get around with.

"The problem was that I did not regard myself as a star"

As a youngster, I had no thought of being a good runner some day in the future. I was satisfied because I had not had that kind of challenges yet. Later, I already was at age 21-22 an international star in Sweden! The problem however was that I did not regard myself as one. I was not running to beat world class athletes. National victories were quite enough for me those days. I finally got the real inspiration in Helsinki during the 1971 European Championships when I saw Juha Väätäinen win the 5000 and 10 000 metres gold medals. It was only then that I realised I also could reach the top. If Juha could it, then why couldn´t I? That became a great challenge for me. I thought I was ready for the 1972 Olympic Games, but I soon noticed I had been wrong. I didn´t know yet the requirements for being a winner. At first it was a big disappointment for me, but I then started to work with my problems because I knew there were quite a lot of them. I did not consider myself a perfect athlete, but I knew I would be a winner as soon as I could get over my problems. Thinking back, I still think I did pretty well in my early career considering the background of my training at that time.

In my top years, I was planning my training for four years ahead, but also for one year, three months and one month. Generally I was able to carry out what I had been planning, perhaps thanks to the flexibility of my programme, which made it easier to follow.

"One gradually learns to listen to one´s body"

Mostly, I enjoyed the training, but there were times when I hated it. It was hard to face the hard slog of several months waiting ahead. But it had to be done. If you don´t do what is required, then you are a loser. In my view, if you are enjoying every workout, then you are a "run-for-fun" enthusiast and not a serious athlete. I think you have to force yourself out on the road every now and then if you want to cultivate your hardness. A single hard training session is no problem. It is the total amount of hard work during a long period of time that is hard to accept. You need an immense will power to manage with it. This is where you will find the difference between a winner and a loser. Everyone is capable of a very hard training session occasionally, but it is another thing to train hard regularly year after year. I can confess now that I sometimes deliberately "improved" my training workouts when writing them down in my diary. If I ran for 80 minutes, for example, I could count it as 22 kilometres - even if the truth may have been 18 kilometres - in order to achieve a certain target of training. It is easy to admit now, but those days - never! As to track training, I absolutely never falsified my times, because that wouldn´t have helped my motivation to continue in the hard way. I think one gradually learns to listen to one´s body. I know, because my body always gave signals. That comes with age and experience. You know what you have to do in training, which means you can be flexible to some extent. When your body says "yes", you train hard. When it says "no", you take it easier. If you then compare what you actually did during the past month with what you should have done, you find out that your plans and the reality actually have been about the same. The only difference is that you have not done your hardest sessions on a certain day, but on the day when your body was ready for it. One of my mistakes probably was not doing enough stretching, which resulted in stiffness, especially in my hamstrings. However, the only longer interruption in my training was in February 1973, when I had an Achilles tendon problem which took one and a half months to heal. In everyday training your body hurts in various ways. You get familiar with these signals, knowing that they are a part of every hard-training athlete´s life.

However, if you have unusual kinds of signals from any part of your body, you have to be careful. Even if they may be weak ones at the beginning, you have to be aware of them and have respect for it. Maybe that was because of some new type of training that you haven´t been accustomed to yet. It is very important to face even unpleasant facts and be realistic with them. In fact it is a must for every international calibre runner to see his situation in a realistic way. Every step on your way forward teaches you something. That means a defeat sometimes is more valuable than a victory, because you then have a problem which must be solved. If you are successful all the time, you may not see your weak sides, which you nevertheless must be confronted with sooner or later.

"You need victories to cultivate self-confidence"

As to one´s rival competitors, they should be considered as enemies before and during a race. Afterwards and in everyday life, however, they certainly are some of your best friends. I don´t think self-confidence is a born thing. I think you need victories to cultivate it. But to be able to win, you have to deal with all the problems which may be bothering you in personal relationships during the preparation for a race. I used to pay all my bills and do other necessary things as well to get rid of all negative thoughts in my mind. That way, I was able to fully concentrate on my task. Every race has a purpose. There are not-so-important races, which are part of your training schedule. In my mind, the races are the best type of training during the competitive season. Important races, however, have another kind of meaning.

It sometimes could happen that if I was not able to win a race for which I had been preparing very well, or was not able to achieve my goal, I was feeling so disappointed that I just gave up.Whenever I was defeated in an important race, my attitude was that I still had many things to learn. What you have to do is to try and see forward. A defeat is a natural obstacle in your way. Your day will come. Continue to work with your problems. Don´t be happy with a second place in a race. Every experience during your running career has a constructive meaning. Try to see it that way. Cheating in sports is something that I don´t like. I know that fair play training methods are good enough for winning in big international races. Those who cheat are just fooling themselves. Imagine living with the knowledge that your wins were achieved with cheating methods!

Publicity never was a problem for me. On the contrary, it was a positive thing because it enabled me to speak my mind and get people to listen. I don´t find it difficult at all to watch my races on video, even the bad ones. Nowadays, I am not annoyed even by bad press, although it was a different thing when I was younger. As to the money, I don´t think that anyone has won big championships inspired just by financial gain. Still, I think the really big money should be available for very top class international runners. The problem however is that many runners get too much money through not-so-good performances. That has a negative effect on such athletes´ development, because they are happy with the times they are running and don´t want to aim higher and train harder.

My advice to the youth: read everything I have written above!

Finally, the best thing in running is the feeling of freedom - in many respects. You have a chance to create great achievements without expensive equipment etc. You are alone and you are feeling free in your running.

GEBRSELASSIE Haile

born 18 April 1973 Arssi, Ethiopia.
The winner of five major 10 000m titles in a row: World champion 1993, 1995 and 1997, Olympic gold medallist 1996 and 2000. World bronze medallist 2001. 5000m World silver medallist 1993. 3000m World indoor champion 1997. World cross country bronze medallist 1994. World Junior 5000 and 10 000m champion 1992. Six outdoor world records: one at two miles, three at 5000m, two at 10000m. Three indoor world records. Improved the 5000m world record by more than 10 secs. at Zürich Weltklasse in 1995. Small runner (160 cm tall) with an astonishingly springy and fluent action.
800m 1:49.35i, 1500m 3:31.76i, 2000m 4:52.86i, 3000m 7:26.02, 2 miles 8:01.08, 5000m 12:39.36, 10000m 26:22.75.

I started running because I was inspired by my brother, who was doing marathons. He gave me the first necessary enthusiasm to train and compete. Also, it was natural for me to run because I was running to school and back every day. Ten kilometres to school, ten kilometres back home, that is twenty kilometres a day. There was no school on Sundays, but I sometimes went to visit my brother, so that was a running day also. Yes, it is true that Ethiopians usually are very fast in the end of the race, but in my case, I think my finishing kick was not made by training; it is a natural gift which I am most thankful for. At first I did not have a coach, because such experts were available only in Addis Abeba. It took three or four years before I had a coach. Nowadays, before a big meeting like World Championships, I am doing a two-month preparation. Usually I have been able to follow my plan just as I have wanted. Sometimes I have to be flexible, but most of the time I try to make it as close to the plan as possible.

Motivational problems? No, I never have any. I always run every morning. Sometimes when in Europe, I do my morning run before 6 o´clock. In Ethiopia it is cold so early in the morning, but in Europe it is easier. Sometimes I don´t do the morning run until 8 or 9 o´clock; those are the days when I sleep longer. I like to sleep (laughs).If I miss a morning session altogether for some reason, I will run in the evening. Training is very important for me. It is a must.

You cannot miss any of it. Nothing must stop the athlete from training, from following the program seriously. Otherwise the results will not be very good.

"You should never do the same mistake twice"

I don´t think I have made any bad errors in my training. Generally, I know why I am doing a specific training session. Usually I don´t train very hard, but with a big race approaching I am doing a little more speed training. I am always thinking ahead to the next competition: how important it is, what kind of tactics it may have...

If I have made a tactical mistake in a race, I later have a deep thought about it, but I don´t let it depress me. I will do my best to correct my error next time. You should never do the same mistake twice. I consider all my rivals as my friends. This is sport, not war. For example, I was punched by Josephat Machuka at the finish line in the 1992 World junior championships, but that did not cause a feud between us. The incident has been forgotten, and we are very good friends. Kenyans and Ethiopians manage well with each other. Machuka made the mistake of punching me because he very, very much wanted to win the race. Self-confidence (looks puzzled)? Oh, that is a very important thing for any athlete before a race, or at any time... One has to know oneself to be able to win a race, and even to be able to prepare well for a race. I think self-confidence is a natural thing, but it also comes from training. Without good training there will be no victories. The most important thing for an athlete is to do the training. The will to train and the will to win have to come from inside a person. It is very difficult to push another person to do the training. The will must come from within oneself.

"I always feel sorry when I hear someone has been using doping"

Doping is very bad for sports. I always feel sorry when I hear someone has been using doping. By taking advantage of illegal means an athlete is hurting himself and the sport. Even if the physical damage may go away, you will never get rid of the mental one. Publicity... If it is good, then of course I like it, but if it is bad, then I don´t. No one likes to hear bad things about oneself. For example, there were many things written about Tanui and me after the 10 000m race in Stuttgart World Championships in 1993. I know many journalists, and O.K., they can write what they want, but the reality is what happened at the stadium. Everybody could see it on television. Most of the journalists wrote how Tanui saw it. They just asked Tanui, but everybody could see that I did not drop his shoe.

Everybody in the world could see that. I was just very sorry. When starting my career I already knew I would be in the limelight one day. I feel happy about people admiring me. It also encourages me to do even better in the future. I have achieved a lot during my career, in fact I have reached most of my goals, but I still have some dreams left. I will not be able to make a full summary until I have reached all my goals. The meaning of money for me? Dollars (laughs)? Oh yes. It is important for an athlete, because running takes so much energy, and you must get paid for it. But when I started running, I did not think about money. I was thinking only about having good results some day. If money comes, that is O.K., but if it doesn´t, that is O.K., too. For me, having a good name has always been more important than having money. No one has been envious about me in Ethiopia. People at home still like me. They are happy about my results. They think my victories are not just for me, they are for the whole of my country. A young athlete should have a clear goal to aim at. You must have that goal before you start training. If you commence training without any deeper thought, without defining your goal, then you will probably meet difficulties. Moreover, it is important to proceed gradually, step by step.

You will always have setbacks both in training and in competition - for instance stress fractures and other injuries. These are difficult things because you cannot foresee them. Everybody has injuries, no matter if you are a top athlete or just an ordinary competitor. You must try and find means to prevent injuries... Having a rest, changing training methods, or cutting down the number of races. Also, it is useful to have some advance knowledge of what the race and track will be like. You should plan your racing tactics well in advance. After racing on a hard surface, I would suggest training only on grass for some time. On a starting line, a young runner usually has two thoughts in his mind - that of winning, and of losing. The hope of winning, of course, is the bigger one. When facing a defeat, some athletes lose their composure and become desperate. They should be able to forget the defeat as soon as possible and aim forward to next races, and to winning them.

Victory and defeat are everyday things in the sports world. You cannot win every time, but no matter if you win or lose, the main thing is that you learn something. My message for youth: Running and racing require a lot from an athlete. It is impossible to win big races without deep personal courage and hard effort. The most important goal for a runner, of course, is to become a champion. Having an aim like that makes it easier to preserve one´s inspiration through the years. For me, the best thing in running is the competition, the feeling of winning. But I also like training. I think most athletes like all of these things. I agree that it is very important to have a love for running, because athletics is a very difficult thing and it takes a lot of time to succeed.

GRAY Johnny

born 19 Jun 1960 Los Angeles.
One of the most legendary figures in the history of 800m running, Johnny Gray was still churning out times around 1.45 in 1999 at age 39 after a career spanning 20 years. The only two-lap man to have reached four Olympic finals: 7th 1984, 5th 1988, bronze 1992, 7th 1996. Six-time U.S.A. champion, Pan-American champion in 1987 and 1999. Ran a sub-1.45 time for 14 consecutive seasons. Gray´s trademark always was to lead the first lap very fast. - In early 2001, Gray was running sub-1.50 800´s indoors at age 40.
400m 46,3 (1983), 600m 1.12.81 (world best in 1986), 800m 1.42.60 (1985), 1000m 2.17.27 (1984), 1500m 3.42.43 (1990). World indoor 1000y best 2.04.39 (1986).

"Set goals and take action"

I kind of stumbled into running. I was a baseball and football player in a California high school. My older brother was a runner, and local coach Merle McGhee noticed me watching by the track. "You want to run, too?" "Sure", I said, and that was it. That was in 1977, when I was 17 years old. I am still coached by Merle McGhee. My coach is a very quiet man, but the good thing about him is that when he speaks, he doesn´t lie! So, when he tells me I am in good shape, that means I am. If he tells me I can do a certain time, then I can. He doesn´t promise me false hopes. That gives me the motivation. One thing you have to remember is "no pain, no gain".

Discipline, for me, is the most important thing for anything you do in life. Any time you have to confront some negative things, you have to try and find something positive in them. Sometimes these things happen for a reason. The good Lord tries to tell me something. I have been running for two decades, and I never have won a gold medal at World Championships or Olympic Games. Yet, I am the most prolific half-miler ever to step on this earth.

Maybe I had a choice: either I had a short career, and a gold medal, or a long career, be respected, be healthy, and accomplish something that no man ever has done before. This latter choice means much more to me, because I know many people who are Olympic champions, and yet they are miserable. I have never won a gold medal, but I know I am a gold medal individual. I am a great motivator. Any time I am in the race, I am motivating the youngsters to run fast. They like me. Most of my competitors like me. As to defeat in a race, there is no such thing as a failure. It depends on how you can proceed a defeat. A defeat is a learning process.

Thomas Edison tried to invent light. 9999 times he failed. "For 10 000 times I am trying to figure out how not to make light", he said. So, he was learning all the time. He did not give up. The same applies to racing. Self-confidence means you go to the track and do what you, as an individual, are capable of doing. Any time you do what you are capable of doing, you are victorious, no matter if you won or finished somewhere else. If you did your best, you were successful even if you didn´t win. Self-confidence also means that you don´t need to belong to the majority.

You can have your own opinions and be part of the minority, if you believe in yourself. I am 38 years old now (in 1998), and I still give a good fight to the youngsters, and I love it. As long as I am doing my best, I am victorious, no matter if it is 10th place. In the 1996 Olympic final I was seventh, but I did my best every step of the way, so I was not a loser. After the race, the gold and silver medallists were thanking me for the effort I put into the race. I have also been motivating a lot of young Kenyan athletes to run fast 800 metres races. My message for the youth: You can do anything in life that you want. Set goals for yourself and take action. If we have a plan, we can be successful. The best thing in running? I don´t want to pinpoint to any specific thing. I really have to think about that one (smiles). When I started running, the best thing was bettering yourself, succeeding. Setting yourself goals.

HÄGG Gunder

born 31.12.1918 Sörbygden, Jämtland, Sweden.
A fantastic middle distance runner in the early 1940´s, Hägg ran 16 World Records at distances between 1500 and 5000 metres, 10 of which came in 1942. Due to World War II, two editions of the Olympic Games were cancelled, which meant Hägg was unable to win the highest honour of an athlete. One of the first runners to train with the famous natural "fartlek" system, Hägg also was the first man to break 14 mins. for 5000 metres; his time of 13.58,2 remained unbeaten for 12 years. In 1945 his career, together with that of his great rival Arne Andersson, was prematurely cut off because of accusations of professionalism. They were never allowed to race again.
800m 1.52,8, 1500m 3.43,0, one mile 4.01,3, 2000m 5.11,8, 3000m 8.01,2, 3000m steeplechase 9.28,4, 2 miles 8.42,8, 3 miles 13.32,4, 5000m 13.58,2.

"My goal was to astonish the athletics world"

I started serious training at age 20 or thereabouts. I was called into Military Service, and there was really nothing else to do. There were no special facilities for any indoor sport, so I thought running would be the only obvious choice for me. I had two idols - the great Paavo Nurmi of Finland, and Olympic medallist Henry Jonsson (Kälarne) from Sweden. I had a strong belief in my abilities. As soon as I started training, my goal was to astonish the athletics world. I was training so hard that I really had just two ways to go: to break down, or run faster than anyone else before. I always did my training in solitude. I had no objections whatsoever from my parents and family; my friends really did not know about my running ambition in the early part of my career. At first, I had no idea of how long it would take to reach the world class level. There was a period when I was feeling so disappointed that I almost gave up, and did not run more than 20 to 25 minutes each time. In my first race I was a complete beginner; I did not know anything about my rivals. I was very nervous before the start, because I was afraid of losing. I never really got rid of that fear of losing. However, with success gradually coming it made me feel much better even if my friends still did not know what I was doing. I think my breakthrough race was a 2000 metres competition in which one of my rivals was Gunnar Höckert, the Finnish 5000 metres Olympic Champion. I never had a coach, but there were many people who thought they were coaching me. In my view, a coach can succeed only if he knows a lot of psychology, of how to handle with people. I usually planned my training some eight months ahead. Generally I was able to follow my plan 100%, even if I had some setbacks, the worst of them in 1939 when I had a lung inflammation. I had no motivational problems even if I did not really enjoy my training. When writing down the training sessions in my diary, I was always honest, not exaggerating times or distances. I always knew why I was doing a training session, and I don´t think I ever made any fatal errors. My simple advice for young middle distance runners (up to 5000 metres): you have to train on shorter than racing distances, but at racing speeds or thereabouts.

Self-confidence is a most important thing for any runner. I never felt an urge to drop out of a race. Whenever I ran badly, I became even more determined and improved my training for the next race. Any kind of cheating - drugs etc. - in sport is, in my view, such a bad thing it should almost be penalised by the death sentence. Things like that ruin the sport. I never sought publicity, but on the other hand it is something that cannot be avoided. I found it a positive thing. I never read anything written about me, except for the headlines. Neither did I collect any clippings. I regard envy as a very bad sickness, and I know people have been envious about my achievements, especially after my running career. Money is a necessary thing even for an athlete, but all I can say is that money never was the decisive reason for my running. I want to tell young athletes that there are more ways than just one to the top. Most of all, you have to avoid long, monotonous running. Running short and fast gives you by far the best results.

HISSOU Salah

born 16 Jan 1972 Kasba Tadla, Morocco.
Ex-World Record Holder at 10000m (26.38.08 in 1996) and 20K road (58.20 in 1994). 5000m World Champion 1999, 10 000m bronze medallist in the 1996 Olympic Games and 1997 World Championships. World Cross Country silver medallist 1996 and 1997, bronze medallist 1995. Like many other Moroccans, reached world-class level very quickly.
1500m 3.33.95, mile 3.52.54, 2000m 5.00.95, 3000m 7.28.93, 5000m 12.50.80, 10 000m 26.38.08, half marathon 1.02.20.

"Sometimes I feel quite tired of running"

Training schedules are not Koran; they have been made by man. It is natural that sometimes you follow your training programmes, and sometimes you don´t. Motivational problems are not unknown to me. I have choosen my sport, which means I have to do the required work. I can freely admit that sometimes I feel quite tired of running, but luckily I am greatly motivated by my family who are backing me in every way. I am not scared by the hard months of training looming ahead. However, I am worried about the years in my life that are passing so quickly. I am not a machine to be programmed. My coach explains to me why I am training the way I am, and I think about it deeply so that I will

understand everything. If I miss an important training session for any reason, I try to do it later as soon as possible. This means that my training schedule has to be moved forward by a day or so. It is absolutely essential that you train with dedication and conviction. You must have an unyielding belief in what you are doing.

Thank God, I haven´t had any major setbacks during my career so far

The rule of the game is that sometimes you win and sometimes you are beaten. This is something that you have to accept. Being defeated may be a hard blow for your ego, but you must put it into right proportion. Your day will eventually come. Winning feels even better when you have been beaten before. Self-confidence is something that you will acquire with time and success. Each time you do well, your self-confidence will improve. On the other hand, defeats may eat your self-confidence away. Your family and friends have a very important role in cultivating your self-confidence.

"I have been motivated by difficult moments"

So far, I have never felt an urge to give up my sport, but who knows if I will experience something like that later. Rather, I have been motivated by difficult moments. I have never cheated in my career, and I don´t want even to think about such things. I am trying to accept publicity, but I am not good in performing in public. I certainly admit that publicity nowadays is an essential part of an athlete´s life. Perhaps I can evaluate this side of my sport sometimes later. Thanks to publicity, people all over the world are able to follow our achievements on the tracks. I always watch all my races on video. I find them interesting due to the fact that I can see myself competing. As a human being, I of course have good and bad days in races, but I don´t let that disturb me.

Money gives an athlete the chance to "make war", i.e. train and live a normal life. Does anyone nowadays manage without money? My message to the young athletes is a simple one. Stay as human beings. Do not allow anyone to turn you into robots. The best thing in running is when you realize you have the same goal as your rivals from all corners of the world: the great honour of the victory.

JUANTORENA Alberto

born 21 Nov 1950 Santiago de Cuba.
Double Olympic Champion in Montreal in 1976, winning both 400 and 800 metres. Ran 800m World Record twice: 1.43.50 in 1976 (Olympic final) and 1.43.44 in 1977. Muscular (190 cm, 85 kg) "El Caballo" is the heaviest middle-distance champion in Olympic history.
200m 20,7, 400m 44.26, 800m 1.43.44.

"Be disciplined, be courageous, be modest"

At first, I was playing basketball in my secondary school in Santiago. I was the fastest runner in my class. I was winning school races at a distance of 600 metres. I decided to become a runner, because I did not have any skill in the basketball. In 1971 I really started to run, but I had always had the ability for running. I have had many setbacks during my career. I had both feet operated on. In a way, setbacks were a normal thing during my career. To recover, you need to follow the advice of a doctor and to be very disciplined with the treatment as well. You have to take care of the injury in a proper way. I had many injuries: hamstrings, Achilles tendons. My ankle was broken during the 1983 World Championships in Helsinki. You can beat the illness and become better if you follow good advice. Don´t lose your temper, don´t lose your courage: that way you will get over the trouble. Defeat is something that just happens. It is a common thing to be beaten in a race. But you need to analyze why you were beaten. What did you do wrong? Was it wrong tactics, or didn´t you train hard enough? Having been beaten, I tried to analyze things. For instance in

1975, when I was beaten by an American runner at the Pan American Games, I watched that race many times over. I had been injured early in the season, and I was not at my best. I never got angry after being beaten; I never got bad feelings about a defeat in a race. It is a normal thing to be beaten in sports. You just need to know why you were beaten, and try and solve the problem for your next race. Helsinki 1983, for instance, was a difficult thing for me. I broke my ankle in the race and was operated immediately afterwards; I had to wear a cast for two months. But I recovered, thanks to my discipline and good advice from doctors. For instance, I was training in a swimming pool, had many kinds of therapy... I managed to come back. It is very important for an athlete to trust in oneself. But to trust in yourself - to have self-confidence - you have to be in good shape. If you are well-trained, that is the first step towards being self-confident. Winning a race also perhaps brings self-confidence, but first you need to be confident so that you can win. As to doping, I am fully against cheating, against use of drugs. If you use drugs, you cheat yourself, you cheat the society, you cheat the sport. Doping is not a good way to be the best, because you know, doping is not something that comes from yourself. It is not about your ability, your strength, your power, your confidence... It is something else. Cheating is a bad example for the young athletes. My advice is: never cheat, never use drugs, never use anything that does not come from your ability, your discipline, your sacrifice, your strength.

Publicity? I had a very good relationship with the media during my career. For me, publicity always was a positive thing. My advice for the young athletes is that you have to be disciplined, courageous, modes. To be accessible all time, because that is the only way you can be the best. Some day, when you are the best, and you behave rudely with people... That is not right. You need to be disciplined in not just one sense, but in every sense. You have to have a good relationship with all the people in the sport. You have to be a modest and honest person, because that is the only correct way to behave in sports. You have to be ready all the time to do the best you can in training. You also need to have a very correct life-style: no alcohol, no smoking, no late nights. You have to be able to train hard the next day.

My best advice is to be disciplined and to follow the advice of your coach

For me, the best thing in running is to run a World Record, to be an Olympic Champion, like I happened to be... Things like these give you confidence, make you happy.

KARIUKI Julius

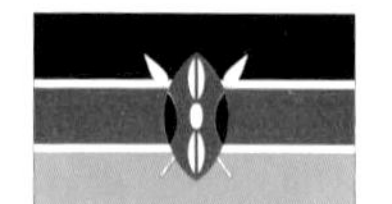

born 12 Jun 1961 Nyahuru, Kenya. Member of Kikuyu tribe.
Steeplechase Olympic Champion in Seoul 1988. 2000 metres steeplechase World Record holder (5.14.43 in 1990). Steeplechase IAAF GP winner in 1988 and 1990. World Cup winner in 1985 and 1989. Had a top-level career spanning more than 10 years.
1000m 2.20.98, 1500m 3.37.79, one mile 4.00.43, 2000m 5.04.71, 2000m steeplechase 5.14.43, 3000m 7.47.35, 3000m steeplechase 8.05.51, 5000m 13.35.72, 10 000m 28.35.46.

"Running must be thought as a career"

When we were in high school, we used to hear stories of runners like Kipchoge Keino, Henry Rono... In the school we had a very good motivation, and I started running well. Then I went up to the national level. In the school we had a teacher who was very interested in the sport. I kept getting better, and in 1984 I was running in the Olympics. The winner came from Kenya, Julius Korir. Then I had a good run in the 1985 World Cup, a very good season in 1986 - although we did not run in the Commonwealth Games because of the boycott -, then in 1987 I went to

America and started training for the 1988 Olympics to get a medal. While in America, I had a coach, but being a distance runner, I had to train mostly by myself. I tried to combine American and Kenyan methods. I was training very hard for the Seoul Olympics, combining these two types of training, and it was O.K.

Difficulties? I really had none... It depends on how you feel. Different people have different workouts. I have an example. When in America, I was training with these high school people, and they could not cope with the workouts I was doing. So, the body tells you what you can do and what you can´t. I have the will to run every day, and if I don´t run, I can feel something in my body. I never have any difficulties to go out and train, unless I am injured. Then I have to rest. If you rest a couple of days, you want even more to go out and run.

If you have been defeated in a race, you should not worry. You may win a few races, then lose a few races in a row. You have no reason to worry about a few defeats, if your training is going well. Forget about it and look forward. In Kenya we have many people running, but the problem is that they just come and go. They do very well, but then they just disappear. I would like to explain that when you are in this sport, you are not running just for today. So many people are running just three or four years. They have the hunger for money, and that is why they are racing too much. The correct thing is to run a few meetings, then stop racing for a while and do the training. You have to think running as a career - that you have something when you retire one day.

There have been some runners who have come to Europe injured, but they don´t tell about it. They just race in spite of the injury, which gets worse and worse. So, if you have an injury, you better take care of it and get it treated. It is better to rest some time and then come back than race injured and destroy your legs.

"You have to know what you are doing"

Self-confidence is very important for a runner, and it has a lot to do with the training one has been doing. If you have been doing very hard workouts and have been feeling fine, then you should go into every race with confidence. You cannot become an Olympic champion without good training. You have to know what you are doing to get self-confidence. It has been said that being a Kenyan gives one lots of self-confidence by itself. I really don´t believe that, because it is not enough being a Kenyan: you still have to do the training. But we Kenyans give moral to each other. We have so many good runners in every event, like the steeplechase, and that is good for competition. Also, we are a very good team in Kenya. There have been no problems, whoever wins. We are friends with each other, and we are helping each other. We are very, very co-operative as a team.

As to publicity, I think in Kenya it is a good thing, because when I walk around, most people recognize me, and it is good for Kenyans to know what we have been achieving around the world. Most Kenyans like sports, but well, of course there are all kinds of people. There are those who like you to win, and those who don´t. I would say it is about fifty-fifty.

God has made us different. God has also made it possible for us to try and achieve things. Athletes have not stolen anything from anybody; they haven´t done anything bad. People who don´t understand about athletics should just keep their mouths shut. If someone doesn´t like me, it means nothing to me. We should forget about those people who have bad feelings.

When I am relaxing and want to show my people what I have been doing in Europe, I am happy to watch the races even myself. It is good being able to show friends how you have been running. I would feel stupid having to run around the world with nothing to show. Yes, it is difficult to watch oneself losing a race, but I have achieved many things, and it is impossible to win all the time. I can bear watching even the lost races, because it is good to know I was there, and there... I have a collection of my races - the good ones and some bad ones.

The best thing in running? You see, competition comes after training, and I love training so much. I like the feeling when training has gone well, and competition is coming near. If I have not been training well, I don´t want to race. My advice to young runners is to train very hard, sit down and plan ahead, to have goals and have a long-time commitment for running.

You have to know what you are doing. You have to plan at least four or five years ahead. You have to pick out the important races, not racing everywhere for two years and then disappearing forever. You have to establish a name for yourself. I have done all the wise things, and now Kariuki is a well-known name in the sport; it is even mentioned in the Guinness Book of Records.

KEINO Kipchoge

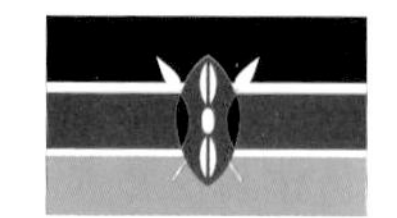

born 17 Jan 1940 Kipsamo, Kenya.
1500 metres Olympic Champion in Mexico City 1968. 3000 metres steeplechase Olympic Champion in Munich 1972. Two Olympic silver medals: 5000 metres in Mexico City and 1500 metres in Munich. Ran World Records for 3000m (7.39,6) and 5000 metres (13.24,2) in 1965. Won his 1500 metres Olympic gold (3.34,9) at an altitude of 2240 metres above sea level, beating silver medallist Jim Ryun by 20 metres. The first great Kenyan distance runner; to many still the greatest.
800m 1.46,4, 1500m 3.34,9, one mile 3.53,1, 3000m 7.39,6, 3000m steeplechase 8.23,6, 3 miles 12.57,4, 5000 metres 13.24,2, 10 000 metres 28.06,4.

Kip Keino´s son Martin Keino (b. 1972) is a top class runner: 1500m 3.33.00, one mile 3.52.33, 2000m 4.53.84 (all in 1996), 3000m 7.35.97 (1997), 5000m 13.30.12, 3000m SC 8.39.14.

"I just wanted to run"

I started running at school for the simple reason that I loved running. I went into serious training at age 19. It did not matter if I won or lost a race. I did not think about the Olympics in those days. I always liked to take part. My international breakthrough took place in the Commonwealth Games in 1962. Although I did not win a medal, I did gain a lot of experience. Of course, the next one was the Olympics in 1964. That was a big thing for me. I was running in two events, 1500 and 5000 metres, at the same time on consecutive days. I think I did pretty well, finishing fifth in the 5000 final, with not much experience. Running just one event, I might have won a medal.

The first Olympic gold by a Kenyan athlete was won by Naftali Temu in the 10 000 metres in Mexico City. I was second in the list, winning the 1500 metres. I think mentally we were well prepared for the games. The Mexicans had been living in the altitude, and they were hosting the games, but they did not win anything in the distance running events.

"Training hard, you cannot avoid problems"

My preparation always started early in the year. I started by preparing for the cross-country. That is the basis, the beginning of it. Generally, I was able to follow the plan I had made. If not, it worried me, because I knew I wasn´t in shape. Unless something else happened, I always made sure I would follow my programme. When I was training very hard, I was sometimes flexible with my programme in order to have more recovery.

Motivational problems? When you are training hard, you cannot avoid problems. I was working, I was employed as a policeman, that was a problem. I could be sent into duty, and I had to take another day to recover, or to do the training. A human being is a human being; you are not always able to do 100% of what you want to do.

Yes, I did make mistakes every now and then. Sometimes I was training with other athletes, who were not willing to do as much as I would have liked, and I did as they wanted. Or I have been injured. Or you are travelling and cannot do the training you have planned. Or your training is stopped by the duties you have been given. I was working for the government, and had to do my duties as ordered. For young athletes, the best advice is that they should enjoy their running. Another aspect is that they should not be forced to do anything that they don´t want to do. Always try to encourage them, to motivate them mentally and physically. They should enjoy competing, whether they lose or win, trying to improve their personal bests. An athlete has to have motivation, self-discipline. That is a key thing, in addition to training; the self-discipline.

I did not have bad setbacks during my career. I did not have many injuries; maybe one or two. I also had malaria and a gall stone (in Mexico City). I had to have a lot of courage to go through it. I was ordered by the doctor not to run. But I went through all the events I had entered in, and got two medals - one gold and one silver. If somebody beat me in a race, I thought the best man had won the race. If someone came at the last moment and went past me, well... I thought "that´s it, I accept it". I was always happy to see my rivals. It has been said that you can judge a man about how he comes in... is he nervous etc? I was always very happy to shake hands with my fellow competitors. We should not be enemies; we are friends. We are going to compete, and and we should wish each other the best. That is the main thing with your rival; even if you lose, make friends with him.

"Self-confidence has a lot to do with courage"

An athlete has to have self-confidence in every race. It is a key thing. He has to make up his mind to fight, and if someone beats you, you have lost to a better man. A runner must go into the race to win. Self-confidence has a lot to do with courage. If a runner is not mentally prepared and has no confidence, then he will have lost the race before the start.

Self-confidence is something that you have to build... By training, competing, by running in the international level. It just doesn´t come by itself. You have to build self-confidence by gaining a lot of experience, by competing for many years. You have to compete in various places, different races. You have to meet and analyse many athletes. You "read" the others, study them. During the race, if someone wants to follow you, let him come. If no one doesn´t, then you go. Most of the Kenyans have lots of self-confidence. "I am better than anyone, but if you are ready, then come and try to follow me!"

Most of the athletes have self-confidence. I would say about 50% of African runners are determined to do anything. They are not worrying, they have decided to run as fast as they can, and then they come and run. A great victory is mainly mental. This is the key thing (points to his forehead). Running is a mental thing. 90% of a great victory is mental. The other thing is the body movement and the physical fitness. You have to build mental strength. Having built mental power, you can run the race the way you want.

There was one race in which I wanted to give up. That was in Mexico City, when I had the gall stone, and during the 10 000 metres race I collapsed. That was the only time. Otherwise, I have always tried my best. I always lost to a better man. If I could see the race in the film, I watched it, and tried to not make the same mistake again. I always liked to see myself run in the film or video - whether I won or lost - and find out where I made a mistake. It was not difficult for me to watch myself losing. As to publicity, it is something that we need in Kenya. It makes people understand how good we are. It gives mental encouragement. It is always good to tell the truth. This way, you can become an example for young runners to follow you. I think publicity is mostly a positive thing. I still have some press cuttings even if I don´t understand all the languages. I collected everything.

"Money doesn´t buy happiness"

In my youth, we were not running for money; we were running for medals and trophies and so forth. And even when the money was there, we were not fighting for money; we were fighting to win. Nowadays, money is good if you can build your life with it, but you can also be destroyed by the money. Money can be a good incentive, but it can be bad as well. Money can tempt you to a bad way in sports, if you are not careful.

Even if you have money, you still belong to a country, Kenya or whatever. But money doesn´t buy happiness. You have to be happy and enjoy whatever you are doing. My message to the young generation is that anything is possible for anybody who is keen for it. There is room for everybody to try. You can become a World Record holder if you are dedicated enough, if you have the self-discipline, if you work hard. You have to earn it all by sweating. There are no short cuts, but anything is possible.

Some day you will be the best runner that you can be. That is the best.

KIPKETER Wilson

born 12 December 1970 (?) Kenya. In 1990 went to live in Denmark, which country he has been representing since 1995.
Two Laps King of late 1990s in spite of finishing last in the 1998 European Championships final after an illness. World Champion 1995 and 1997, missed Atlanta Olympic Games, his entry denied by Kenyan federation. In 1997, he first tied Sebastian Coe´s 16 year-old WR of 1:41.73, then broke it twice with 1:41.24 and 1:41.11. World indoor record 1:42.67 in 1997. An exceptionally fluent and light-footed runner, who so far has been world class at 800 metres only.
400m 46.85, 800m 1:41.11, 1000m 2:16.29, 1500m 3:42.80, mile 3:59.57.

"You have to race according to your own standard"

In Kenya we have a lot of running in school, and I started racing in primary school, against other schools. Now, thinking about young generation of runners, in training you have to pay attention to what you are doing and believe in it. When you are training, and you get tired, you may think "maybe I am training wrong", but at long last you can achieve more than before. You have to believe in your training system. However, at some point you will reach the breaking point, and you have to know where it is so that you don´t overdo it. Even I have had some setbacks during my career. In 1991 I had a problem with my left foot and Achilles tendon. Early this year (1995) I had a problem with the other leg. I was not able to start hard training until April and May.

These injuries have taught me to be careful, especially when coming from Kenya, because if you train outdoors and then go straight into indoor competition, for instance, it will be very hard for your muscles. You have to take care of your legs and muscles. However, I don´t use lots of massage, because I believe in controlling my muscles myself. Massage may be good, but it may also have a bad effect. When I am training the correct way, the muscles will stay good and loose. But people are different in this respect. Sometimes, when your muscles are feeling painful, it may be good to have them massaged. As to the racing situation, I think that at all times an athlete must concentrate on himself - not just on his rivals, looking around to see what they are doing etc. When you are racing, you have to race according to your own standard, your own limit. If you are going to run your best, you have to do it in your own way.

You have to realize that Mercedes and Toyota will not be driving at the same speed. In a race there always will be someone who runs a fast 200, and another who runs a fast 600, but I have to run my own race all the way round. I am racing against other people, but I have to make my own race smoothly the way I want it. Speaking on self-confidence, it sometimes comes from winning, but sometimes you first have to believe in yourself, no matter how the race is going to be. It is both a physical and mental thing, and a question of training. The thing is to be able to train let us say five months without doing anything else, then compete for two months without doing anything else. In a race, I think self-confidence comes from controlling yourself and your pace, not looking at other people.

With Kenyans, the thing is that most of them are racing 10 000 and 5000 metres, which you cannot race more than four times a month. They are long distances. Between, you have to relax and get back more energy. But if you race every day, you get exhausted and there is no more energy. I think drugs in sport are something that some people are taking to earn quick money. If you want to have a long career, to stay in sport for ten years or so, you won´t make it if you are using drugs. Maybe you can do well a couple of times with drugs, but after that you will be unable to repeat your performance without them.

Publicity, for me, is a negative thing, because I like to be the way I am. There is nothing special in me. I just happen to run fast. People nowadays pay more respect to me, but I want them to pay respect to me for what I am, not for running fast.

I do preserve some of the press cuttings, and so does my girlfriend. However, the bad thing is that sometimes the press writes things that I did not say, things that are not true. They don´t listen to what I say. It is a negative way of getting more popular, because the press so often turns the story upside down. Watching my own races on a videotape, I like to see all of them, no matter if I have finished tenth or first. I like to see how it was when I was losing, and how it was when I was winning. When I have seen my mistakes, I may learn how to correct them. I can understand some runners not being able to watch their bad races, but for me it is a good thing because I can compare what I was like when I was a slower runner, and what I am like now, when I am doing better. Nowadays running is like a job to me. It is like working. You have to train, you have to compete. So money is O.K., but I think no one really lets other people know how much they are earning. I like to progress in my life like all people do. I have my own plans. With running, you never know what is going to happen tomorrow.

"You have got to have the balance in life"

My personal message to young runners: The only thing really is to train very hard and have the discipline, because running has to be disciplined. Young runners have to build up slowly. Some people want to come fast, and they also go away fast, but I think it is better to understand what this sport is all about. You must also go to school and take care of your life that way. You have got to have the balance in life (points to his brain).

I love running, and training, too. In order to succeed, you have to know exactly what you are doing in training. Training is a combination of many things. Some people say training is just going out on the track, putting spikes on and running some intervals. I think that is a wrong story. Some people say you have to run this and this distance to be good, and that is another story. You have to listen to your body. Every day you have to be aware of how you feel, and train according to that feeling.
The main thing is that you have to train every day, unless you are feeling sick.

"I convinced myself to go on"

After being seriously ill with malaria, Kipketer again spoke with Seppo Luhtala in April 2000:

In the European Championships in Budapest I could really feel how weak I was. It took me more than five months to be myself again, and originally I had decided not to race during the 1998 season.

I have been in Kenya many times during the last few years, and I have always stayed healthy. This time it was raining so much that the enviroment was exceptionally favourable for mosquitoes, but not for a human being with fresh blood from Denmark!

When I think now about my situation, it was really very serious, but I convinced myself to go on. I knew I was going to run again, but how good was I going to be? That was something I didn 't know. It took big effort to start running after three months without exercise. That I made it, I now think was a miracle.

My confidence was developing through winning competitions, and by how I was feeling after every race, and by watching other runners. But the most important thing was that I took every race in a different way, each one at a time.

My severe sickness taught me at least one million positive things about my life! Because of the disease, I can now see myself better and see where I am. I am really motivated again to challenge everybody on the track.

KIPTANUI Moses

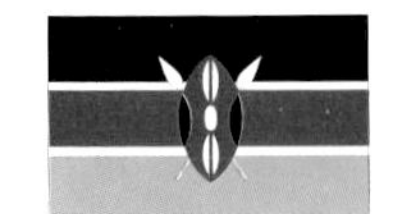

born 1 Oct 1970 (?) Elgeyo, Marakwet area, Kenya.
Three times 3000 m steeplechase world champion 1991, 1993 and 1995, silver medalist 1997, Olympic silver medallist 1996. Four world records: 3000m 7:28.96 in 1992, 3000m steeple 8:02.08 in 1992, 5000m 12:55.30 in 1995, 3000m steeple 7:59.18 in 1995 (first man to break eight minutes). IAAF Grand Prix overall winner 1995. Ran his fastest 3000m steeplechase time 7:56.16 behind countryman Bernard Barmasai´s world record (7:55.72) in Köln in 1997.
1500m 3:34,0, mile 3:52.06, 2000m 4:52.53, 3000m 7:27.18, 2 miles 8:13.40, 5000m 12:55.30, 3000m steeplechase 7:56.16.

Usually I am in a good shape. After one month of programmed training, I am ready for top-class racing for another month. I always follow my training programme closely, without missing a day. If I have to miss a training session, I do not feel good. For instance, during the endurance base training I am still trying to train according to my plan even if my muscles feel somewhat stiff.

I have no motivational problems thanks to the fact that I generally do not train alone. Accordingly, thanks to the help from others I am able to train hard even when I am not feeling at my best. When in the midst of a two-month training period before a big race, it feels very difficult especially when I am tired. In this kind of situation I usually don´t force myself to train three times a day; one session a day may then be enough.

I never deceive myself with my training diary. I am always honest, no matter if I have been running 2 hours or 20 minutes, or 15K or 10K. I don´t see any reason to add imaginary kilometres, because I know I will follow the same plan the next year. I always know why I am doing a certain training session. If I miss training for some reason, I will do something extra next time, or perhaps do a third session instead of the two I had planned. As to young athletes, my advice is to train hard, eat properly and follow your training schedule. Also, it is important that you have respect for your rivals and people generally. Never lose hope even if you are injured or ill. Wait until you are healthy again, then start training for the next racing season. Whenever I am defeated in a race, I am not surprised, because every competitor has been preparing as well as he can. I am trying to find out what went wrong and do it better next time. In my view, videotapes are very helpful when analyzing a race.

"Some people have a born will to win"

In my view, self-confidence comes from winning and good performances, but it also comes from a successful training program. Some people have a born will to win, which can be developed further by training. Some other athletes don´t have this natural will to win, but they can cultivate the necessary mental properties by hard work. Publicity does not bother me. Usually, I will help media people in every way they wish me to do. I tell them exactly what I have been doing. I think I should give them what they want out of me. There are athletes who try to avoid publicity, but I don´t have the need to be like that.

Of course, there can also be negative publicity. It sometimes happens that sportswriters - after having an interview with me - go and write things about my training that are not true. I do not like that kind of writer.

Yes, I do collect newspaper and magazine cuttings and preserve them. In fact I have had some of them framed. Younger generation, perhaps including my own children, may some day be willing to have a look at them. I have noticed some people being envious about my success in sports.

That bothers me. Money, however, is for me something that makes life more enjoyable. When you have money, you can eat well and travel. In fact, I think money nowadays is the main motivation for racing. Without money you cannot succeed. I wouldn´t mind racing even without the incentive of money, but nowadays - with financial matters so relevant everywhere - I am racing also for the money. My advice to young people is, in order to succeed they have to train hard. Also, they have to realize that not everyone can reach the top in sports, but sport is something through which everyone can develop as a person.

When children are in school, it is a hard program because of studying, but we do some light training. Of course they will not be at the top because of the small amount of training they are doing. But after finishing school, when there is not that combination of studying and training any more, they can train very hard. From then on, it is full time training. When young people are growing, it is not good to give them lots of training which maybe spoils their sleep, or hampers growing. There should be an age limit after which one can start training hard. In Kenya this age normally comes when a person finishes high school, which means it is at 18 years. When a child is still developing, it is good for that development to grow in a very natural manner, not to be disturbed by hard training. Doping? Some athletes perhaps don´t train hard enough and therefore have to use illegal means. In my view, the most important thing in international sports is to get rid of doping. This should be done to assure the right direction of the sport in the future. It is not right to cheat with the people you are running with. I cannot support doping, because I don´t think it is right to use drugs or other substances in sports.

"10K is too long a race for me"

Many Kenyan athletes like the middle distance races, in which we have a long tradition. When you see a countryman of yours running well, it is natural to think that you can have success, too. The most significant difference between Kenyans and Ethiopians is that the Ethiopian runners concentrate on the long distance races - 5000 and 10 000 metres, and the marathon. Kenya, however, has good athletes in the 400, 800 and 1500 metres as well. At the moment (1993), distance running is in the midst of strong developing period in many countries. Ethiopia has some very good athletes in the long distances, and Kenya also is progressing well. The strength of Kenyan runners is due to the fact that we train very, very hard. When you can punish yourself in

training, you can do that in a racing situation as well. When you train three times a day, it is much more strenuous than a race, which may take just a few minutes. I do not race much in cross country, because to succeed in World cross country championships I would have to do too much endurance-type training to my liking. That is also why I cannot take part in the Djakarta money race: 10K simply is too long a race for me.

"I felt comfortable all the way"

To be the first person ever to go sub-8 minutes in the 3000m steeplechase was very important to me. I had been planning to break 8 minutes since 1992 when I first time broke the world record. After that I was thinking nearly every day what I can do to be able to run a sub-8. But it was too early for me, and when I trained hard, I got injured. There was a time when I was not in good shape. But this year (1995) I was very confident. I knew that I could do 8.01, 8.02 but it was not enough for me to break the record. I wanted to go sub-8. I felt comfortable all the way. I didn´t have problems like last year. All went perfect, running and going over the barriers. Also, I didn´t want to have a pacemaker, because sometimes pacemakers can go very fast and sometimes very, very slow, and sometimes it is very difficult to judge the distance at the barriers. So I felt that it is good for me to run, when I can take the barriers clearly.

KOMEN Daniel

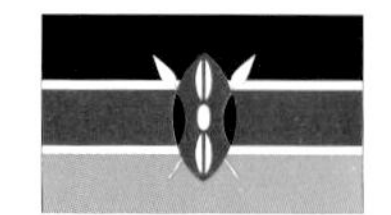

born 17 May 1976 Elgeyo, Kenya. Member of Marakwet tribe.
On 1 Sep 1996 in Rieti, after having missed the Atlanta Olympics due to a bad run in the Kenyan trials, Komen ran one of the most astonishing World Records of all time with a 7.20.67 in 3000 metres, having passed one mile in 3.55,0 and 2000m 4.53,4. In 1997, he ran a 5000m World Record (since broken by Haile Gebrselassie) and became the first man to run 2 miles in less than 8 minutes with a time of 7.58.61, averaging approximately the same speed as Roger Bannister in his epic sub-4 minute mile 43 years earlier. An unusual talent, Komen won the junior 5000 and 10 000m World titles in 1994 and ran junior 1500 and 5000m World Records in 1995. Winning the 5000m World Championship in Athens in 1997 in 13.07.38 he sped the last 3K in 7.34. Komen´s first ever indoor season in 1998 was highlighted by World Records at 3000 and 5000 metres.
1500m 3.29.46, one mile 3.46.38, 2000m 4.51.30, 3000m 7.20.67, 2 miles 7.58.61, 5000m 12.39.74, 10 000m 28.12.79 (1995), 3000m steeplechase 8.54,5 (1994).

"Self-confidence comes from how you talk with people"

I started running because I liked sports. I did not run because some other people were running. I did it because I enjoyed it. I was running five kilometres to school and five kilometres back, but sometimes I also ran the same distances during the lunch hour. That might have been as much as 20 km a day. However, I did not start organized training until in 1994, after finishing school. For me, the most important thing for a runner is to train hard so that when you are racing, it feels easy.

At first, when I was training at home, I was getting advice from my neighbours Joseph Chesire and Susan Sirma. Later, when I came to race in Europe, I was following the programmes they had given to me. Back home in Kenya I have a coach, a man in my school, who has brought about more than ten international class runners. Yes, if I miss a few days of training and then

have to come back again, it bothers me because I may have some pain in my legs at first. I have had some minor injuries and illnesses, usually during my travels. When you are injured, it is no good to continue training. You have to take care of yourself and get healthy again. When you get back into training, you must do it very easily and carefully.

When someone comes and beats me in race, it is not a difficult matter for me at all. I cannot be the number one all the time. There are other guys who have been training hard as well. It is easy for me to accept a defeat because even if I was beaten, perhaps the next time I will be the best. This is life.

This is only sports. As to self-confidence, it is very important for a runner because in a race you have to be in control. You have to know what you are doing, and at what time. These are very important things. I think self-confidence comes from how you talk with people, with a good manner. You have to believe in yourself. Self-confidence also comes from training, when you are aiming at something that is good.

"...drugs just aren´t the right thing to do"

Cheating in sports? I think, coming from a community where I come from, that is something that is not good. Someone like me is just not thinking about drugs. There have been rumours about people who may be taking drugs, but I am not thinking about things like that. For me, it is just hard training that matters. People should understand that there are communities where drugs just aren´t the right thing to do. John Ngugi case? (Thinks deeply.) Well, I think that people coming from another culture did not understand that it was not right to ask for a doping sample from a Kenyan immediately, without any other witnesses, in the middle of his working day.
I am sure that John Ngugi has never taken any drugs.

As to newspapers, I always read everything written about me and preserve the cuttings. I have a lot of them in my place, at home. I like to have them filed. Yes, I have a TV set, but I am just planning to get a video system. I know that the whole school of mine will come and see my races over the season. A bad race of mine? (Smiles.) No, I don´t mind watching it afterwards because good or bad, you may learn something about it.

Maybe I wasn´t fit at the time, or the other guys just were better than me. I am always happy to see my performance even if I finished last. I have never noticed people being envious about myself in my community, but perhaps somewhere else somebody may not be saying so good things about me. In my community, people are always happy when I come back home from Europe. Especially the youngsters, who want to know how I have been doing.

For me, the meaning of money is being able to support my family back at home. When I get enough money, we will be able to get a good accommodation for them. I am running for my family and for my country. When I am running in Europe, I am proud of the fact that I am representing my country and my community.

My message to the young generation of runners is that hard training is what matters. You should be in self-control, you should know what you are doing. You should be planning your races, not racing too much. The best thing in running? (Thinks deep and long.) I think the best thing may be the fact that I am able to travel, to see all the places around the world, and then go back and be able to tell all about it to my family. I am also getting lots of friends from various parts of the world. Even today, I have met you, and you are now my friend. That, for me, is the best thing in running.

KONCHELLAH Billy

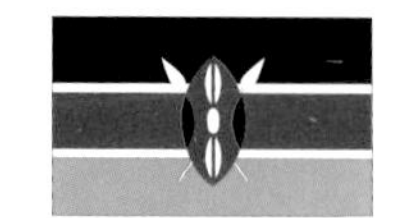

born 20 Oct 1962 Kilgoris, Kenya. Member of Masai tribe.
A great two-lap runner: 800m World Champion in Rome 1987 and Tokyo 1991, bronze medallist in Stuttgart 1993. Due to persistent asthma, various allergies and TB (in 1985) Konchellah had to miss half a dozen seasons in his career, including those of Helsinki World Championships in 1983 and two Olympic Games. 188 cm tall, Konchellah was at his best in the finishing straight, where he was able to change gears in an irresistible way. After a 20 year career, Konchellah was still running respectable times in the late 1990's. As a young man in 1981, he paced Sebastian Coe to an 800m World Record (1.41.73) with 49,6 sec. first lap.
200m 21,2, 400m 45.38 (in 1979, at age 17), 800m 1.43.06, 1000m 2.16.71, 1500m 3.41.80. - Younger brother Patrick Konchellah (b. 1968) won 800m Commonwealth title in 1994, pb 1.42.98 in 1997.

I started serious training at age 16. I think that was a bit too late. You should probably do some kind of training from age 10 or so. When in the secondary school, I had a coach, who was interested in training me. He thought I had some speed. I knew I could be a good runner, because I always was the fastest of the kids. Unlike many other Kenyan youngsters, I did not run to school. I was living in a city, Nairobi, and I took the bus! Earlier, in the primary school, I walked about 2 km to school and the same back. My parents never supported me in athletics in spite of the fact that they were told by my teachers about my talent.

My parents did not think I would become an athlete. They wanted me to become a pilot. The first time I saw a competition in TV was in 1979 while in England. I had heard about Kipchoge Keino, but I never really had any idols due to the fact that I got into serious athletics in a reasonably late age. My way of coming into running certainly was very unique and different, but I think it is good for a young athlete to have idols. I never planned to become an idol myself (laughs), but I now know I am one of the idols in Kenya. When spending the last two years there I was quite surprised to notice that people still remember me and my achievements. I am not bragging, but it may be that I am the most popular runner in Kenya ever, with Kipchoge Keino perhaps.

I enjoyed most of my training except the track work. In fact I hated running on the track from the beginning, but I always loved long runs. I enjoyed being out in the nature - the longer the run, the better. That was why I trained a lot with marathon runners in New Mexico. I never enjoyed training with milers, because they always ran fast, but what I did enjoy was running long and slow. Between the long runs I did some fartlek for speed. I never really concentrated on speedwork on the track.

The speed just comes naturally for me. I always found my speed back very quickly. I usually planned my training on a monthly basis. When healthy, I was able to follow my plans, but if not, it did not bother me. I have always been very flexible with my training methods anyway. When I thought about my good races, they gave me the inspiration to train harder. I did not think very far ahead and never took any worries about the long months of training waiting for me. I never compensated for anything I may have missed: I just started all over again and did what I had started earlier that week. The most important thing in training is the discipline. In spite of being flexible, you have to be focused on what you are going to do. Discipline means so many things - what you eat, how you sleep, who your friends are, whom you hang around with. Relax as much as possible and try to be happy. Have a lot of friends who have their lives in order and have a positive outlook towards life.

Without all this discipline, you better forget the whole thing and throw it out of the window. Also, it is important that you don't let anybody push you. Just do what is necessary for that particular day. Also think about your coach - what does he/she want you to do in the long run, perhaps years later. Don't stress yourself worrying about the great runners. You have to remember that they all started just like you. As to running styles and ways of running, each runner is unique, and you should not try to emulate others. Yes, I have had motivational problems, especially when I was living in America for nine years. That was difficult time for me. Loneliness was the worst thing for a Kenyan. We are very social people and like to be together all the time. Due to the loneliness in the U.S.A., it was sometimes difficult to motivate oneself for training. The biggest adversity in my career has been the asthma, but I have learned to live with this continual setback. I also take my medication regularly and exactly as the doctor has told me.

Self-confidence is important for an athlete in the way that you need to be confident without being cocky. There is a difference. Confidence doesn't mean arrogance. Where one gets the self-confidence is a long story (laughs). I could spend the whole day telling about the history of Masai tribe. I think it is very much social. If you look at the Masai, who ruled East Africa for a long time before the British came, and even later, our self-confidence has always been so strong that it is no wonder that we have some of the best runners in the world. Confidence, in this case, means that you race to be someone in society. With Masai, everybody is equal. We don't say "you are a beggar, you are well-to-do" etc. No one can say "I am better than you" in our social life. But we also have to pay our dues to society from small kids to old people, and I think that is what makes the Masai so self-confident.

I do not think self-confidence is a born thing. It is a social thing. It is very difficult in the western world when you have to find your self-confidence by your own means through reading and so on. You may get your self-confidence from your parents, but in Kenya it comes from the whole society. Young athletes must have their dreams, and they must continue their dreaming. My first dream was to be the best in Nairobi. After achieving that, I thought "what is the next step?" I wanted to be the best in the secondary schools in Kenya. Then colleges, Kenya championships and so on. Don't talk about too big goals - that may eventually frustrate you. It is better to think year by year rather than ten years at a time. You don't go to the track for the first time and think "I will win". You have to lose first. In Swahili we have a saying, "if one doesn't accept defeat, then he or she will not be a winner".

I thought about this all the time when I lost. Nobody is perfect, so you have to go back to your usual training and and then analyze why you lost that race, making the necessary changes to get you back. Don't make any dramatic changes - only small ones, like, if you have been doing too many long runs, cut back a little and then do more speedwork. When you have done some kind of hard training and you then lose a race, you are not happy and you are wondering what will happen to you. I have had that feeling so many times, but after a few hours I get over it and will go to a dance or have a few beers with good friends.

Winning is not the most important thing! What is, is the progress with your running. You don't need to win to be a winner. You can excel by doing your best. You need parents to be very good role models and supporters.

Unfortunately, in the western world people nowadays are in such a hurry making money that all they do is work. When they come home, they are stressed and tired. Yes, I did drop out of many races because at times I was so far behind the rest of the pack that it is impossible to make up so much distance. So I thought to myself, "next time I will be healthy and will challenge these guys". But when I was in shape, I didn't drop out. I fought to the very end. It's a good thing if you finish all races that you start, because that builds your confidence. What did I like about running? Everything! It has been my life for 20 years. I like every bit of it. I liked beating people in races. I liked being beaten every now and then, because then I could think about what went wrong. Being beaten, I never buried my head into sand like an ostrich. I gave compliments to the people who beat me.

I like publicity anytime because it makes me believe I can still do it, and it also lifts my self-esteem by making me think I'm important. I also like criticism when it is meant to help you. Positive publicity certainly is a good thing, a negative one can be damaging for an athlete in the long run. Videotapes are good. It is good to see your races again, even the bad ones, even if you sometimes wish they would repeat the race and call us back to our marks (laughs). I see many people behave differently when I am running well and when I am not. Sometimes I feel painful for the fact that people are hating each other because of sport. Cheating in sports should not be allowed. If one cheats, he or she should not be allowed to compete any more. After all, this is supposed to be fun, just a race among many other races.

Money is important in a way that without it I don't think I would have been able to do the necessary training to become a world champion. To be able to train hard you have to have a good apartment, a sport club with weight lifting facilities, swimming pool... Why are Kenyans so good at distance running? I will tell you. That is because slavery was created to get the best individuals of our race to America. The weak ones died and were thrown overboard from the ship. The strong ones made it, and you can see how tough they are now in every way.

One hundred years ago Africa was just bush and animals, with people living only to about 45 years of age, maybe older if they were lucky. Either malaria killed you, or other diseases, or animals. So it was survival of the strongest as well. If you look at our landscape in East Africa, it is not very hilly and not very flat. I think that when our ancestors were hunting, they were in fact doing serious training on foot. The strongest ones survived, and that is what made us so unique. I think it is not the food or the climate. It is in this special breed of people that has been bred for many years by nature, without anyone knowing it. You have to remember that not everybody in Kenya runs. We have some tribes who probably cannot run 100 metres or even 50 metres. The good runners are tall and leggy and they come from this special area in East Africa... Kenya, Tansania, Ethiopia. As to young athletes, everything in sports is more scientific today, so my advice to young athletes is to equip himself or herself with modern technology and a good coach. The best thing in running is to enjoy it, to listen and learn from past champions.

KOSGEI Reuben

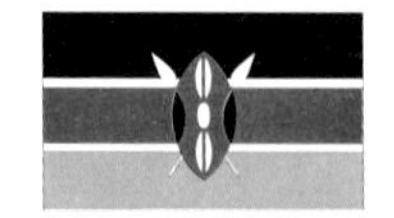

born 2 Aug 1979 Kapsabet, Kenya. Member of Nandi tribe.
A small and light-footed runner and born steeplechaser, Kosgei reached the top quickly, winning the African junior title in 1997, World junior title in 1998 and finally becoming an Olympic Champion in Sydney 2000. He went on with his series of big titles by winning the World Championship in Edmonton 2001.
1500m 3.37.24, 3000m 7.41.86i, 3000m steeplechase 8.03.92.

"Perfectly normal to be beaten"

Yes, I was surprised to win in Sydney. At that time I still was just 21 years old, so no way I could be sure that I would so soon become an Olympic champion. I started training in 1996, but I did not go into real hard work until I represented Kenya in the World Junior Championships in 1998. So, I started training at age 17 and the hard work two years later. My school was some distance away from home, about 6 kilometres, which I covered by running because that was the only way to do it. If I was too slow and missed the start of the school, I was punished by my teacher. He either reprimanded me or sent me back home (laughs heartily).

If you came late to school day after day, you were not a good student!

It is true that sometimes there are days when you really don´t want to run. Mostly, however, I do enjoy my training - all types of it, especially the steeplechase athletics without training regularly from day to day.

You have to believe in yourself, in what you are trying to achieve. I do! Someday, perhaps, the day will come when I move up to the marathon, but for now I am happy with the usual type of track and distance training. There have been occasional days when I have not been feeling well and have decided to postpone the training session until the following day. After extra recovery, I have usually been doing fine the next day.

As to myself, I try to train every day, even on Sundays, when I do an early morning run before going to church. My worst setback so far was in 1999 when I was in a good shape and ran 8.12 in Hengelo. I then went to Kenyan trials for the World Championships in Seville, and somebody stepped on my Achilles tendon. It took me many months to recover from the injury. What I learned from my setback was that it is absolutely no use to train when you are injured. After being patient and training hard again for less than a year, I became an Olympic champion. It is perfectly normal to be beaten in a race. It is not possible to win every time when you go to the starting line. What you have to do after a defeat is to not get discouraged. You have to train harder for your next race and try to run better. Self-confidence is good, because it makes you to relax and to believe in yourself. And if you believe in yourself, you are going to win. In my opinion, you get the self-confidence from training. Whenever you train well, you are in good shape, and that brings you the self-confidence. If you are training very well, it is possible for you even to predict your time in the upcoming race.

I do not believe in getting self-confidence from winning. It is possible even to win a race accidentally! When you get your confidence from winning and you then lose a race, where is your confidence? What I like about running is to be able to travel to far-away countries, meeting interesting people, having so many good friends. It feels good to be a big name (laughs)! I like running so much because it has helped me into better life, bringing money and higher living standards... (thinks long)... Why I run every day, of course there are World Records and big championships to aim at, but there is something else as well inside myself, making me run daily. As to my coach, I meet Bernard Barmasai about twice a week, but the rest of the time I am training alone.

KRISTIANSEN Ingrid

born 21 Mar 1956 Trondheim. Née Christensen.
One of the true pioneers of women´s distance running, Kristiansen is the only athlete to have broken world records at 5000m, 10 000m and marathon, and the only world champion at track, road and cross-country. 10 000 m European champion in 1986 and World champion in 1987, 15 K road World Champion 1987 and 1988, World cross country champion 1988. Won several prestigious marathons, including Boston twice, New York once and London four times (1985 with a world best of 2.21.06). In the 1988 Olympic 10 000m final she had to drop out when leading the race, due to foot injury. As a cross country skier, Kristiansen represented Norway at the 1978 World Championships before starting a serious running career. She gave a birth to a son in 1983 and to a daughter in 1990 and was still racing occasional marathons in the late 1990s.
800m 2.09,7, 1500m 4.05.97, 3000m 8.34.10, 5000m 14.37.33 (World record in 1986), 10 000m 30.13.74 (improved her own World record by 45 secs. in 1986), 10K road 30.39, 15K road 47.16, half marathon 1.07.59, marathon 2.21.06.

"Sport is universal"

I started training at age 15, first in cross country skiing. I did not choose running as my number one sport until I was 24 years old due to the fact that I had finished my studies and started to work. It was easier to be a runner with an 8.00 to 16.00 working day than to be a skier. I had a training plan for one year ahead, but it was then done separately for every week. I was generally able to follow the plan with some exceptions.

Yes, I think I was flexible about my training schedules. I have always loved to train and compete and I was always looking forward to every training session. I still do love training. I always knew why I was doing a specific training session thanks to the fact that I was listening to my body. Whenever I happened to miss a session, I never tried to compensate for it later. You cannot do your training when you have already lost it.

I think the most important thing in training is that you like to train and sometimes also are willing to accept the pain. You have to love to train and have fun with mixing hard and easy training.I had more or less no setbacks until I was 27 years old (my first pregnancy), but I had variation in my training, doing cross country skiing in winter and running in summer.

I think that helped me to keep away from injuries. Coming back after a pregnancy, of course, was hard enough. The most important thing is to take it easy in the beginning, and so I came back step by step after having children three times, and it was harder and harder every time. Also I had a very serious injury in the 1988 Olympic Games. That experience taught me not overdo things in my training.

A defeat in a competition always is a positive thing if you really want to become a top athlete. You cannot become a good winner before you have learned how to lose. After a defeat you have to try and find out why you were tired or what you did wrong in the days before the race. Then, you can start looking forward to the next competition.It is easy for me to face the facts. If I want to be the best, I have to analyse my life and training very carefully.

It is essential for an athlete to have self-confidence. When you are confident, you can do what you believe in - almost everything. In order to reach a great victory you first have to believe that you are the best. You can build self-confidence by working with your faults, especially in your head. You can work with your mental preparation, telling yourself that you are the best and will like to win this and that race. After a while you will do it.

Money means a lot in sports, which is both good and bad. Money is necessary for an athlete at top level for arranging her or his training and for helping going on a few more years. The bad side of the money is the cheating in sports. Nowadays, due to all the money in the sport, cheating is a very big problem. I do not need publicity any more.

When I was competing at the top, I never read anything about myself before important races. Afterwards it is no problem for me to watch my races on video, no matter if it was a good or bad performance. An untrue comment in a paper, however, can hit me very hard.

My message for young runners: Young athletes of today have to be patient. If you will become one of the best runners in the world, you have to train seriously for some years.

There are no shortcuts. Keep going, have fun in training and competition. Do not be afraid of losing. It is only then that you can win. Do not cheat!

The best thing in running is that the sport is so universal. Everybody in the world (poor and rich) can do this sport. I have got a lot of friends from all over the world. If you run long distances as we are doing, you can run in the country, on the road, on the track, everywhere. It is great to compete and feel that one is in good shape.

LANDY John

born 4 Apr 1930 Hawthorn, Victoria, Australia.
Second sub-4 minute miler in history, Landy ran a World Record of 3.57,9 in Turku, Finland in 1954 (1500m intermediate time 3.41,8 also was a World Record). In 1956 Landy won a 1500m bronze medal in Melbourne Olympic Games, in which he also took the oath in behalf of all participants. Landy´s career was a short but exciting one - only about four years.
800m 1,49,8, 1000m 2.20,9, 1500m 3.41,8, one mile 3.57,9, 2000m 5.12,6, 3000m 8.09,4, 2 miles 8.42,4, 3 miles 13.27,4.

"I was an intuitive trainer"

I started running young, winning races in Melbourne as a schoolboy. Then I gave it away to university and I was really a footballer. I wanted to get into the league team. Later, when I was in Agricultural College during one year of my course I did some running and was winning events, but I still was a better footballer than a runner. Then, over the summer I decided to do long and slow

running one day and running sprints the next, and I improved my times so much that when I came down to Melbourne I was picked for the state team. So all of a sudden I was a runner and gave away my football career. The 1952 Olympics were coming in about a year´s time, so I just might get fit for that. Prior to that I never ran better than 4.20 at the 1500 metres, but I then reduced my time to 3.50 in less than a year. I really got into running almost by accident in that sense. If I had had very good performances in football, I would have gone on with that. When I was training in the 1950´s I had plans but they weren´t fixed.

I tended to change them. I did three different periods of running and training. The first one, I did very little lap running with a clock. I just went out and ran. In 1953 I tried an interval system in which I used to run around the track, recording all the times I ran. I would run 400 metres in 60 seconds and rest half a minute and and run another 60 seconds. I continued to do something like that when I came to Finland in 1954.

My plans were not made by a coach, because I had none. I made them up myself. I was an intuitive trainer. I thought of things, then I went and did them. If I tried something that did not work out, I tried something else. In the last stage of my running, when I ran very well in Melbourne in early 1956, on my way to the Olympic Games, I abandoned using a clock at all my training stages. What I did was a plan that made me able to run long distances like 5000 metres effectively and also improve my fast work.

All I did was very short burst of sprints and long easy runs. I did no lapwork at all in a normal sense. I noticed I got better results doing that. When training, I had to be adaptable. If I did not have a ground on which to train, I would go and train in the woods. I didn´t get very upset about it. But when I intended to do timework and couldn´t get to the track, that would upset me. I just wasn´t flexible enough, but when I was training without a clock, it didn´t matter.

I never had any motivational problems. I was a very self-motivated person. I could run fast times in training or in solo racing because I could motivate myself to run fast without any competition at all. When I decided to do something, I was even too obstinate. I didn´t need anyone to tell me what to do. I trained nearly always on my own. I used to run at night, but if I trained during the day, a lot of people came and joined me, in which case I didn´t mind if they came or didn´t. I didn´t need people to run with. I could always do it on my own. Yes, I enjoyed my training very much. I liked the idea of training hard, the feeling when I got myself going. I always set myself goals, wanting to see what I could do. I had a goal of running an hour, perhaps an hour and a half, and I was able to enjoy it. You found it difficult in the start, but once you got a habit of doing it, it got easier and easier.Occasionally I did it to the point of exhaustion, but I didn´t have any fear for that. I can´t remember any problem whatsoever with that.

"I never saw my notebook again"

I usually didn´t keep a book of mileage except when I came to Finland. For a period in 1954 I kept some notes and gave them to somebody. I never saw them again. My keeping book wasn´t really part of the plan. I recorded what I was doing for a while, but by the time it was circulated to all different athletes, I was already doing something else anyway. I only kept a book for about a year. The rest of the time when I was running I did not write anything down at all. I had broad principles. I usually knew why I was doing various types of training. I was trying to look closely at the three different aspects of my programme. I was trying to do a bit of the racing speed to get the idea of rhythm for the race which usually was 1500 metres or a mile.

I would also go out and specifically train my speed to get myself into the frame of mind that I was a sprinter. I had to learn to sprint. When I practised fast running I would think that way. Then another day I would go out for a long run, sometimes in the woods, sometimes in an oval. I might run 1-1,5 hours at steady speed as if I was a 10 000 metres runner. The three things to aim at were to improve your speed, to improve your stamina or staying power, and to have the sense of lap training, in other words to get the rhythm of running faster than 60 seconds laps. If you had all these, you were right, but you couldn´t mix it up together. When you got out for speed work, you could only do speed work. I´m sure they do much more sophisticated things nowadays, but at my time that was all I knew.

When I went out for my long run I would think I was Emil Zatopek. The next day I would go out and run not laps but bursts of maybe 300-400 metres at 1500m pace. I could also do quite a bit of stretching exercise before I went out because I thought it was important especially in speed work to be flexible.

The only times when I missed my training sessions were because of injury. I had a lot of tendon trouble, which I tried to compensate for, and that would cause more injury. My idea was that consistency was the most important single thing in training. To be able to go out and do it was more important than the amount. You did that for two reasons. First, you got better results. Secondly, it was terribly important from the point of view of discipline. If you are going out regularly, it is much easier to do something. During the last year at the University I was very hard pressed and could train only every second night during the winter, which was a very hard thing to do. To be honest, when I was running we did a lot of blind-folded work. We weren´t quite sure what we were supposed to do.

"I was never one to get emotional"

Yes, I had quite many setbacks, especially in 1956 when I was in huge trouble. I damaged my Achilles tendon trying to do too much fast work on very hard tracks with very bad shoes. In retrospect that was a bad mistake. I think I didn´t balance my training well enough, lacking the work in speed stamina. I was concentrating on making fast 300 metres bursts and having a longish recovery period. When I watch the athletes training today, they get their recovery right down, running another burst very quickly afterwards, and that´s something we didn´t understand. If you look at the present day runners, they ran a lap of honour immediately after the race, whereas we used to be really tired. We weren´t as fit as the present runners are.

When you are pushing yourself to run, one of the most difficult things is not to overtrain. If you have a high conscience, it´s certainly not a problem of undertraining. Particularly Achilles tendon troubles are very difficult because they get chronic and they are extremely hard to get over. They undermine your mental confidence because if you are an athlete who trains consistently, and suddenly you cannot do it, then your confidence is gone. As to defeats during my career, I was more or less deterministic. I would always accept the things that were going to happen. I was never one to get emotional. My reaction always was to get over it. It shouldn´t take very long.

I was never a person who could hate or dislike. I liked Chataway, Bannister. I was mostly very friendly with the people I ran with. I still see a lot of Bannister. People were really good fellows to me. It was in the race where you tried to win. If you lost, so what? It´s almost impossible for most runners never to be beaten. For me, problems were there to be solved. Adversity will not be the end of the world. Problems are an opportunity, a learning experience. When a problem comes along and you get beaten, it´s telling to you that you could do something better. If you are not performing to the level people think you should, you should be able to work out a way of overcoming that. There are advantages in analyzing today when you can use a video especially in tactical things. If you are not relaxed in your running, you can see that sort of thing.

"There is a limit for what you can lift"

The meaning of self-confidence for me is that I can only have confidence if I know a certain amount of my performance. That would come out of the fact that I had won races against people. If I hadn´t run races against them, I would want to be sure that I could have the equipment to beat them. I would want to know that my own distance ability was as good as theirs and that I was always well trained. Any confidence that I had was based on knowledge that within a reasonable degree of certainty I had the necessary elements to beat those other people. In other words, I was fitter, I was more relaxed and rhythmical, and I was hopefully faster. At that stage I would be totally relaxed and confident, but if anything less than that, I would be a little uncertain.

Yes, winning brings confidence but it depends on what you win. The ultimate is to win the Olympic Games, and if you do that, I suppose that´s something you are not going to reproduce. When you win an Olympic final, most people do not win another one. Some do. Viren did, but it is unusual.

With all respect, you can´t alter facts. If you are running against Said Aouita, you are not confident because he has got an arrogant attitude. Aouita has all the basic facts in abundance. He has got the rhythm, he has got the staying power, and he has got the speed. He is a better mixture than anyone else. Aouita knows that if he has trained well, he beats those people, but the other people who run against him haven´t got that confidence even if they trained harder than Aouita does. No amount of training will change the fact that Aouita is faster than they are or he has got over-distance ability or that he is a combination of all these. That´s a physical thing in my opinion.

Training builds your confidence, and that can be proved scientifically nowadays. However, with a weight lifter there is a limit as to what you can lift. Confidence can be all sorts of things but there is a point at which no amount of confidence counts. You can only work within your physical limits.

van LANGEN Ellen

born 9 Feb 1966 Oldenzaal, Netherlands.
A talented but injury-ridden athlete, van Langen had her Day of Days in Barcelona 1992, winning an Olympic 800m title and improving her personal best by more than two seconds during that amazing season. After having finished 4th in the European Championships in 1990 she had an Achilles injury, which she got rid of in time, but which later destroyed her career again. In spite of these difficulties, van Langen had seven seasons running faster than 2.00.
400m 53.66, 800m 1.55.54, 1000m 2.35.21, 1500m 4.06.92, one mile 4.31.88.

"... achieving things you never thought would be possible"

I did not start serious training until I was 20 years old. I was studying economics and sometimes we had sport lessons. My sports teacher thought I had some talent for running and asked me to join the local track and field club. Actually at first I didn´t want to because I didn´t have much time. I was studying hard and also spent lots of time with friends. But I then joined some workouts and liked it a lot, after which I gradually got more and more serious about training. I had always liked running very much, but my home town had no track and no club. I then lost my interest for many years until I happened to meet the sports teacher who convinced me it was worth trying. From

the moment I became seriously involved with the sport, I never had any motivational problems because I liked it a lot and I just wanted to be the best. I always enjoyed my training sessions. I liked to do the long runs in the woods as well as the weight workouts. But what I liked most were the workouts on the track, especially those in which I had to concentrate very hard to be able to finish well. Only at times when I was injured and had to do alternative forms of training like aquajogging or cycling, I got impatient because I didn´t like these types of training. I just loved running. There are so many important things in training, but what seems to be most vital for me is to listen to oneself. Your body is not a machine, it has different reactions every day. Of course you need to have to drive. You shouldn´t stop training for stupid reasons. And yet you are the only one who knows your body best, so you always have to heed its signals seriously so that you can avoid injuries as much as possible.

As to myself, I have had lots of serious injuries, and that is why I have missed some important championships. Of course I have learned a lot from them! As an athlete you always want to win even if you well know that isn´t possible. You can learn something from every defeat. Think about what went wrong and what you can do about that in training and in your next race. As long as you have been able to do whatever you can, there is reason for some satisfaction. Self-confidence is important because it can make the difference between winning and losing a race. Your rivals will see and sense your self-confidence. However, don´t confuse it with arrogance, you just need to be aware of your capabilities.

The way to acquire self-confidence is to think about all your strong points before a race. You have to tell yourself literally that you can do it! Think about all the things that can happen in a race and what your reaction to them will be. So when these things then happen, you know exactly what to do. This way you will feel confident and more relaxed before a race. A career as a competitive runner is just wonderful. It is a very good feeling to work very hard towards a goal and to give everything you have in order to achieve it. Whatever the result might be, the fact that you have dedicated yourself to something is very worthwhile. The best thing in running is the feeling of winning, achieving things you never thought would be possible.

LIMO Benjamin

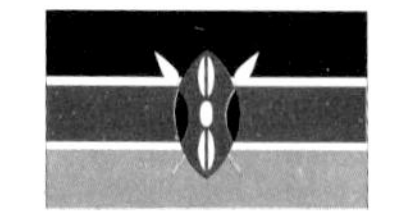

born 23 Aug 1974 Kaptagat, Kenya.
Limo made his big breakthrough in 1999, winning the World cross country 4K title and - after an astonishing finishing sprint - taking the 5000m silver at World Championships in Seville. During this great season he broke the 13 minutes barrier four times.
3000m 7.28.67, 5000m 12.55.82.

"I had a dream of flying in an aeroplane"

When in primary school, I just ran to please my teachers or to have some fun, but I later realized I could see the world if I became a good runner. I started serious training in 1995, after my military training. At one time I had an injury problem which put my running on hold for a couple of years until 1997. In fact the main goal of my running originally was to travel in an aeroplane even once in my life! I knew many people who had been able to do that, and they told me what a great feeling it was to be in the air.

Training really is very hard. At first I had no clear idea of what I had to face.

Competition can be even harder than training. When training, you can control what you are doing in intervals etc. Competition can be very tough because you have to be all out. I know many people who say training is harder than racing, but for me it is another way. Sometimes there are days when I am so exhausted that I don´t want to go out and train. These things happen. Generally, however, I enjoy my training because you are not able to do things very long if you don´t enjoy them. I enjoy all kinds of training sessions. The most enjoyable training is the type that I am doing with my friends. Group running is good. It is good for competition as well - for instance cross country racing - because then you know these guys and how they have been doing in training, what kind of shape they are in. The most important thing in training is to know what you are training for. You have to know your aims. You need to aim at somewhere - national or international level.

I got my bad injury when I perhaps did something that I was not supposed to do. I should say that the way you train decides if you get injured or not. You need good shoes, you need a level surface to run on. My philosophy on a defeat is, "may the best athlete win!" You need not be too much affected by a defeat. If you are beaten, the other guy has been stronger than you. What you need then is to train harder. I find it good to watch any race of mine on videotape. It is good! No matter if I ran good or bad. It always teaches you something when you see it. You need to be confident for what you are going to do. You need not worry about when you are confident with yourself.

I have the self-confidence. I can feel it. Maybe it comes from training and the way you have been competing. It gives you the self-confidence you need. But if you are not performing the way you expected, that can affect you. You should not be over-confident either. The good thing is to know what you are capable of. Confidence certainly mostly comes from training. When you have been training well, that gives you much more confidence than winning a race every now and then. In Belfast (World Cross Country 1999), before the race I never thought I would be the winner. I was running my own race. At the very end I saw I was still leading! Tergat is very confident on what he is doing. That is why he is so good.

My message to the youth is that when you have been training hard enough for many years, you can then resist any pace your rivals are running. The best thing...? Apart flom flying (smiles) and seeing the world, maybe the Worlds or the Olympics. The feeling of being a champion.

LIMO Richard

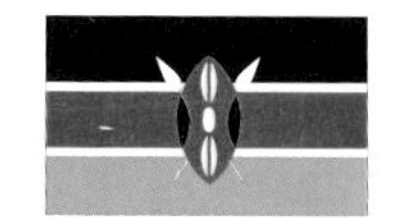

born 18 Nov 1980 Cheptigit, Kenya. Member of Kalenjin tribe.
An unusual talent even by Kenyan standards, Limo ran third in the 1998 Commonwealth Games 5000m final at age 17 and twice finished second at World Junior cross country championships. After a 10th place in the Sydney Olympic final, Limo´s fantastic finishing sprint carried him to a 5000m World title in Edmonton 2001.
1500m 3.37.59, 2000m 5.00,6, 3000m 7.33.71, 2 miles 8.13.47, 5000m 12.58.15, 3000m steeplechase 8.20.67.

"Self-confidence means that you are happy with whatever you are doing"

I started serious training at the end of 1997, when I was 17 years old. Maybe I started a bit early. Every young child can do some running, but it is another matter to train hard. When you are young, the level of the competition should be low. What made me start training was the fact that I was living near a forest some 1900m above sea level, and many runners from all over the country came to the area to train there. I saw some of these guys running and thus became interested in the sport. Motivational problems? Of course, that is a normal thing in sports.

It is easy to train when you are feeling fresh and well, but naturally it cannot be so every day. You have to to know yourself to be able to steer clear of injuries, or of punishing yourself too much. When I am training, it is not something easy, so I have to learn to enjoy my running even when it is hard. Nowadays I can say I am enjoying it, as hard as it may be. In training you have to push yourself even when you don´t like it. The important thing when you are motivating your athletes is to tell them to be patient. Running hard isn´t easy. You have to go a long way to become an Olympic or World champion. When you are young, you feel anything is possible. Running is not something that is a must for you, nor a mandatory thing. It comes from your heart.

KENYA
TDK
684
EDMONTON 2001

Of course I have had setbacks. At the end of the season, most of all, I often have the feeling that I have been overloading my body. That is the time when you get easily injured unless you slow down for a while! When running, you are using your legs and arms, and your head as well, and at the end of the day you can feel very, very tired. If you are racing for six months without a break, as some people are doing, you will certainly get problems.

When training hard, you have to use your reason as well, because otherwise you might get an injury bad enough to stop your career forever. When loading your body, you have to be careful and patient. If you do too much too soon, you are going to damage yourself. My message for a young runner: after having started, you are gradually rising from a low level to a higher one. At the same time you are growing up. I know, because when I was young and I was far away from winning a race, I was beaten by runners older and more experienced than myself. When developing, you have to climb so many barriers. One day, if you have been patient enough, you will beat those who beat you before.

What you have to remember is to always be friendly with your rivals, even those who have defeated you. After winning many races, some day the moment will come when you have been at the top long enough and you start losing again. That is the nature of the sport. You have to enjoy your running and be friendly with everyone, no matter if you are winning or losing. Self-confidence first of all means that you are happy with whatever you are doing. That means when I am doing it, I will make it! I don´t get the self-confidence from others; I get it from myself.

When I am training, I am responsible for it only to myself, not to other people. Running is something that I am doing for myself. For me, self-confidence comes from training. Everyone is training in his or her own way, and every one of us is different, but you have to have faith in your own system.

There have been runners who have lost their ability to win because they have lost their self-confidence. When you are ill or injured, you are not feeling well and you know you don´t have the self-confidence. But when you are feeling good and your body is responding to your training, your mind is in tune as well, and you are feeling confident.

For young athletes, I would say that all of us have happened to come across running, which is a very fine sport, but sometimes also a difficult thing to do. We always have aims and dreams, but it is not always possible to reach them. Maybe you will become a great runner, or maybe not.

The best thing in running? Whew... (sighs and laughs). I can say that running has brought me away from Kenya, to Europe, to faraway places. Without running, it would not have been possible.

Also, I am running because that is something important for me, a very deep feeling inside me. If you want to have a long career, you have to be careful with yourself. Most of the Kenyan runners reach the top quickly and then disappear after two or three years. So I repeat, you have to be careful.

You have to remember that you are doing the sport for yourself, not for anyone else. No matter if you succeed or don´t, you have only yourself to thank or to blame. When I went into the 5000 metres final In Edmonton, I knew it would be a very hard race. We had planned beforehand to do it as a team work, in a hard way. We didn´t want an easy win. We wanted to feel that at the end of it we had done a lot of hard work. We actually sat down and made a plan. It went exactly as we wanted it to happen.

LOPES Carlos

born 18 Feb 1947 Viseu, Portugal.

Lopes crowned his long and difficult career with the marathon Olympic gold medal in Los Angeles in 1984 at age 37, and the following year ran a world best time of 2.07.12 at Rotterdam. He also won the World Cross Country title three times in 1976, 1984 and 1985. In his big-meet debut race at the European Championship 10 000 metres in 1971 Lopes finished last, but in 1976 he was good enough for an Olympic silver medal in Montreal behind Lasse Viren. After several injuries he came back again and finally reached the top echelons of the sport.

1500m 3.41,4 (at age 35), 3000m 7.48,8, 2 miles 8.25,0, 3000m steeplechase 8.39,6, 5000m 13.16.38, 10 000m 27.17.48, 20 000m 59.44,2, one hour 20 158m, marathon 2.07.12.

"A runner did not need shoes"

I started training just before my 18th birthday. In fact I was more interested in soccer, but due to the poor background of my family I finally chose running. Soccer certainly is the No. 1 sport in all Portuguese-speaking countries. All sportsminded youngsters are dreaming of becoming professional football players. My parents, however, could not afford buying me a pair of football shoes, which meant I had to stay away from official matches. Running, on the other hand, was something that I was able to do without shoes. I always had talent for endurance sports. As a young boy, I was thin and weak, but I had lots of guts. After getting some inspiration from my uncle, a running enthusiast, I soon noticed I had found my ideal sport. I had no idea of how long I would go on with this running, but I never seriously considered quitting either.

"I never had a feeling of fear"

In 1977, I had a serious injury which almost destroyed my career. I already had achieved quite a lot by then, including an Olympic silver medal and World Cross Country title, but I still had a burning desire to go on. I knew I had not reached my limits and I had decided to give everything I had. Luckily I still had eight more years left to reach even higher. In my early years I did not enjoy all my training. Speed training, most of all, was something that I detested, but I well realized I had to do all kinds of training sessions so that I could develop as an athlete.

I never had any special feelings towards my rivals. I never thought of them before races, and not much during the competition. I always aimed at running my own race. I generally knew what I was capable of and raced accordingly. Whenever I was performing according to my plans, I was happy. Everyone is feeling some degree of nervousness before a race. That is nothing to worry about. I never let my excitement take control over myself during my career. All I was thinking about was my own performance.

What the others did was of no concern for me. I never had a feeling of fear - not even the fear of losing. Being beaten in a race was no shock for me especially if I had been performing as I had expected. In fact, sometimes it was good to be beaten. Those were the days when you noticed you couldn´t relax in your preparation. That was a good lesson. As to my countrymen generally, I think they were more disappointed than I was about being defeated by Lasse Viren in Montreal. I am sure most Portuguese people had been expecting me to win.

There are people who don´t like an athlete to succeed. There may be various reasons for that: perhaps they don´t like somebody´s coach or whatever. In sport, there have always been cliques, the members of which like one athlete and don´t like another. In Montreal, I suppose my supporters were more disappointed than I was. I did not have my first races until at age 18.

They were at Viseu district cross country meetings, which were followed by national championships. I was very happy to finish second and first in the district races, then third at Portuguese championships. This was followed by 15th place at World Cross Country Championships. All this success gave me great encouragement on my way forward as a long distance runner.

It took me nine more years to reach the international top level. That was in 1975, when I realized I had the capability of becoming an Olympic medal runner. Before me, no Portuguese runner ever had achieved international honours, but now - together with me - many other runners in my country began to believe they had a chance. In my early years there was practically no coverage on track and field athletics in Portuguese press. Later, with success coming, there was gradually more interest in our sport. As to myself, I never bothered reading the stories and never preserved them. Later, it has turned out that some of friends have kept a kind of scrapbook of my achievements.

Whatever there has been written about me, I haven´t worried about it. Of course I have wished the stories to be truthful, but if not, that hasn´t ruined my day. The most important thing is I know what I am and what is the truth. That is enough. Whether I have succeeded or not, I have always remained the same. I have always been myself.

"It took me 20 years of running"

I never took any pressure about the eventual performance. I never worried about whether I would be running well or not. I never let defeats depress me, whereas I liked to celebrate success. Whatever the result, I always tried to see the better side of it. Of course I was getting more and more hungry! But even if I wanted more, success did not come easily. It took almost a decade until I started to believe I might be good enough for the highest honours of the sport. In spite of my success, I did not make any radical changes in my training. Why to change, because I was running so well? This is something on which I have been criticizing some coaches. If an athlete is having success and getting better, there is no reason to try some radically other type of training. If you do well by a reasonable amount of training, you should beware of doing doubly more.

I find it extremely valuable to analyse an athlete´s training in great detail when he or she has been doing well. My advice is to continue in the same way even if someone in the coaching fraternity would like to do otherwise. Training is an individual matter. What suits someone, doesn´t necessarily suit someone else. That is why I never have liked to tell about how I trained. It would be stupid to try and emulate what I was doing. You have to remember that it took me 20 years of running before I won an Olympic gold medal. Even if it is true that the training of the last 12 months was the decisive factor, that wasn´t all of it. I had been building background and gathering racing experience for my big race for two decades. Whatever training method you are using, the essential thing is to listen to your body. In other words, you have to rest when you are tired, and train hard when you feel good. As to myself, I did not learn these things until one year before the Los Angeles Olympic Games, with excellent results. The only adversities I had during my career really were the knee and Achilles tendon injuries, which took a long time to recover from. I did not allow these problems to knock me down. As bad as adversities are, they also usually teach you something. You have to stay in a positive frame of mind in every situation. When you learn to do that, nothing will stop your progress.

My school teacher, Sarmento, was the first coach I ever had. He was one of the very few track and field enthusiasts in Portugal those days. A year later, I moved to Lisbon, where I joined Sporting Club de Portugal and was being coached by Raimondo Mendes. In the early 1970´s this task was taken over by the head coach of the club, Mario Moniz Pereira.

In the early part of my career, I received useful advice from Spanish runner Javier Alvarez Salgado in various topics. I am most thankful for him. He was an enthusiast, who gave me much needed encouragement. My breakthrough year - also a breakthrough year for the whole of Portuguese athletics - came in 1976. A whole generation of runners was inspired and encouraged by my Olympic medal. Also, it helped to bring more young talents to the sport.

"The belief must come from inside"

However good a coach you may have, you have to take part in planning your training schedule. An athlete knows himself or herself better than anyone else - better than any coach. When an athlete is planning the training schedule together with his coach, there will be no need to ask why something is being done in this or that way. In big championhips meetings, most of all, it is an essential thing for an athlete to believe that what he has been doing, has been right. In the Olympic Games, a coach cannot be there at the last moment, encouraging and giving advice.

The belief must come from inside the athlete. Nowadays there are many coaches to choose from. In my youth, you had to take the coach who happened to be there. All my coaches have been valuable persons for my career, each one of them in a different way. It is very important for any athlete to have a coach. Coaching is a difficult task, because it is not always easy to see what kind of person an athlete is and what may be the best for him.

"A coach is an educator as well"

In addition to building an ordinary athlete into a world-class athlete, a coach also must be an educator. It is a pity - in some cases a crime - if a coach is not able to think of his athlete as a human being. Sports is just a part of an athlete´s life. There are other things as well - studying, family, work and emotional life - which have to be taken into consideration as well. The best results in sports and life are achieved, when these various aspects of life are synchronized so that an athlete´s life is in balance. As important as sports may be for a world-class athlete, it must be kept in mind that it is, nevertheless, a short period in one´s life. Both a coach and an athlete must take care of not ruining the other parts of a well-balanced life.

As to self-confidence, the better results I achieved, the more I trusted myself, and yet it took almost 10 years before I realized I might be able to climb to the very top. As a person I have always been an anti-star. Life goes on whether you succeed in sport or don´t. The fact that my personality has not been changed in any way by wins, defeats, money or publicity is, for me, perhaps my greatest achievement as an athlete. I still am the same Carlos Lopes as I was before becoming a runner. To me, everything came very slowly. I was training regularly for 22 years, improving all the time. The first half of it meant striving to the top, the second half was trying to stay there. For a country boy, the first trips abroad naturally brought impressive memories, but it was not my way to gape at everything with mouth open. The more I was travelling around the world, the more I got used to it. I always longed to get back home to Portugal. I haven´t been much impressed with any other runners. I was afraid of no one. For me it felt natural to step inside a stadium in order to race. It was just a part and parcel of any athlete´s life.

"An athlete is not a machine"

In my view, it is not advisable to plan one´s training too far ahead. If your main goal is to get through your training schedule no matter what, you may forget the truth. You will carry out your training plans perfectly, but you don´t get the performances. To avoid that, you must listen to your body. An athlete is not a machine. There are too many variables in every athlete´s life. I always did serious training sessions whenever I felt "this is the day".

But it also could happen that I was not feeling as good as I wished, which necessitated some changes in that days´ training. If you have a bad race, the reasons behind it have to be analysed. In my mind, however, it is not enough that your coach tells you what went wrong. You must get hold of the situation yourself and be responsible for it.

There were times when I trained more than planned, but sometimes I did less. I trusted my feelings. When your ambition is in order, there will be no problems. All you have to remember is your goal. If you are aiming at an Olympic gold medal, it takes a lot of training. I never wrote down my training sessions, but to put it simply, sometimes I was running faster, sometimes slower. Generally I was averaging 17-19K an hour, occasionally as much as 20. Towards the end of my career I preferred training alone.

I had a principle of never compensating anything that I may have missed. It is no use doing a week´s workload in four days. For instance, if you have missed a week of training due to illness, it is pure madness to start training hard as soon as you are able to run again. How can you train more if you are not healthy? I don´t think I made very bad errors in my training. I am reasoning this by the fact that I was improving steadily year after year. I always had the feeling of staying in balance. In my firm opinion, very few runners in the world ever made so few mistakes in their training as I did. That was the basis for my success. A young athlete must be a realist, and he or she must be coached in a realistic way. The requirements of useful training are balance, patience and progression. In endurance events it takes quite a long time to reach the top. Young athletes mustn´t hurry. Winning at a young age is not relevant. Once again, I want to stress the meaning of patience.

"For two days I didn´t talk with anyone"

In my view, the most important capacity for an athlete is to be a master of himself. There is no need to see rivals as enemies. When you believe in yourself, you have a firm feeling that no one is better than you. I always went to a race with the attitude "I will make myself noticed", but the first time I really went to win was in the Olympic marathon in 1984. I was so sure about my fitness that I believed I would win even with a 90% performance. In a way, I was aiming lower than usually at Los Angeles. On the other hand, if I had lost, I would have been very, very disappointed.

At Los Angeles, I was much more nervous than normally before a race. For two days I was practically by myself, talking with no one. All I was doing was concentrating for the most important race of my life. I got rid of all nervousness during my warm-up, and stepping to the starting line I was feeling completely calm. No athlete can succeed without self-confidence. You will become mentally stronger through good performances in racing as well as in training. Consequently it is important to plan training sessions in a way that allows an athlete to get through them and enjoy a feeling of satisfaction. Winning a race of course is a source of satisfaction as well. My guess is that mental toughness is a born thing, which, nevertheless, it is possible to cultivate through experience of an athletic career.

I never had an urge of giving up in a race

Anyone taking advantage of drugs in sports is a cheat. These kinds of people never can enjoy their achievements in the way we, the clean athletes, can. They are machines who have offered their self-consciences, their souls, their whole lives to foul play. They never can enjoy their lives as champions. Publicity is something that I don´t look after nor avoid. Publicity in itself has no meaning for me, but there have been occasional untrue comments which have harmed my nearest people. Unlike most athletes, I have never been unjustly criticized in public. If I had, I wouldn´t have let it bother me. The main thing is that I know the truth.

"You should have respect for each other"

Money doesn´t always bring you happiness, but it certainly helps. For me and my family, the money that I have got through sports has meant a lot. If you have no money, you will not develop as an athlete. As to marathon running, for example, the level of the sport has reached new heights thanks to the money. To succeed in long distance running takes at least 10 years of hard work. I think it is right to get some compensation for it financially.

My advice to young athletes is that they, like all people, should have respect for each other. They should know what they are doing, not letting themselves become arrogant with success. You always have to keep your feet firmly in the ground.

The best thing in running is the simple enjoyment it brings to one´s life. Moreover, my long career has taught me a great number of things.

LOROUPE Tegla

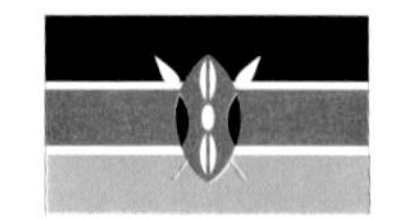

born 9 May 1973 Kapsoit, Kenya. Member of Pokot tribe.
A sprightly and diminutive athlete (153 cm tall) living and training in Germany, Loroupe in April 1998 became the first black African woman to break a world best time in an Olympic event when she won Rotterdam marathon in 2.20.47, collecting a 150 000 dollar bonus for the race. She improved her World Best by four seconds in Berlin in 1999. She also won in New York in 1994 (debut marathon) and 1995, Rotterdam in 1997 and World Half Marathon title in 1997, 1998 and 1999. As a track runner, Loroupe was a World Championship 10 000 metres bronze medallist in 1995 and 1999. She has been racing very frequently with amazing power of recovery.
3000m 8.30.95, 5000m 14.45.95, 10 000m 30.32.03, half marathon 1.07.12, marathon 2.20.47.

"It is hard to get away without setbacks"

The most important thing in training is to set the desired goals with your coach and establish a program for the standard of an athlete you would want to be. When planning my training, it depends on what kind of races I want to compete in. If it is a 10K or a marathon, workouts may differ a bit. Anyhow, in order to run a good race, one has to put in long term training which should last for several months - not just weeks or days.

Generally speaking, as a serious athlete I try my best to maintain the training plan as much as possible in order to achieve the desired goal. Any serious runner will not improve when his/her training plan is not adhered to. Since I tend to set goals, it sometimes gets hard to be flexible unless something serious happens, e.g. an injury. Once I have set my goals, I try to stay motivated as much as I can to see that nothing comes in my way to distract my motivation. I know that training is not an easy task, therefore I try to stay motivated, aiming for my desired goals towards the next race. As to setbacks, it is quite hard to get away throughout one´s life without them. Things like sickness and injury are hard to escape. In my case, I and my coach try to adjust to the training program despite setbacks and see to it that we remain focused on our goals.

My advice to young runners: Work everything out with your coach and know that any setback is not the end of the world. A defeat in a race is not anything bad to worry a motivated athlete. In fact it is a measurement of some sort. A defeat makes an athlete know her own standard, and what kind of runners she competed against. Somehow that is a motivating factor. Yes, it is possible to acquire self-confidence. If the athlete has done enough training, following her program, then self-confidence should have been attained. Cheating in sports is not good because it gets to a point whereby the cheating becomes unfair to the other athletes. The publicity factor is there, but I tend to try and stay as before as much as possible. Actually, I never need publicity when I am preparing for a big race like the Olympics.

I watch videos of my bad races as well because in some way they help me to learn from mistakes that I might have made in a previous race. I don´t know if people are envious of me but you never know. Anyhow I haven´t noticed anything like that so far.

The financial factors of running are something that remain to be looked upon by my manager and me. My personal message to the young generation of runners is that running is there to stay. Just set up your goals and focus on what you want to achieve in running. You have to put lots of emphasis on running before you can look at the money factor which many young runners today tend to think about too much.

Finally, the best thing in running is that one gets to be physically and mentally fit, and one gets a general wellbeing in life.

MEYER Elana

born 10 Oct 1966 Albertina, South Africa. Née van Zyl.
Half marathon World Champion 1994 and silver medallist 1998, Olympic 10 000m silver medallist in Barcelona 1992, World Cup 10 000m winner 1994. Road world bests of 46.57 at 15K (1991) and half marathon 1.07.59 (1991). A somewhat enigmatic but beautifully fluent-striding runner, Meyer ran a former African record of 2.25.15 in her marathon debut, placing 3rd in 1994 Boston. She was still racing strongly all over the world in the early 2000´s.
800m 2.06.23, 1500m 4.02.15, 3000m 8.32.00, 5000m 14.44.05, 10 000m 30.52.51, half marathon 1.06.44, marathon 2.25.15.

"Running is such a beautiful and natural sport"

We do some long term planning for races four years in advance, but the shorter-term planning of my training is 4-6 months (up to a year). Generally I have been able to follow the schedule, but we do make slight adjustments whenever necessary. I always try to listen to my body as well. No, I don´t have motivational problems. I simply love running. As to the long months of strenuous training, I am looking forward to it. I rather try to put in some good training over several months than just focusing on individual sets. I am well aware on why I am doing various types of training sessions. I try to never skip a session. I don´t think I have made serious mistakes; this is because my coach is very good in planning the programmes. I have had some minor injuries in the past - Achilles tendon etc. -, that have kept me from running for a while, but nothing permanently serious so far. Also, I have been lucky not to get sick in the past very often. Sometimes an injury is a way that nature looks after your body - a way to tell you that you should slow down a bit.

After an injury you usually appreciate the fact that you can run again and enjoy your running. A defeat really motivates me. I find it easy to analyze a defeat, because I don´t like excuses for running a bad race. You can almost always learn something from being beaten in a race - and that is nice. As to young runners, I think it is important to set goals in terms of your own potential. That is why I believe it is better to set goals in terms of times and not

in terms of competitors. So, this way you can be defeated in a race but still "win" in terms of your own goals. If you fail in this respect, then you can use it as a motivation for the future. I always greet my rivals in a friendly way, at the same time focusing on my own race. Afterwards - friendly as well, but on the track during the race we are competitors.

Self-confidence to me means believing that you can achieve your own goals. You can cultivate self-confidence by training and achieving what you have been aiming at. The premises for a great victory are that you believe that you can do it - that you have the will to win. You have to be able to adapt and not to be upset when things don´t go your way all the time (like waiting at airports, bad weather etc.). I am quite relaxed before a race because by that time you have done all the hard training - so then I know I can do it in the race as well. As to cheating, I think it is wrong. It is important to keep our beautiful sport clean.

Publicity is part of being a top sportsman, but it must not influence your focus on training and definitely not let it rule your life. Publicity is good for informing general public about our sport. It is good also for your sponsors,

which makes it possible for us to be athletes. For me, publicity has been mainly a positive thing. I read the newspapers to be informed, but I don´t like reading about myself. I don´t collect clippings, but I get them from an agency. I think it is good to preserve these things. I don´t like watching myself on a video in front of other people, but to analyze a race it is good to watch it on my own (or with my husband or coach). Negative remarks really don´t bother me because it happens so often. If it did upset me, I would be an unhappy person all the time. What other people think about me doesn´t really worry me, because it is impossible that the whole wide world will like me.

To be myself is very important, and not to be what others may expect of me

It is good that running has made me independent, but for me money isn´t the motivation behind running. It is a good incentive, but what rather motivates me is excellence. Running is such a beautiful and natural sport. All you need is a pair of running shoes and you can do it anywhere. There is no short cut to success. You have to be consistent over years in your training in order to deliver results. But you must enjoy running, otherwise it is not the sport for you. For me, the most difficult part of running is just putting on my shoes. The rest I just love. The best thing in running is that great feeling after a run.

MILLS Billy

born 30 Jun 1938 Pine Ridge, South Dakota, U.S.A.
10 000m Olympic Champion in Tokyo 1964. Lakota Sioux Indian, Mills´ victory was one of the biggest sensations in Olympic history; his name had not been mentioned in any experts´ forecasts. 6 miles World Record in 1965.
One mile 4.03,5, 3000m 7.56,4, 2 miles 8.41,4, 5000m 13.41,4, 6 miles 27.11,6, 10 000m 28.17,6, marathon 2.22.55,4.

"A tale of a warrior"

I started serious physical training at the age of 19. However, I started visualizing winning the Olympic Gold Medal at age 21. But, because of food allergies I was not able to become consistent in my training until the age of 24. When I was 12 years old my Dad gave me a secret on how dreams come true. He showed me a paper with the following written on it:

Find your desires, know yourself, and succeed.
With desire comes self motivation.
With self motivation comes work.
With work comes success.

It was signed anonymous. He said, "You find your desires in sports, drama, dance, music, reading, creative writing, student leadership, the arts etc. I hope you try sports, son." Running was my desire; it unleashed the passion within me. The Olympics became my dream. Following the secret, my dream became my reality. However, I always had motivational problems. Because of food allergies I frequently found myself having hypoglycemic symptoms, and because of pronation I was subject to injuries. From the age of 15 to 23 I ran about eight to nine months out of the year, averaging 40 to 45 miles a week.

I enjoyed my training very much but only after I was able to address the allergy problems and have a major input into my training. Two years before the Olympics I started coaching myself. For me the most important thing in training was focus. When I was able to balance my life physically, mentally, socially, culturally and spiritually, I was able to develop incredible focus. The ability to focus provided the motivation and consistency needed to pursue excellence at a world class level. It also empowered me with my visualization training. I visualized hundreds of times a day the last lap of my race at the Olympics. My race turned out just as I visualized for a number of years, except for being pushed twice during the last lap.

In 1964, from April 40th to September 1st, I missed 30% of my training because of injuries. What I learned from this experience was the value of cross training and visualization. I would swim and take easy, long, slow runs with an occasional walk to keep my fitness. I also would review my workout book, the training I already did to empower me, and help to keep the confidence I had.

This was overlapped with the constant visualization of winning the Olympic 10 000m Gold Medal. Your subconscious mind can´t tell the difference between reality and imagination. It will respond equally to both.

In regard to a defeat in a race, if running is truly your passion you can accept defeat - not failure -, and continue to pursue excellence while all the while being defeated. Ultimately the pursuit of excellence will take you to victory. Your victory may not be winning the race, but something even more valuable and and empowering. Your victory may be being able to reach within the depths of your capabilities and competing against yourself to the greatest extent you are capable of. This is the greatest level of competition and provides the most cherished victory of all... personal happiness through the pursuit of excellence. The meaning of self-confidence for me was realizing I could compete against myself to the greatest degree I was capable of, and on a given day I could achieve one or all of four goals:

1. **Win an Olympic Gold Medal.**
2. **Set a World Record.**
3. **Beat the greatest runners in the world.**
4. **Compete with character, compete with dignity, and compete with pride at the level of fitness I was at the moment and so finding personal happiness.**

I believe it is possible to acquire self-confidence, and how you do so is also my personal message to the younger generation of runners. I challenge you to live your life like a warrior. The Olympic circles represent the continents of the world. Every continent has its male and female warriors.
A warrior lives his or her life centered around four values:

1. A warrior assumes self responsibility. As you become responsible for yourself you reach out and help others become responsible.

2. A warrior assumes humility. You humble yourself to all creation. We are no better or no less than one another. As we find the balance of humility we never lose sight of the passion that allows us to accept defeat but no failure. We continue to pursue excellence, being the best we can be.

3. A warrior learns the power of giving and generosity.

4. A warrior takes responsibility, humility, the power of giving, and centers it around his or her core of spirituality.

There are also four spiritual needs we all seek to fulfill. If you are atheist, then call them human needs, but fullfill them.

1. We all want to be unique.
2. We all want to belong.
3. We all want to make a creative difference to society.
4. We all want to understand.

Whether it´s running, creative writing etc., unleash the passion within yourself, pursue excellence, and achieve. Your achievement is your uniqueness. You have met the first step. Take your uniqueness to the group, empower the group. The group empowers you. From this dual empowerment you make a creative difference to society. This brings you understanding and self confidence. You are a warrior! The best thing in running is the expression of freedom and being as one with Mother Earth.

MIMOUN Alain

born 1 Jan 1921 Telargh, Algeria (then belonging to France).
Marathon Olympic Champion in Melbourne 1956 at age 35 in his debut race at the distance, beating among others Emil Zatopek, behind whom he had already won five silver medals at two Olympic Games (10 000m in London 1948, 5000 and 10 000m in Helsinki 1952) and one European Championships (5000 and 10 000m in Brussels 1950). Four-time winner of "Cross International" (forerunner of World Cross Country Championships) in 1949, 1952, 1954 and 1956. Ran his fastest ever 3000m at age 41 and went on competing until his 60´s. Alain Mimoun certainly is one of the most famous and beloved French athletes of all time.
1500m 3.57,0, 3000m 8.22,0, 5000m 14.07,4, 10 000m 29.13,4, one hour 19 364m, 20 000m 1.01.56,4, marathon 2.25.00 (his winning time in Melbourne).

"I started running just for the heck of it"

I got interested in distance running at age 25. Before that I had been playing soccer, doing bicycle races and so on. I was a soldier for seven years, from the start to the end of WW II, always in the front. Then I started running just for the heck of it, inspired by people whom I had seen running in the forest. I had no training whatsoever under my belt, but I had lots of natural endurance and I was immediately doing well. I realized I was a born runner. I always ran alone and never had any kind of training schedule. Two years later in London I was an Olympic medallist. In Helsinki 1952 I got two more medals, and finally in 1956 I became an Olympic Champion.

In my view, it is not wise for a young runner to start competing at age 10, 11 or 12. You shouldn´t start until you are 15. Before that you can do any sport you like for fun - running, playing soccer, bicycling. The most important thing for a young athlete is to enjoy his sport. If you take it seriously too early, you may also drop out of the sport too early. I was very sore after the 1954 European Championships. It took me a year to get over my sciatica problems. I got fat, and people were saying, "Mimoun´s great career is finished". I did not believe that. Healthy again, I started gradual training, and after eight months I

56

was as fit as I had ever been in my life. In 1956 I won every major race I entered, including the Olympic Marathon! No matter if I won or lost, I was always happy. It was just sport, but it gave me fantastic joy and enjoyment. Sometimes it could happen that I had not been sleeping enough, or I had stomach trouble, and did not race well. I did not worry about it. I just said to myself, "next time I am going to win". Which I usually did.

I always had high respect for my rivals, especially for Emil Zatopek. We had some fantastic races, after which we always congratulated and hugged each other. We have been friends for half a century since then. Self-confidence, in my opinion, comes from the following: you have a peaceful mind after being well-trained, well-slept, well-eaten - but not well-drunk!

My usual way of preparing for the summer races was to race cross country through the winter. In April I did not compete; instead I went to the mountains to do some training. For three months I was doing training and more training, after which I was ready to climb onto the medal podium in August. In October I had another spell of altitude training, starting my preparation for the cross country.

Cheating in sports makes me very sad. Whoever is cheating, cannot have inner peace. Doping is cheating in its extremity. Anybody who has been using drugs is a crook. Nowadays, publicity brings an athlete lots of money, but in France in the 1950´s Olympic Champion Alain Mimoun got very little publicity and no money at all. However, I and my wife were not seeking publicity. We had a home of our own to live in, and enough food to eat. I don´t know why we would have needed any publicity. There can be negative publicity as well. Many things can be written about Olympic Champions, not all of them good. Today, I am being interviewed more than ever.

It looks like television is more interested in myself nowadays than in the ministers of French government. At the time when Emil Zatopek and myself were racing, we never got paid for it. I don´t criticize that fact that athletes are being paid today. The fact is that athletes have to live and eat as well. Many of the present champions come from poor backgrounds and try to improve their lives through sport.

I just cannot imagine that a top marathon runner of the 1990´s would be working in a factory. It is impossible for a marathon runner to be an amateur these days. All children and young people should do some kind of sports in order to keep active and healthy. It is not necessary to have success in sports, but even if it comes, the main thing still should be health and fitness.

The best thing in running, for me, was the simple enjoyment it was giving me every day. It was a great feeling to win for France. I love my country. I am a very patriotic person. It was absolutely wonderful to run for France.

MORCELI Noureddine

born 28 Feb 1970 Tenes, Algeria.
One of the most successful milers ever: 1500m Olympic Champion in Atlanta 1996, three-time World Champion in 1991, 1993 and 1995, five-time World Record breaker at 1500m, one mile, 2000m and 3000m in 1992-1995. Started his international career with a 1500m silver medal at the World Junior Championships in 1988, then studied in the United States. Had a 45-race winning streak at 1500m from the 1992 Olympic final (7th) until the Grand Prix final 1996, when beaten by Hicham El Guerrouj. Ran the fastest ever last lap of 52,2 at 5000m when winning in Zürich in 1994 in 13.03.85. Worlds leading miler for seven years 1990-96.
400m 46.85 (in training), 800m 1.44.79, 1000m 2.13.73, 1500m 3.27.37, one mile 3.44.39, 2000m 4.47.88, 3000m 7.25.11, 5000m 13.03.85. - Elder brother Abderrahmane Morceli ran 1500m in 3.36.26 in 1977; younger brother Ali Morceli has been a "hare" in Noureddine´s many great races.

"Running is like raising fruit trees"

At maybe 6 years of age, I remember racing a distance of 600 metres with one of my brothers - three years older than me. At age 8 I started doing some runs with another brother Abderrahmane, who was a world-class miler those days. I ran my first official race at age 12 in school. It turned out that I won. It must have been in 1981 or 1982. This early success encouraged me to start some kind of regular training.

Thanks to my brother, who was racing all around the world, I was well aware of Sebastian Coe´s World Record performances. Said Aouita´s Olympic gold medal in 1984 also helped me to get more insight into top class athletics. I was 14 years old and I had a dream of becoming some day a great runner myself. You may have adversities in the early part of your career, and that is why it is extremely important to have dreams to carry you over difficult times. Top class athletics is very hard work, but I am thankful for having received my gift for running from God. I have not hesitated in sacrificing my life to sports. My dream of becoming the best in the world was finally realized, but not

adidas
ALGERIA
TDK
108
GÖTEBORG '95
adidas

without lots of patience. You may have to work 15 or 20 years in order to run World Records. It is like raising fruit trees. You must give them water, take care of them every day. In my view, whenever an athlete starts to think he has reached the top, he will stop developing. I don´t think I am anything special; I am still aiming at better and better results. I want to show the whole world what I can really do. A sportsman always must retain his dreams. Religion is a very important aspect in my life. Through it, I suppose I get 40% extra strength for racing and training. I am getting help from religion 24 hours a day. Thanks to my faith, I am eating the right foods, sleeping nine hours every night and so on. Thanks to religion, I don´t celebrate, I don´t drink alcohol, I don´t go to discos. I don´t do anything that might be bad for my sport. As with all other Muslims, Ramadan is an essential part of my life as well. We fast for God, not for ourselves. We sacrifice our lives fo God. He knows what he wants from us.

Your body may be in bad shape every now and then - suffering from various troubles and wounds. Your digestion doesn´t work as it should. What you need then is Ramadan - an excellent course of treatment. I have been following it rigorously since age 7, without any problems. I always have fantastic races after Ramadan. People should try that so they would understand. If a child of 7 or 8 years is capable of following Ramadan, then why not grown-up people? Ramadan is a mental thing. If you are mentally strong, you can fight with anything in your life.

In the early part of my career I had some difficulties with my federation, the people of which were not willing to help me. I had a discussion on this with my brother, after which we decided to do something about it. It was a great idea from us to go to the United States in 1988. While there, I learned many things and was able to improve my training in excellent conditions. I started my career as a cross country runner, representing my country at the World Championships in New Zealand in 1988. Even later, in spite of making the decision to concentrate on track races, cross country running still is an important aspect of my training. Nowadays I am coaching myself, yet not forgetting any advice I may have received from others. To be able to run very fast some day requires a base work of maybe 10 years - a mixture of speed, speed endurance and endurance training. The biggest difference between myself and other runners, in my view, can be found in self control. I have sacrificed my life to my sport, which is something you have to do in order to reach the highest honours. It is impossible for an athlete to train and to celebrate at the same time. It just doesn´t work that way. If you are an athlete, you have to be an athlete 24 hours a day.

If I have planned a track session of 10x400 metres in 54-56 seconds with a 60 second recovery, I may feel tired after the very first run. I may have an urge of giving up, but that is the moment of decision. What you have to do is tell yourself, "Try to go on! You have to do what you have decided!" To succeed in any profession takes a lot of effort, a lot of courage. Every one of us sometimes feels lazy, but that is when you have to fight it and defeat it.

"I always know ´what´ and ´why´"

I always do separate training for indoor and outdoor seasons. I usually plan for something like three months ahead. I like to have discussions with my brother over the schedules. It is good to have someone to check these things with. Yes, it bothers me a lot when my training, for some reason or another, doesn´t go according to the plan. It is essential to be aware what you are doing. I always know the answers for "what" and "why". I am training so hard that it takes a lot of concentration. Whenever I have to back out due to illness or injury, I take care of starting very, very carefully when I am able to train again.

In winter I do lots of quantity, running as much as 200-220 kilometres per week, including fartlek in a hilly terrain. I lift weights twice a week for about four months before the start of the track season. The weights are very light, but I am doing all the movements dynamically, with explosive speed. I try to take care of both upper body and leg muscles. I do the squats with perhaps 20-30 kilos with many repeats. This improves leg coordination. If I were lifting weights of 80-100 kilos, I would soon become a weightlifter - too heavy for middle distance running. Athletics is an individual sport, which suits my personality very well. I like to do long runs by myself, whereas I need other runners to help me in track sessions. In training, I want to stress the co-operation of mind and body, without which you cannot defeat the difficulties that everyone sooner or later has.

Before every race, I go through the list of competitors, trying to figure out everyone´s strengths and weaknesses. It is essential to be aware of fast finishers so that you can start your own finishing sprint at a correct point in the race. I always keep my rivals in high regard because of the fact that I know they have been preparing very well. If I am beaten by them, that is O.K. This is just sport.

After a defeat, a runner must be able to have a deep analysis of why it happened. You have to aim at doing better next time. Everyone of us is beaten sooner or later - that is a law which you cannot help - but luckily it doesn´t matter if you lose in a minor competition. What counts are the Olympic Games and World Championships.

"Europeans have it too easy"

African runners are so good because their life has been so hard. They live in severe conditions. Europeans have it too easy. They have not been used to suffering like the Africans have. On the other hand, climate in Africa is good for running training, especially at altitude. No runner can have success without self-confidence. You have to be able to believe in what you have been planning. I get self-confidence by training well. I never lose my faith in myself. Injuries, however are bad because it is very difficult to race when you are injured. I had a horrible race in the Olympic Games in Barcelona due to the fact that I was virtually running on one leg. My injury was finally examined and cured in Switzerland, but before that I had been able to do just six repetitions on the track instead of the usual 35.

Sport has been changing a lot in recent years. We cannot be compared with the past generation. We are professionals and we are able to train full-time year round. Top athletes are born talents - having got their gift from God -, but everyone has to train to become even better. Whenever I am beaten, it strengthens my motivation to get back and succeed again.

I see publicity as a positive thing. Also, I don´t mind watching any races on video. That way you get to know more about your rivals and how to race with them. For any runner, money is a stimulating factor. Money makes you strive forward. Thanks to the money in sports, you can become a professional runner. However, you always have to remember that success comes first and money second.

My childhood was a tough one in a family of 10 people. There were many times when I had to go to sleep on an empty stomach. Nowadays I am living another life, being able to train harder and harder. Nevertheless, I have to be thankful of everything and remain the same person I always was. If not, then God may take away everything He has given to me.

My advice to young runners is to have a deep love for your chosen sport. You have to do all the training required from you. The only way to reach the top is to train hard for many years. If you are younger than 15, you have to do short and fast runs. You have to sleep well, eat well. It is essential to build a solid background for the demanding years to come.

MOTA Rosa

born 29 Jun 1958 Foz do Douro.
Diminutive Mota won 14 of her 21 marathons, including Olympic gold in 1988 and World title in 1987 plus three European Championships in 1982 (her marathon debut), 1986 and 1990. She also collected victories at Rotterdam, Chicago, Tokyo, Boston, Osaka and London.
800m 2.10.76, 1500m 4.19.53, 3000m 8.53.84, 5000m 15.22.97, 10 000m 32.33.51, 20 000m 1.06.55,5, one hour 18 027m, marathon 2.23.29.

These answers have been given by phone to Miguel A. Mostaza.

"You have to study hard if you want to make a career"

I started serious training at age 14. I used to run from place to place all the time, feeling better and better. Then one day I went to a race with a friend of mine. I was fifth and immediately realized that with a little more training I could be first. In my daily training I never had any motivational problems. For instance, even nowadays (1998) I still like training very much and try to do my best every day. I just love to train. I think that for an athlete, the training sessions should be the most important item, and he or she must like doing them.

Without preparation, nothing in life is possible. You have to study hard if you want to make a career. In terms of training, what you put into it will determine how good you will become. I didn´t have too many setbacks during the years when I was competing on the top level. Actually I had just one setback towards the end of my career. Illnesses and injuries are part of our short lives. The most important thing is to try and take good care of them as soon as they show up, and also try to prevent them in advance.

Do not overtrain. Don´t drink alcohol. Don´t smoke. Do a lot of stretching. Do eat good and healthy food. Go to see your doctor as soon as you have problems. Listen to your body every day, especially before and after training.

When you are defeated in a race, remember that in sport there will always be another chance. Try to learn from your mistakes and try to do better next time. Self-confidence is a very important issue. You have to think that you are as good as the others and that with your confidence you can be as strong as the best athletes in the race. Of course it is possible to build one´s self-confidence. Experience is vital in order to increase your faith in yourself. The more experience you have, the better you are going to be.

My message to you and the whole young generation of runners is, don´t go too fast too soon! Don´t think how much money you can make. You have to become a good athlete first. The best thing in running is that it is a sport in which the most important person is you. With good training and good habits in life you can go very far.

MUTOLA Maria

born 27 Oct 1972 Maputo, Mozambique.
800 m World Champion 1993, fourth 1991, silver medallist 1997 and 1999, dq´ed in 1995 for accidentally cutting in too early in the semifinal. Four-time Olympian, taking part in Seoul in 1988 at age 15; then finished fifth in Barcelona in 1992, then won a bronze medal in Atlanta in 1996 and finally became the first ever Olympic champion of Mozambique in Sydney 2000. Four-time World Indoor Champion at 800m in 1993, 1995, 1997 and 2001. Ran 1000m World Record in 1995. A pioneer of women´s athletics in Mozambique, Mutola owns all the national records in her country between 200 and 3000m. Started sports as a soccer player, has been living and studying in Eugene, Oregon, U.S.A. since 1990 thanks to Olympic Solidarity scholarship programme.
200m 23.86, 400m 51.37, 800m 1.55.19, 1000m 2.29.34, 1500m 4.01.63, 3000m 9.27.37.

"One must accept that it is all right to lose a race"

I started running in response to the influence of the poet laureate of Mozambique, Mr. Jose Craverinha. He observed my football skills while I was participating on a boys´ football team in Maputo. He came to me and told me that he thought I possessed the skills to compete at a high level in women´s track and field. I don´t know if I really like training or not. That is a difficult question. Some days you enjoy training, some other days you don´t. What I know is that to be good at this sport you have to train. Further, not only to train, but to train hard. The approach to important training sessions is to make hard efforts, not just to get them done. Youngsters must know that training must be done on a consistent basis.

When I first started running I was doing about 2.10 in the 800. I then went to Portugal, where I trained consistently for four months, improving my time to 2.04 at the 1988 Olympic Games. After that experience I returned to Maputo and trained sporadically for the next two years and did not do better than 2.08. Early in 1991 I moved to the United States, training there with more diligence and consistency, improving regularly, finally to 1.57 later in the same

year at the World Championships in Tokyo. I have experienced only one injury in my career. What I learned was that it was possible to compete well under adverse conditions. I just refused to let the injury take over my mind. I was able to put the injury aside even if I am sure it had some negative effect. I did establish a new Junior World Record at the World Championships when the injury was the most intense.

One must accept that it is all right to lose a race. Your rivals are talented and train hard as well. By accepting it is all right to lose you will not lose sight of your goal which is to win. You have to go back to training, as training is the key to success. You also have to take the trouble to analyze your losing effort, as a lot can be gained in establishing new racing tactics for the future races. For me, self-confidence is created by the preparation (training) for races. If I can train better this year than last year, then I will feel good about my chances when I toe the line.

To a young runner I would say, "Training is the key to everything. Try to push yourself to new levels. Keep records of your training so that you will be able to follow your improvement. Also, it is very important to enjoy what you are doing. For me the best thing in running is the things that it has brought to my life. Certainly it has provided me with health, financial security and a great deal of self-confidence and self esteem, as I have had some degree of success at this sport.

NGENY Noah

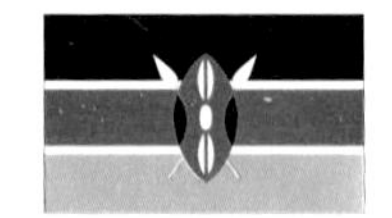

born 2 Nov 1978 Kenya.
After finishing 8th in the 1996 World junior 1500m final (almost falling twice), Ngeny made astonishing progress, breaking Jim Ryun´s 31 year-old mile World junior record with 3.50.41 in 1997. In 1998 Ngeny paced Hicham El Guerrouj to a 1500m World Record, himself running 3.30.34. In 1999 he was the most prolific miler in the world, breaking 3.30 at 1500m six times and taking the silver medal in the Worlds. An absolutely fearless runner, his greatest race so far was the mile in 3.43.40 behind El Guerrouj´s WR 3.43.13 in Rome. In September, Ngeny broke Seb Coe´s 18 year-old 1000m World Record in Rieti. - In Sydney 2000, Ngeny´s magnificent run brought him an Olympic 1500m gold medal - Kenya´s first big victory in this event since Peter Rono in Seoul 12 years earlier.
800m 1.44.49, 1000m 2.11.96, 1500m 3.28.12, one mile 3.43.40, 2000m 4.50.08, 3000m 7.35.46.

"I don´t want to set any limits"

The summer of 1999 was a bit surprising for me, but I had been in such good shape that I kind of knew I would be doing very well. I am 21 now. I started running in 1994 and went into serious training two years later. I became a runner because I had seen many famous Kenyans competing in Europe, and I wanted to be like them. I was there in 1993 when Kenyan runners were celebrated after returning home from World Championships in Stuttgart. That was a great occasion for me. I also thought I could get money from running and become a well-known person. Starting training always is a bit hard, but when your body responds, it is going smoothly. My coach in Britain is Kim McDonald, but in Kenya I am training with people like Moses Kiptanui, Daniel Komen etc.

In training there are many problems that you may encounter. Injuries... It is hard. Maybe you feel lazy sometimes, but it is a must that you go out and train. You can feel tired, but you have to do it anyway. To become a top runner, self-discipline is the vital thing. To be able to control yourself. You need to be serious in order to succeed. Self-discipline is something that comes when

you are young. It should be in your mind when you start training. Self-discipline often comes from your parents. They should know how you are doing at school. Last year I was training hard and yet was beaten in almost every race. What I thought was "I will learn from these defeats, I will train even harder and be the winner next year". Don´t worry about your position in the race, whatever it is. Try to run faster times so that you can see you are progressing.

I do not want to set any limits. Last year, when I was pacing El Guerrouj to his World Record 3.26.00, I thought no one else could run that fast. But now, having run 3.28 myself, I know I can run 3.26 or even faster. I have seen my times becoming better and better year after year. I don´t really feel pain even when I am running 3.28, yet in spite of the fact that I put everything into the race, I couldn´t catch El Guerrouj. I really don´t think about the pain before a race.

When I watch a bad race of mine on tape, I don´t press the fast-forward button (smiles). I have had races in the past in which I was really struggling. I want to find out the reason why that happened. That is why I like to watch any race of mine. I think it is good to have self-confidence because it makes you run faster. I am confident now because I know I am in shape. You cannot be confident before you have trained well. Training gives you the confidence you need. When you are good in training, that means you are good in racing as well. Somebody can win every now and then without being in good shape, but the next day he can finish last. Then you cannot be confident any more. Young runners should realize that training is hard. To be an international runner is not something easy. But when you make it and reach the top, you will be a well-known personality. Have self-discipline, train well, then you will be a good runner. The best thing is that running has made it possible for me to see the world: London, USA, Australia, Sweden... If I had not run, I wouldn´t have been able to do this.

NGUGI John

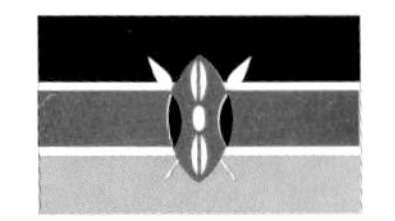

born 10 May 1962 Nyahuru, Kenya. Member of Kikuyu tribe.
A wonderful runner who liked to lead, Ngugi won World Cross Country title five times in 1986, 1987, 1988, 1989 and 1992. In Seoul Olympic Games in 1988, Ngugi put in a 58,2 seconds lap in the early part of the 5 000 metres final and managed to hold on to win the gold medal. In 1992, after refusing to undergo an out-of-season doping test at his home in Kenya, Ngugi was banned for four years from the sport, after which he was not able to reach the top again.
1500m 3.37.02, one mile 3.56.75, 3000m 7.45.59, 5000m 13.11.14, 10 000m 27.11.62, half marathon 1.01.24.

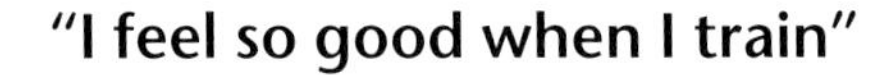

"I feel so good when I train"

I started running at school at age 15 because I enjoyed running. I saw Henry Rono´s and Kipchoge´s success which inspired me. I wanted to become as famous a runner as they were. However, when I started running, I never knew that I was going to reach such heights one day. I trained hard and finally became successful. I have also realized that running can make you rich.

Many runners don´t like cross country, but I was good at it because I enjoyed it. Later, I lost some of my interest in cross country. I wanted to concentrate on track running, but I also still wanted to defend my cross country title.

All I can say about self-confidence is that I get it by training hard

My message to young athletes is that if you want to win a gold medal you have to work hard for it. You have to set your mind to your goal. The best thing in running is training and winning. I feel so good when I train. Sometimes I like running alone, but some other times I enjoy training with company.

NIYONGABO Venuste

born 9 Dec 1973 Vugizo, Burundi.
5000m Olympic Champion in Atlanta 1996 (his first season at the distance), 1500m World Championships bonze medallist 1995. Burundi´s first ever Olympic Champion.
800m 1.45.13, 1000m 2.15.62, 1500m 3.29.18, one mile 3.46.70, 2000m 4.48.69, 3000m 7.34.03, 2 miles 8.17.56, 5000m 13.03.29. Missed part of 1997 and the whole of 1998 season due to illness and injury, then made a tentative come-back to racing in 1999.

"To run is one´s own choice"

At school I was playing soccer, volleyball and handball. I enjoyed those sports, but as I wanted to see more of my country and meet more people and friends, I started to practice athletics. I did that only because I wanted to be the best in my school and because I hoped to get more friends. I did not know anything about international competition, because we had no television. Being the best runner in my village, I was given a chance to join a club in our capital - the only club in our country. I had been practicing for four years, but my parents really did not want me to join the club because they thought that wouldn´t be a good thing for my studies. It wasn´t until 1991 that my parents gave me the permission to join the club, because I had been doing so well in my studies. That year, at age 18, I was the second-best miler in my

country. In 1992, I went to World Junior Championships in Seoul, where I got the silver medal. Soon after, I had a contact with some American universities and was waiting for answers from them, when my federation told me about Dionisi, from Siena in Italy, who wanted to contact me. I went to Italy in March 1993, but it was so cold I couldn´t train for a month. When it finally got warmer, I started to train and ran many personal bests. At first, the only runner whose name I knew was Dieudonne Kwizera, our own 800 metres runner. In my country, every student is practicing sports because they think that way they may be able to get abroad. Kwizera was our first runner to get a scholarship in the U.S.A. The first time I heard about Morceli was about 1993. That time I was thinking perhaps I might be good enough to get into Grand Prix races some day. Yes, I have met Morceli many times later. We have taken the same aeroplanes, but we haven´t had time to talk very much. (After a switch into a written interview, Niyongabo gives the rest of his answers on a sheet of paper decorated with a symbol "SPORT AGAINST DRUGS".) When planning my training, I usually look for two weeks ahead at a time. Before planning the training schedule, I have to see when I have competition and when I need hard training or a specific training programme. I don´t think I have made any major errors in my training thus far.

I have had setbacks during my career, but it is not so easy to learn from them because they may be different from what they were earlier. After being beaten in a race, I am capable of facing the facts. Either, I was beaten by a better runner, or there may have been some other reason, which I have to think about. My advice is that a defeat may mean many things: somebody has been stronger than you; you have to have a close look at your training schedule; the defeat also may have had something to do with a lack of experience.

The way for an athlete to acquire self-confidence is through a good training programme and striving after victory. I don´t think self-confidence is a born thing; an athlete can cultivate his mental strength year after year. Sometimes I have had an urge of giving up in a race because the athletic season is too long. Sometimes it has been difficult for me even to warm up for a race. Publicity, for me, mainly is a positive thing. I like to read the sports pages in detail because I have to know what they are saying about me. I also enjoy watching any race of mine on video; that is because I need to know what I may have done wrong and what I have to correct. I want to tell the youth that to run is one´s own choice. After you have chosen to become a runner, you are responsible for what you are doing. That means that you have to be honest about yourself. You have to train your self-confidence, your mental power for winning.

ONDIEKI Yobes

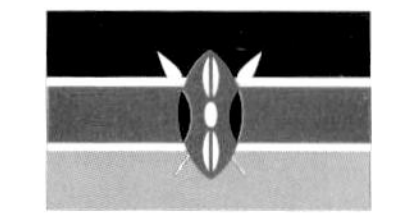

born 21 Feb 1961 Kenya. Member of Kisii tribe.
On 10 July 1993 in Oslo, Ondieki crowned his long career by becoming the first man in history to run 10 000m in under 27 minutes (26.58.38) in his second ever track race on this distance. 5000m World Champion in 1991, having led the race from the second lap on. A tough competitor, who used to prepare for big races with extremely hard track sessions.
1500m 3.34.36, one mile 3.55.32, 2000m 5.01,6, 3000m 7.34.18, 5000m 13.01.82, 10 000m 26.58.38, half marathon 1.01.41.

"I never felt I was burning myself off"

All pupils in my high school in Kenya had to take part in sports. Moreover, we had to participate in various competitions after school. That was when I noticed I was better in running races than the others. After doing some races, I was selected to take part in bigger meetings representing my school in other parts of Kenya, which made me start regular training. Yes, I have had periods of motivational problems. There have been times when I have been feeling tired and worn-out. For instance, in 1992 I was suffering from sciatica during the Olympic Games. Only a few weeks earlier I had been running well, but suddenly I was in big trouble. Not being able to do any fast workouts was very frustrating.

Also, when I was studying hard I was not able to concentrate on running as much as I wanted. Physically everything was O.K., but mentally I was lacking the vital spirit. When healthy and injury-free, I always enjoy training. Every workout is a new challenge for me. I enjoy setting new goals and preparing for them. The most important thing for a young distance runner is to avoid training too hard. The correct way is to develop oneself gradually, with small steps, year after year. It is not wise for a young athlete to aim too high too soon. Training levels must be synchronized with an athlete´s age and maturity.

I don´t believe I would have become so good if I had not been saving myself in my youth. Even the many injuries I had eventually helped me to reach higher. I never felt I was burning myself off unlike so many other talents you never hear again about later. It is natural to feel bad after being beaten in

race. What I have learned, however, is that every race has many competitors who have the will and the ability to win. You always have to remember this is only sport. There would be no sense in sport if Ondieki always won everything. Even after being defeated, I am always able to think analytically. It is no problem for me to watch a hopeless race of mine on video. On the other hand, I think that analysis by video is even better for sprinters or field event athletes who rely more on technique than distance runners. In our sport, what counts is what is happening inside your body. For me, self-confidence means being able to look forward to a close race with people like Said Aouita or Noureddine Morceli. An athlete can look forward to a race when he or she has been training well and when he or she can consult a capable expert who is able to tell you what you can expect with this kind of training. In my view, European runners pay too much importance to tactical and technical aspects of racing, instead of just going out and running as fast as they can. It is a kind of dangerous trap for an athlete to think too methodically, for instance "I am able to run 62 second laps, but no faster". What you must do is to forget about limits and convince yourself you will be a hard competitor for anyone in the world.

"No one can race forever"

Running is good in teaching you to deal with life. Everyone has to understand that it is not the end of the world to be beaten in a running race. A person must have other things in life as well: home, family, playing with children... All this is extremely important. Young people should be happy and avoid drugs at all costs. Training should be a gradual process. You should never copy anyone else´s schedules. You should find out what is good for you, preserving your energy for the important years to come. The best thing in running is when you win. The winner always gets his or her prize. Nevertheless, you have to keep in mind that running takes a lot of effort, and no one can race for ever. Everyone has to face the day when your legs are starting to feel old.

It is important for sports federations in all countries to help their athletes. If you want your runners to succeed, you have to assist their training financially. Any athlete working from 8 a.m. to 5 p.m. for his or he living cannot train as well as is needed for world class results.

I don´t want to hide the fact that one of the main reasons for the African runners being so good is simply the money. When Africa was boycotting the Olympic Games, it was a very bad thing for the enthusiasm for the sport in our continent. On the other hand, when IAAF started the Grand Prix circuit that was a great motivation for us to reach as high as we can. I think it is right to reward top athletes with money; that is the only means for us to be able to train. No one wants to see a 5000 metres race won in 14 minutes in a big meeting.

I did my first real racing tour in Europe in 1988. I had been there five years earlier, after which I had injuries and was studying hard, which was why I did not return until 1988. During that season I had a dozen 5000 metres races, and I ran every one of them hard. Yet in 1989, starting my indoor season, I overheard my agent say "Ondieki will never reach the top". That was when I decided to show them. I went back to Kenya to train very, very hard at our private training camp with Peter Koech. He made me run faster and still faster during our 800 and 1000 metres repeats. I was the one always to lead, and I soon realized Peter was in great shape as well.

Back in Europe, I won my first race. The next one in England was against such guys as Steve Cram and Eamonn Martin. I knew they were excellent kickers so I had to run their legs off. No one knew me, so I thought "so what if I am playing with fire". I decided to run so fast from the start that Cram and Martin would feel it. Everybody in the stadium was excited about my tactics, and I decided to make it as my hallmark. Very soon I noticed some other people had started racing in the same way.

O'SULLIVAN Sonia

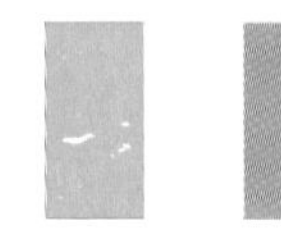

born 28 Nov 1969 Cork, Ireland.
5000m World Champion 1995, 3000m European Champion 1994. 1500m World silver medallist 1993. Overall winner of IAAF Grand Prix 1993. 2000m world record 5:23.3 in 1994. 3000m European record 8:21.64 in 1994. 5000m indoor world record 15:17.28 in 1991. Best non-Chinese runner in the 1500 and 3000m at World Championships in 1993.
Made a remarkable return to the top after a couple of lean years in 1998, winning both distances at the World Cross Country Championships in Morocco and winning both the 5000 and 10 000 metres European titles in Budapest, the latter in her first ever try at the distance.
800m 2:00.69, 1000m 2:34.66, 1500m 3:58.85, mile 4.17.25, 2000m 5:25.36, 3000m 8:21.64, 5000m 14:41.40, 10 000m 31:29.33.

When planning my training I usually have a general idea of what type of training I will be doing throughout the year. From October to March I am usually doing a lot of distance work, with a lot of long runs, hills and cross country type sessions. Then around the start of April I begin to include some track sessions which become more frequent and intense as I get closer to the summer track season and the major races that I am preparing for. Inside each of these segments I like to have a basic plan of action for each week, so I normally plan a week ahead at a time. I always like to know exactly what I am going to do before I go to sleep at night. I find it difficult to rest if I don´t have a specific run in my mind for the next day.

I really enjoy training each day, especially when the weather is good. I always feel good when I return from my morning run in the Park. I also like to run with my friends and have a chat. Sometimes we have such interesting conversations that when we return home we are still talking and could continue to run for many more miles without any effort.

The only times that I lack motivation are if I am extremely tired or if I have any aches or pains which I can´t seem to shake. If I ever have a problem getting myself going on any particular morning, I always ask myself the

question: What would I rather be doing at this moment? I rarely have an answer at 9 a.m., so I figure I am better to be out running than doing nothing. After taking a break in October, I am always ready to start back into the long weeks and months of winter training. After reviewing the previous season and finding any mistakes I have made, or areas where I know that I can improve, I set about my training with a new motivation to be better and faster than the year before.

"I might have got out of the wrong side of the bed"

I don´t always look forward to a very hard training session, but somehow I always take myself into working hard once the session gets started. If I lack concentration during a session, there is usually a reason. I might have something on my mind or I might simply have got out of the wrong side of the bed. Sometimes, rather than struggle through the session, I might change it to a shorter session or go for an easy run and come back to the track when I am in a better frame of mind. I never add extra miles to my training diary. I possibly write less than the truth sometimes, because when I run for time I tend to divide the total by a 7 min/mile estimate. I have been told that I regularly run a lot faster than 7 minutes per mile.

Also, I never falsify the times I have been running. You only cheat yourself since you only get out of a race what you have put in on the training track. If I don´t know why I am doing a particular training session, I have a hard time putting all my energy and concentration into it, because the whole time that I am doing the session I am trying to figure out why and what benefit it is to me. Sometimes if I miss training for reasons other than illness or injury, I will do a lot of sit-ups, push-ups, leg exercises and stretching before I go to bed. Sometimes I just accept that I am not going to get a session in and take the day off and enjoy my rest. The only errors I have made that affected my training and racing plans have been when I have felt any slight injuries and I have continued to train until the injury is so bad that I have to take time off and do alternative training on a bike or in the pool. I think that the most important thing in training is to train consistently each day, to train sufficiently hard that you improve gradually and consistently each day, week, month and year.

"I would definitely advise young runners to stay off the road"

When I was 17 years old I had a lot of stress fractures in both of my legs. Each time I had to take off at last 4 weeks from training. I think that because my bones were still growing and while I was training hard my body couldn´t cope with the extra stress of running each day. At this time I also did a lot of running on the road. Nowadays I train on the grass and through parks as much as possible. I think it allows me to train harder and farther because the soft ground doesn´t take as much out of my legs and allows me to recover faster. I would definitely advise young athletes to stay off the road, especially when they are still growing. Sometimes when you are younger you should train with a greater emphasis on quality than quantity. I now realise that at the slightest pain I should have my physio or massage therapist check it out and suggest whether I need to take a day off or continue running. I have also been receiving a regular massage to make sure that everything is in order each week. The thing that I have learned from my mistakes is that it is better to take one or two days off than to continue training to the point where you are forced to take a few weeks off training.

"After a defeat, my first reaction is always emotional"

If I am surprisingly defeated in a race, my first reaction is to be upset and disappointed with myself. I think my first reaction is always emotional and therefore I find it hard to control my feelings. Also, it is hard to accept a defeat without analysing the reason, which is why I like to talk through the race, possibly watch it on video and discuss the errors I may have made during the race. I am always able to accept the hard facts of a bad race, and once the problem has been found and analysed I like to close the door and start again tomorrow, trying my best to never make the same mistake again.

As an advice for young runners, the first and most important thing is to realise that being beaten is not the end of the world. It is only one race, and there is always another race within a week or two. There is nothing wrong with being disappointed but you must not be devastated. You must put things in perspective and always remember that it is a sport that you are taking part in, so you should enjoy what you are doing. As soon as running begins to lose the enjoyment factor, it becomes twice as difficult to work hard in training and racing.

Before a big race I try to be as relaxed as possible. Therefore, to create a normal atmosphere I tend to act the same towards my main rivals both before and after the race. I may be a little bit tense before the race, but I greet my friends and rivals as I would at any other time. We may even sit and stretch together before warming up.

Once the race gets started I find a wall forms around me and I focus and concentrate on what I have to do and block out everyone else in the race, instead focusing on doing everything possible to win the race against everyone else in the field and also against the clock. After the race I will congratulate my fellow athletes and more than likely go for a warm-down jog, discussing the race and various other topics. After the race the wall around me disintegrates, and I am a lot more relaxed and talkative. I think that self-confidence for me as an athlete comes into the play when I step on the starting line and know that because I have put in plenty of testing track sessions I am ready to run my very best. Self-confidence is a belief in the training I have completed over the past few weeks and months. If I have any doubts regarding my training and why I am doing any sessions, it is difficult to find the races easy.

I also feel that no matter how much confidence athletes have in themselves, they must have somebody else, such as a coach who instills this confidence in their minds before each important race and even during a difficult track session. When the coach speaks to the athlete, doubts and fears are often eliminated and never discussed. Together they must always think positively and move forward to a higher level. Ever since I finished 4th in the Olympic Games in 1992, my manager Kim McDonald has always been there to make sure that I have no doubts or fears in my mind before each race. He is rarely surprised by any fast times that I run or races that I win, because he is aware of what training I have been doing and he knows when I am ready to run my best race. He also has an explanation if I don´t feel as good as I would like. It also helps that I am never afraid of training and racing up to his expectations because I see it as a challenge. Other than winning, an athlete can gain a lot of self-confidence by competing in every race for as far as possible.

To be competitive is the most important thing in a race. Especially for young athletes it is not possible to become a winner before you are fully developed as an international athlete. There are stepping stones to be taken every year, and as long as an athlete´s performances continue to improve, then their self-confidence in their abilities should also be improving with each race.

Once an athlete is physically ready to achieve a great victory, there are a few other factors to consider in order to win a race. The athlete must:
- Feel relaxed and confident.
- Be nervous but in full control of the situation.
- Be well rested, and have slept well in the days leading up to the race.

Always picture a positive outcome of the race. It is good to run through the race in your mind a few times to prepare yourself for every possible situation. Go through the race as you would a normal training day, eat foods you are comfortable with, and warm up as you would before a track training session.

"Every race is really a game"

It is always important to feel that you belong in each race that you run. If an athlete´s mind is not focused, then it is very difficult for the body to co-operate and run the best possible race. The mind and body must work together. If one aspect is lacking, it is difficult to be successful. Once you are in control of your mind, then it is also important to always have a look of confidence, especially if you are going into the race but not feeling 100%. Your rivals do not need to know that you are below par!

As an athlete´s training and racing move to a new level and his/her confidence grows, then the mind also becomes stronger. So just as an athlete develops physically, the mind should also move to a new level of thinking and a greater ability to concentrate. I have never wanted to drop out of a race or give up. I think it is easier to recover mentally from a bad race than from an incomplete race. When I was younger, my club coach always said that if you drop out of a race, it only makes it easier to drop out of more races in the future. It is when athletes lose control of their minds that they allow negative thoughts enter and begin to physically feel bad. At this point your mind has won the "mind over body" game! Every race is really a game. You should be physically fit enough to race, but if your mind starts to play games during the race and if you lose control of your positive thoughts, then negative thoughts begin to take over and you either lose the race, drop out or quit. It is important to prepare yourself mentally for winning. Before any major race I try to visualise the race with a number of different scenarios. I picture how I should deal with any situation I may be faced with. When I have run through the race in my mind and resolved each challenge positively, then I know that I am ready for anything in the real race. I try not to think about the race for any great length of time, because if I start picturing it in my mind over breakfast and I don´t run until 9 p.m., then I find that I get too nervous too early. It is better to set a time later in the afternoon when I begin to channel all my energy towards focusing on the race and the positive result that I can expect. Of course every race will not work out perfectly even if you imagined it would, but I don´t think anyone should prepare themselves for a negative result.

"Somehow we need to eliminate all the cheats from the sport"

I think that when people have to cheat to win, they are really only cheating themselves. They must live in fear of being caught and find it difficult to look their hardworking opponents straight in the eye, if they have any conscience. Everyone is different, we have different levels of ability, we are born with different talents and some people have the ability to work harder than others. People who cheat are looking for a short-cut to the top. Most people who take short-cuts anywhere find themselves turning around and starting again. Somehow we need to eliminate all the cheats from the sport and play fairly and honestly. Hard training is not recognised if you have a group of chemical creations winning all the medals.

"We all need supporters and fans"

I think it is important to be seen by the public as both a person and an athlete. I am willing to co-operate with the media as long as it fits in with my training schedule. I always believe that my training should come first, because if I get too involved with publicity, then my training will suffer. So will my races, and then the reason for publicity vanishes. I don´t try to avoid publicity but I do like to have some time to myself to be a normal person occasionally. We all need supporters and fans. However too many times a negative aspect such as a great athlete being defeated or an athlete with a positive drug test will make headlines rather than a great performance. I don´t have a problem reading about myself. I like to read any athletic stories and learn more about other athletes that I may be competing against. I think it is good for me to watch a video tape of a bad race that I have had. I can be very critical of myself, but I also like when other people point out what went wrong. I listen and remember any advice I am given, which I then recall if I am ever in the same situation again. Video tapes are great for pointing out errors and thinking of ways to overcome them, but also good as a confidence builder before a race, to watch what I have already run before. It is also good to have a look at my main rival and pick out their good and bad points.

If I read something about myself that is untrue, then I let anyone with me know that, but I don´t dwell on it and usually forget about it before I have finished reading the paper. I don´t believe everything that is written in the papers. Sometimes people don´t get a true picture of an athlete. I read the papers for enjoyment, not for the true facts. When I am training and racing I do not think about money. I feel very grateful to the people who support me and know that if I were not being paid to train hard and run races, it would be very difficult for me to be as committed to my daily training schedule as I am.

With regard to financial factors and which races I choose to run, I leave that in the hands of my manager Kim McDonald. I trust him to make the best decisions for me, and I just concentrate on the training I have to do in order to perform my best in the races.

Sometimes when I go out for a run in the morning, I think to myself how lucky I am. I have the best job in the world, for me, and there is nothing else I would rather be doing.

My personal message for young runners: Consistency is the most important thing in training to be a great athlete. Nobody can become a world champion overnight. It takes a lot of years of consistent commitment to training that build upon each other each year and raise you to a new level. There are no short-cuts! To be successful you must enjoy what you are doing. You must feel good after a training session and look forward to the next one.

Running is a great way to relax. You can go for a run and clear your mind. After a run I always find myself refreshed and in a great frame of mind. There is nothing I like better than going for a run anytime, any place! For me, that is the best thing about running.

OVETT Steve

born 9 Oct 1955 Brighton, England.
One of the most versatile middle distance runners ever. 800m Olympic Champion and 1500m bronze medallist in Moscow 1980, 1500m European Champion 1978, European 800m silver medallist 1974 (at age 18) and 1978. 5000m Commonwealth Champion 1986. Ran one mile in 4.00,0 at age 17. Five World Records (two at 1500m, two at one mile, one at two miles) in 1978-81. Had a string of 45 consecutive 1500m/one mile wins in 1977-80. A happy-go-lucky character who never took his running deadly seriously.
400m 47,5, 800m 1.44.09, 1000m 2.15.91, 1500m 3.31.36, one mile 3.48.40, 2000m 4.57,8, 3000m 7.41,3, 2 miles 8.13.51, 5000m 13.25,0, half marathon 1.05.38 (two weeks before World Cup 1500m win in 1977!).

"... to lessen the feeling of futility"

I usually planned my training for two or three weeks ahead at a time. However, Olympic Games and other big meetings were a different matter. The truth is, generally I was not able to follow my plans, but it did not worry me. There wasn´t always enjoyment in my training. On the contrary, quite often there were days when it was very boring to go out and do it. I can´t stand it! There must be better things to do! I found it was best to do it with someone else to lessen the feeling of futility.

I always wrote down my training totally honestly - of course! I always knew why I was doing this or that type of training and never tried to compensate later anything that I might have missed for one reason or another. I don´t think I ever made any grave errors in my training schedule. For me, the most essential thing in training is continuity - to keep it going regularly, week after week, month after month and so on. Yes, there were quite a many setbacks during my career - too many to mention. Whatever adversities you may have, you just have to go on. On the other hand, I never let defeats depress me: it was just a running race, not a matter of life and death. My way of getting over disappointments was to cry them away - I cry a lot! - and then to make up my mind to win my next race. Winning is easy, whereas losing is something that usually needs working at. A few drinks usually helps a lot!

In addition to great fitness, a big victory requires simple luck as well. You don´t win a race by mental power alone. The decisive thing is the physical fitness required in your event. As to self-confidence, for me it means just honesty allied to competence. I have to admit I had the feeling of wanting to give up almost in every race, usually on the second lap of the one mile race.

There will always be the problem of doping in sports, and you have to live with it

I never had any problems with publicity whatsoever. Publicity may be good or bad, depending on how you use it. I used not to read the stories written about me nor collect clippings. I also find it boring to watch in video something that is past. Yes, I have noticed people being sometimes envious about my achievements, but I never let it bother me. My advice to young runners? Well, I think it is a good job to be a runner if you do it well. However, I would say, pack it in and take up golf!

The best thing in running is the finish line!

PIETERSE Zola

born 26 May 1966 Bloemfontain, South Africa. Née Budd.
A fantastic and controversial athlete in her youth - often racing in barefoot -, Budd broke through in South Africa in early 1980´s, setting several world bests, which were not officially approved due to the apartheid policy of her country at the time and its exclusion from IAAF. She was granted British citizenship in 1984, finishing 7th in the dramatic Olympic 3000 metres final in 1984. Won the World Cross Country title for Britain in 1985 and 1986, then returned to South Africa where she got married and became a mother. She has run some excellent times in the 1990´s and represented her country in Olympic Games, World Cross Country and World Half Marathon Championhips.
800m 2.00,9, 1500m 3.59.96, one mile 4.17.57, 2000m 5.30.19, 3000m 8.28.83, 5000m 14.48.07, 10K road 32.20, half marathon 1.11.09.

"Your mental attitude is what matters"

I started running due to the fact that I was not good at any other sport. I couldn´t do any ball games. I just didn´t have the ability in any sport except running, which is the easiest sport in the way that you don´t need any equipment for it. I sometimes do have motivational problems when I am feeling tired, not very often though. Whenever I miss a training session, I tend to feel guilty and try to fill it in later somewhere. Your mental approach is the most important thing in your training. It is not so important what you do, but your mental attitude is what matters. You have to believe that the training works. As to getting over a defeat, I am still looking for the formula myself. I just train harder which is probably not the right thing to do but it motivates me after a bad race. I think that for every athlete, self-confidence probably means something

different. Some get it from the training session they have done, some from the races they have won and from the natural abilities they have. For me it is the combination of good training and the good races I have had. Self-confidence comes not only from training but if training goes well, it helps. Yes, there have been quite a many times when I have wanted to drop out of a race, for example in the 1984 Olympic 3000 metres final. I am probably one of the few athletes who have excelled as a junior and still run as a senior. My message to young generation is that it is important to pace and plan your career on a long term which I did not do. Put your goals far ahead and don´t be disappointed if you don´t succeed at first. The best thing in running simply is the feeling that I get from it.

PUTTEMANS Emiel

born 8 Oct 1947 Leuwen, Belgium.
In addition to Olympic 10 000m silver medal in the 1972 Olympic Games, Puttemans broke world records three times outdoors (2 miles 8.17,8 in 1971, 3000m 7.37,6 in 1972, 5000m 13.13,0 in 1972) and five times indoors, including an unusual feat of 28.12,0 at 10 000m in 1975. His indoor world record of 7.39,2 at 3000m in 1973 had a lifespan of 19 years, and that of 8.13,2 at 2 miles in 1973 still remained intact at the start of the new Millennium (broken in 2000). Puttemans - a gardener by profession - had a long career, running a sub-13.30 in the 5000 m for 12 years in a row.
1500m 3.40,4, one mile 3.56,0, 2000m 4.59,8, 3000m 7.37,6, 2 miles (indoors) 8.13,2, 3000m steeplechase 8.27,8, 5000m 13.13,0, 10 000m 27.39,6, marathon 2.12.27.

"A young athlete must have big dreams"

At 15 years of age I was training once a week. At 16, there were two training sessions a week. By the 1968 Olympic Games, at age 21, I was training six times a week, which means I had been adding a little bit every year. Thanks to Gaston Roelants, distance running was quite popular in Belgium those days. He was 10 years older than me and 12 years older than Karel Lismont, the great marathon runner. We had to train hard, because there were 6 to 8 world class distance runners in Belgium those days. That was very good for our motivation. The most important thing in running is to enjoy it. As

well as you have been doing, you have to aim higher and higher all time. A young athlete must have big dreams. I did my first runs together with my brother, eight years older than me. He was training with Gaston Roelants, and every now and then I could join them, which made me very happy. That was how I became a distance runner. I had no problems with finding a good coach, because I was lucky to have the same one who had been guiding Roelants and Ivo van Damme forward. I was lucky in another respect as well. I did not burn myself off as a youngster.

If you train too hard when you are young, you will have had enough of running by the time you are 23 or 24. You have to train in a way that allows you being hungry for more and more. The ideal age for hard training is that from 28 to 29 or even to 32. I was putting in my hardest training from age 23 to 29. I had three distinct racing seasons per year. First, I was racing cross country until the end of January. I then moved indoors, aiming at the European Championships. Finally, after a pause of a couple of weeks, I started training for the summer season.

I had no chance of beating Lasse Viren in the Munich 10 000m Olympic final. All I could do was to try and follow him during the last 400 or 200 meters. He was faster. I couldn´t do anything about it. When you are beaten fair and square in a race by a better athlete, it is useless to look for any explanations. No runner can succeed without self-confidence. The way to build self-confidence is to train hard. As soon as you can do good times in training, you can be sure about yourself. The best race of my career was the 5000m in Brussels (13.13,0), but I perhaps have even fonder memories of my indoor 2 miles, which still has not been bettered. My 3000 m indoor time also was something about which I really cannot complain.

QUAX Dick

born 1 Jan 1948 Alkmaar, Netherlands. At 6 years of age moved to New Zealand.
At his favourite distance 5000m Quax was an Olympic silver medallist behind Lasse Viren in 1976 and ran a world record of 13.12.86 at Stockholm in 1977. His long career included world class times in everything from 1500m to the marathon.
1500m 3.36,7 (3.35,9 relay leg), one mile 3.56,2, 2 miles 8.17,1, 5000m 13.12.86, 10 000m 27.41.95, marathon 2.10.47.

"A runner cannot rely on team members"

The most important thing in training is to have a sensible plan. There is no single recipe for succeeding in sports. Everyone is an individual being, which means it is wrong to think you will become a great runner by imitating the training schedules of Dick Quax, Lasse Viren or Peter Snell. Every athlete has to find out a training programme suitable for his or her needs, and that is something that takes its time. Consequently, I wouldn´t like to emphasize any single detail in training, because there are so many things to be worked out before having success. Even if it is true that you have to train hard, it is even more true that you have to follow a training programme based on sound physiological facts. An athlete aiming high just cannot do any idiotic things in his training. Long distance running is a sport that takes immense amounts of energy and mental concentration. A runner cannot rely on team members. What he has to do is to take care of his training every morning and evening. It is quite natural to feel somewhat tired most of the time. A distance runner´s schedule may require running as much as 250 km per week, which means he is not feeling very fresh. Consequently, my answer to the question on motivational problems is "yes". Every runner training hard occasionally has motivational problems. It is difficult to flog oneself for daily training, for concentration, for continual motivation. In my view, the most important thing for an athlete is to feel that he is progressing. This means he has to follow a sensible training program thanks to which he is progressing - perhaps not every single day, but gradually nonetheless. Progress brings you more motivation at all levels of the sport. Peter Snell once said his self-confidence could have been better. I think I understand what he means. To a certain extent we are striving forward because we want to show it to ourselves and to our peers. A person having high goals in life may have an unusual mental and psychological build. Anyone succeeding in sports, business or politics probably is very much different from an ordinary man of street.

To reach the highest honours in any field you must have exceptional amounts of ambition, determination and ability to concentrate on a task waiting ahead. A person like this usually has a deep feeling that there is always something to improve at in regard to tactics, training and so on. Wanting to get better and better, he very seldom is happy with himself. In my mind, this fact certainly has something to do with self-confidence. There is a certain difference between a bitter defeat and a poor performance. If you have had a poor run, you have to analyze what went wrong. In case of a defeat, you have to understand that it is part of sport, part of life, part of the sum of experiences. You may have raced poorly due to bad preparation, wrong training or unsuitable tactics. On the other hand, if you have been training as well as you can and have raced your best possible race, then you should not let a defeat ruin your spirits. On the day, there was another competitor who was even faster, even better prepared. Everyone will be beaten sooner or later. No one is able to go through a running career without experiencing some kind of defeat. By this I want to emphasize that a defeat and a poor performance are two very different things. Every athlete should try and avoid poor performances, but you cannot avoid defeats. Sometimes you may have to take lots of criticism in spite of having had the race of your life. What you have to do is to learn to accept these things without becoming disheartened.

QUIROT Ana

born 23 Mar 1963 Palma Soriano (suburb of Santiago de Cuba).
One of the greatest 800 metres runners in history: World Champion 1995 and 1997, silver medallist 1991, Olympic silver medallist 1996 and bronze medallist 1992. A fluent and powerful stylist, Ana Fidelia Quirot had a winning streak of 39 consecutive victories at 800 metres in 1987-90. In her prime, she was emulating her compatriot Alberto Juantorena as a world class 400 and 800 metres runner. Pregnant in early 1993, Quirot was severely burned in an accident in her kitchen, sadly losing the child she was expecting. Her subsequent come-back to the tracks after 12 operations, culminating in two World titles was no less than a miracle. Quirot became a mother in 1999 and then announced her retirement from the sport.
200m 23.07, 400m 49.61 (49,2 hand timing), 600m 1.22.63, 800m 1.54.44, 1000m 2.33.12, 1500m 4.13.08. - Ana Quirot´s older sister Maria was a basketball player in the 1980 Olympic Games.

"Nothing in life is perfect"

The most important properties for an athlete are the desire to train hard; toughness of mind; determination and will power - most of all the mental strength for enduring physical exertion year after year. Yes, I have had an innumerable amount of various hardships during my career, but luckily - thanks to my mother, sister, coach, doctor and psychologist -, I have always managed to overcome them. Of course it has been essential as well that I have had the will to come back again and again. Whenever you have been beaten in a race, the reasons for your defeat must be deeply analyzed. Nothing in life is perfect: sometimes you win, sometimes you lose. As well as you may have trained and prepared for the race, and as fit as you may be both mentally and physically, you still may be beaten. That is the time to put forward some serious questions, trying to find out what went wrong. No one likes to be defeated.

In my view, the best way to build one´s self-confidence is to train hard. When you have a feeling of having done all you can and prepared for the race as well as you can, that is a solid confidence-builder, certainly bringing good results. My message to the young generation is this: The only valid reason for doing sports is for the enjoyment of it. Don´t start serious competition at too early an age. As to myself, I started athletics for the simple reason that I liked it. Even without ever reaching international level I am sure that I still would have been running for health and enjoyment. One of the positive sides of my sport are the people; all those people who are collecting signatures and who have a high regard for what you are doing; those people who come and watch you race. I find it extremely rewarding to get acquainted with people, to get new friends; to see many kinds of countries. The best thing in running - speaking of my own career - is that I was able to come back after my accident, reaching the very top of the sport again.

RADCLIFFE Paula

born 17 Dec 1973 Northwich, Cheshire, England.
A fearless runner who likes to lead, Radcliffe is enormously respected by her rivals from all over the world. A major force on the track as well as on the roads and cross country, she has very gradually climbed to the top. After posting the fastest ever 10 000m debut time of 30.48.58 in 1998, she finally climbed onto the medal podium in the 1999 World Championships in Seville, taking the silver. After finishing 4th in the Sydney Olympic final - having led most of the way in one of the greatest races ever - she finally fulfilled one of her dreams, winning the 2001 World Cross Country title nine years after her victory in the Junior race in Boston. She also won the World Half Marathon title in 2000.
400m 58,9, 800m 2.05.22, 1500m 4.05.81, one mile 4.24.94, 3000m 8.27.40, 5000m 14.43.54, 10 000m 30.26.97, half marathon 1.07.07. - Married to Gary Lough (1500m 3.34.76).

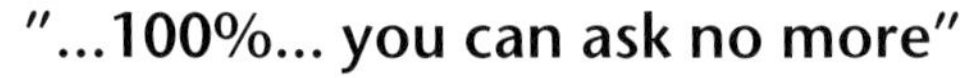

"...100%... you can ask no more"

I first started to get involved in running when I was 9 years old, but it wasn´t until I was 12 that I had any type of structure to what I did. At that time I ran three times a week, which progressed to four by the age of 15. I was training six times a week when I won the World Junior Cross Country in Boston in 1992.

My father used to do some running to keep fit, and often I would join in with him, for short distances, if he ran past. I also walked in a local forest with my mother. I found running enjoyable, but my parents were conscious that I shouldn´t do too much.

Some days it is easier to motivate yourself than others. The weather can be a factor, it is easier to go out when it is warmer or at least sunny. I find it easier to motivate myself when I have a major race approaching. I enjoy doing workouts more than steady running. I like the intensity that a workout can bring, although when you are running in beautiful surroundings time can pass by without you even noticing it.

To me the most important thing in training is to enjoy it. I feel that you get the most out of something when you are happy doing it. I also think that quality is very important, but everything must be tailored for individual needs rather than doing it because someone else does. As to injuries, in 1994 I had a stress fracture in my foot as well as in 1996. In 2000, I had to have a knee operation in June. I have learned that you have to listen to your body and also to respect it. I take my resting pulse every morning to monitor how my body is coping with training, and if it is not, I have to give it extra rest. I think that rest is very important to maximise one´s training.

While evwerybody wants to win, there can be only one winner. I think that while winning is very important, young runners should think about other things like progression, improving one´s personal bests. The most important thing is to give 100% of yourself - you can ask no more.

Self confidence is very important. How can you expect others to be confident in you if you do not have confidence yourself? Athletes can gain confidence from training and also from racing. It is very important to believe in yourself and your ability. This confidence does not have to be left on the sportsfield. I have found that the confidence I have gained from running has carried into other aspects of my life, making me a more confident person.

What I would like to say to young runners is to enjoy our wonderful sport and appreciate the gift that you have been given. Train hard and believe in yourself. Talent is important but it is not as important as hard work.

The best thing in running is the freedom that it brings. When I run, it is my time, there are no phones ringing, it is just me and the road ahead. Running has enabled me to travel all over the world and meet lots of new people, and I have a great time doing it.

RIBEIRO Fernanda

born 23 Jun 1969 Penafiel, Portugal.
More than a decade after running a 1.24 half marathon at age 11 and making the Portuguese national team at age 13, Ribeiro collected a hat trick of great 10 000 victories at European Championships in 1994, World Championships in 1995 and Atlanta Olympic Games in 1996. She also has a World Championship 5000 metres silver from 1995, 10 000 metres silver and 5000 metres bronze from 1997, and European 10 000 metres silver from 1998. She briefly held the 5000 metres World Record in 1995 and won the 1994 European 3000 metres title in her first ever indoor race. Sydney Olympic Games in 2000 saw Ribeiro running faster than ever, being rewarded with a 10 000m bronze medal. Ribeiro has participated in most of the big championships since the Europeans in Stuttgart in 1986, when only 17 years old. In late 1998 and early 1999 she again successfully tried the half marathon distance on her way to an eventual marathon debut .
800m 2.05.71, 1500m 4.05.97, 3000m 8.30.66, 5000m 14.36.45, 10 000m 30.22.88, half marathon 1.08.23.

"Whoever runs for the love of it, never gets bored!"

I got my first pair of running shoes from my father when I was 9 years old. We travelled together to Lousada, where I entered my first race, finishing in 2nd place behind a girl from Lisbon. My first coach was Luis Miguel, also well-known as the successful coach of the Penafiel soccer team. Thanks to him, I won the Portuguese junior cross country title at age 11 from rivals who were as much as seven years older than me. I also tried long road races at a very young age. In 1981, I took part in the Nazaret half marathon, finishing in 2nd place not far behind Rosa Mota. Due to a mix-up I did not do any kind of a finishing sprint in that race. Only a year later, Mota became the inaugural European marathon champion in Athens.

At age 16 I was asked if I was planning to become as good a runner as Rosa Mota and Aurora Cunha were. I still remember my answer: "No! I want to become even better!" Please don´t think that I was cocky or that success was going to my head. The plain fact is that I have never wanted to copy anyone. I

have wanted to be myself. I always knew I would have my future in long distance running, and I always was dreaming of big victories. For me, that is the very best thing in running: to fullfill one´s goals and dreams. After breaking many records and winning many national titles as a junior, I found it extremely difficult to have success among grown-up women. For a time it seemed I was not able to get rid of injuries. After many years of disappointments I finally made it, thanks to Joao Campos, my coach for the past decade or so. He has an excellent psychological eye, coupled with wide knowledge of the coaching aspects. I often train with Campos´ wife Elsa Amaral, but there is no exact programme; I always am free to improvise. Whenever I am feeling tired, not having the inspiration to train, then I will have a rest day. I never have any motivational problems. It is always a pleasure for me to run with someone else. Whoever runs for the love of it, never gets bored! The most important thing in training is to never give up. You should train not suffering a lot, but being happy in every training session. You have to like what you are doing.

What I have learned from my injury problems is that you have to comply with medical advice: if doctors tell you to stop, then you have to do it. This is my advice even if sometimes I am not doing that myself! It was very, very difficult for me to miss the 1997 World Cross Country Championships in Turin, but according to my doctor, it was a must due to the injury in my thigh muscle. All I could do was to have a complete rest. What made the decision even more difficult was the fact that my coach Campos was the leader of the Portuguese team, and my staying away from the race would diminish our chance to a great extent. Nevertheless, my coach did not want to risk my future.

After winning the Olympic 10 000 metres gold medal in Atlanta I was able to experience the immense joy of my fellow Portuguese people. For the whole way from the airport to my home village Novelas, I was standing in an open Jeep with the flag of my country in my hand, waving for the thousands of onlookers. At home, I followed my usual custom of placing a bouquet of flowers at the statue of Virgin Maria. For the next several days all I wanted to do was to sleep and eat the excellent meals cooked by my mother, something that I had not been able to enjoy in Atlanta.

By the way, my parents dared not watch my race on television; what I did was to phone them the great news after the race, and it was only then that they went and saw it on videotape. I really don´t enjoy watching my races afterwards, no matter how good they have been. Instead, I like watching the soccer matches of my home team FC Porto at Antas stadium. The problem is I always feel so nervous then that I am biting my fingernails! Consequently, I have had to limit my visits to these matches even if the club has asked me to come because - as they tell me - I am bringing luck for them!

Being asked things like that is a big honour for me. I have strong feelings about FC Porto, and I just love its blue and white colours. Also, after my Olympic victory I have visited many schools, giving signatures to children, encouraging them to start sports and emphasizing the meaning of honesty in all things in life. Cheating: results achieved by illegal means aren´t meaningful for an athlete, because they have not been done by yourself. It means that sooner or later an athlete will be cheating himself.

I like children very much. Whenever I see children playing, or kicking a ball, I enjoy joining them for a while. I have always been like that, and I haven´t been changed by success in any way. If I had not become a runner, I would have studied to be a kindergarten teacher. I still have many years to give to my sport, but sometimes later the time will come when I will work for my town, taking care of children.

RODAL Vebjörn

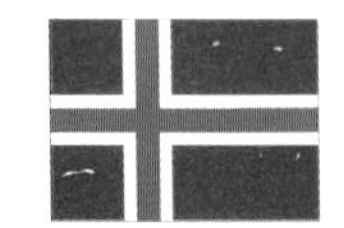

born 16 Sep 1972 Berkak, Norway.
After making the final only as the fastest loser, everything klicked with Rodal in the decisive race in Atlanta in 1996 as he won the Olympic 800 metres title with the fastest time of his career - 1.42.58. European silver medallist 1994, World bronze medallist 1995. A powerful runner who trains more like a quarter-miler and yet enjoys autumn treks of several hours in the Norwegian fjords and mountains.
400m 46.56, 600m 1.15.29, 800m 1.42.58, 1000m 2.16.78, 1500m 3.37.57.

"I have a very solid winner´s instinct"

I feel very flexible about my training programme. Every autumn I and my coach discuss what we shall do during the winter, but we never plan the training for more than a week ahead. We do this because it is impossible for us to say how my body reacts from day to day. It is my body which tells how much and what kind of training I shall do. I usually don´t have any motivational problems. If I do, or if I am very tired, I ease down the training load for a day or two and try to do something that I like. I have a very solid winner´s instinct. To be a good runner you have to endure pain, so pain is a daily event for me; in fact I enjoy the pain of the training.

If I miss a training session, I have a very good reason for it - something that certainly is more important that day than the training. So far I haven´t made any big mistakes in my training. I have been lucky, perhaps smart, too. Young runners´ training: have fun, think more about quality than quantity. It is important to be a fast runner, and it is easiest to be fast when you are young. Having variation in the training programme is important for young runners. In spite of being just 23 years old I feel I have a lot of experience. I have been running in two World Junior Championships and two Olympic Games, one European and two World Championships.

In the semi-final of the 1994 European Championships in Helsinki I got a stress fracture in my leg - my worst injury up to the present day. It was painful, but I nevertheless chose to run in the final and managed to win a silver medal. I have learned that it is very important to listen to the signals my body gives me. My body tells me when there has been enough training and when something is wrong. Listen to the body, not to the technical machines! If someone beats me in a race, he is a better runner than I am. If I have been able to do my best, then a defeat is O.K. If I feel I have had a bad race, I try to analyze it and find the reasons for the poor result.

You have to be able to deal with the facts. You have to be honest about everything. Honesty never is an unpleasant thing. It is fun to win, but you also learn by losing. About my rivals: Before a race we are saying hello, and perhaps shake hands, but nothing more. After the race we can relax and have a talk. I never hate any of my rivals, but I like beating them.

No, I never have had an urge of giving up during a race

You get self-confidence through experience. If you set yourself a goal and then reach it, it brings you more experience and self-confidence. Some runners behave in an arrogant way, but that has nothing to do with self-confidence. Arrogance is negative. Self-confidence is positive.

"No one should cheat when having fun"

As to the morals of sport, the most important thing is to be happy when you know you have run your best. It is also important to realize that running is not the most important thing in your life. Sports should be fun. No one should cheat when having fun. I don´t like cheating, which, in my view, also includes drugs. Without publicity there would be very little sports, but it is important that an athlete knows when to say "yes" or "no". The Press always wants more, so you have to tell them where the limit is. My coach says "yes" to what he thinks has to be done, but he also says "no" when he has to.

I see publicity more a positive than a negative thing. If journalists take my job (=running) seriously, then I´ll take their job seriously. If they are impolite to me, then my door will stay closed. Yes, I do read articles about myself, but not every one of them. In Norway we have a serious Press. I have no problem with watching my races on video, no matter if they are good or bad ones. I always learn something by having a look at them.

Yes, some people are envious, but it is not my job to change them. It´s their problem. Money: This is a hard world. If you are good, you get paid well. If you are bad, you can stay at home. Therefore it is better to be good than bad. Finally, the best thing in running for me is feeling happy after a training session that almost no one else in the world could have managed. Also, reaching a goal, like becoming an Olympic Champion or the first athlete ever to run a sub 1.40 at 800 metres.

adidas
Atlanta 1996
2009
Atlanta
KENYA
180
adidas

RODGERS Bill

born 23 Dec 1947 Hartford, Connecticut, U.S.A.
A great marathon runner, four-time winner at New York in 1976-79, four time winner at Boston in 1975 and 1978-80, winner at Fukuoka in 1977. 25 000 metres World Record 1.14.11,8 in 1979. Without American boycott, Rodgers would have been the number one favourite at the 1980 Olympic marathon in Moscow. In spite of starting serious training late - at age 25 -, Bill Rodgers became the inspiration for a whole generation of American road runners in the footsteps of Frank Shorter.
5000m 13.42,0, 10 000m 28.04.42, 25 000m 1.14.11,8, marathon 2.09.27. - Rodgers went on racing successfully in Masters competition at age 50 in the late 1990´s and early 2000´s.

"The continual renewal of your physical and spiritual self"

I started running for fun in informal races around our school. I then ran in a Parks & Recreation track meet one mile race which I won in 5 mins. 20 secs. I also played other sports for fun - baseball, swimming, badminton, basketball and so on. I admired Abebe Bikila, Ron Clarke, Jim Ryun and Gerry Lindgren in youth - and still do! My goal at the beginning was to win and to set records which I found I could do. I often ran alone but also with my brother Charles and friend Jason, joining our school cross country team with them. My friends realized I was serious about my running and were very encouraging to me. However, I had no idea of it becoming a lifetime sport.

After graduating from college I quit running for two years. I was in a state of confusion over possibly being forced to leave the U.S. due to being asked to join the army for the Vietnam war, and I was a conscientious objector. Even later I was many times considering retiring from racing (not from running), but I solved the problem by cutting back training. Training can be dull (very!) and boring, so you have to find the ways to make it easier - like training with friends, rewarding yourself for your "work" in some way etc.

Yes, I was in awe of my rivals sometimes but still tried to beat them. I was afraid of losing and still am, but the intensity of the feeling varies. In some of my early races I really did go out too fast for my conditioning due to self imposed pressure. I still occasionally lose my temper or have tantrums after losing to someone I feel I should have beaten, but get over it quickly. I immediately started having success in cross country and two mile track races against other high schools. I won nine races out of ten. I saved some clippings, and I loved the success!

In my early years my training was inconsistent, but I thought that was normal. In winter I ran indoors at school or jumped rope and lifted weights in the basement of our home. My biggest disappointment as a youth was losing the state championship title (I was 2nd) in X-country in my senior year. I realized I went out too fast for my level of strength. I also was bothered to be beaten by a younger runner than me in High School. This happened two or three times. My first real coach was in X-country and track in High School. His name was Frank O´Rourke. He went on coaching me for three years. I have had two other coaches since then.

The most essential thing for a coach is to understand all the practical matters concerned with the athlete such as his job, family situation etc. and factors such as the athlete´s response to constructive criticism, fatigue, losing, in addition to appreciate the athlete´s physical & psychological capacity. Of course it is difficult for a coach to do a successful job in every area of concern. Understanding the emotional side of a person probably is the most difficult thing. I was confident at a certain level but did not think beyond that in terms of my future. I only raced one year at a time. My breakthrough came in 1975 when I won a bronze medal in the World Cross Country Championships in Rabat, Morocco in 1975 and then won the Boston Marathon the month after in 2.09.55. My first trip abroad felt very exciting. It is another thing nowadays because I don´t travel much abroad any more. Of course I was excited about racing with and sometimes beating "star" runners. It was new to me and I didn´t believe I could do it!

"Every runner has motivational problems"

I usually plan my training several weeks or months in advance, occasionally even longer. Usually I have been able to follow my schedule. If I wasn´t, it bothered me in my prime, but not any more! In my view, flexibility to a minor degree with the program is a good thing. Every runner has motivational problems sooner or later! I do enjoy training under the right conditions (enough rest, decent weather etc). When keeping a training diary, I am always honest with writing down times and distances. I pretty much know why I´m doing this or that type of training. If I miss a workout, I will try and do it later, following my plan as much as possible.

I have occasionally overtrained (too much mileage) and overraced. Sometimes I have also done too little anaerobic work. The most important thing for young athletes is to not overdo their training at any single workout or short severe training periods of a few weeks. Young runners never must lose sight of their most important goals.

I´ve been lucky with no serious injuries like broken bones but I´ve had frequent achilles tendonitis, allergies, colds etc. When ill, you have to give yourself a set time to recover, say three days´ complete rest, then ease back to your training. You also have to analyze why you got hurt or sick. You have to remember that everyone gets laid low at some time. As to self-confidence, the way to build it is by solid training! You will become confident by progressing step by step. In our sport the progress can be seen for example in track workouts and long runs. Every athlete consciously is following his or her progress. You always know if you are going up or down. Winning edge in my view possibly is a born thing but which still can be trained.

Have I ever wanted to give up in a race? Of course!

Cheating in sports is A BIG PROBLEM, not seriously addressed by IOC, IAAF and other federations. In addition to athletes, also doctors and officials participating in cheating must be penalized. I´m very happy never to have cheated. I think most top athletes and beginners can say the same. As to publicity, I don´t enjoy having 12 hours of it before a race! Generally, however, I see it as a positive thing. I do read most stories written about me and preserve them, but don´t enjoy watching bad races of mine on videotape: it is not worthwhile because I usually know what went wrong!

Yes, I am annoyed by untrue comments about myself in media, but luckily that is very rare. I also have noticed some envy in people, to the extent of feeling a bit isolated. Money is a very big thing in today´s sport - it wasn´t in my top athletics years. There wasn´t much money around then. Money is a factor that must be understood by the athletes. My message to the young: I´m glad for you - running is great! The best thing in it is the continual renewal of your physical and spiritual self.

RONO Henry

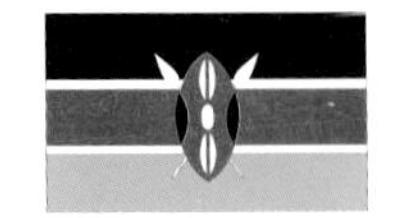

born 12 Feb 1952 Kaprirsang, Kenya. Member of Nandi tribe.
During 80 days in the summer of 1978, Henry Rono made running history by demolishing four world records - 5000m 13.08,4, 3000m steeplechase 8.05,4, 10 000m 27.22,5 and 3000m 7.32,1. One of the pioneers of Kenyan distance running glory towards the end of the century, Rono missed both 1976 and 1980 Olympic Games due to African boycotts. After a couple of leaner years he again astonished the world with his 5000m world record of 13.06.20 in Norway in September 1981. Henry Rono was a man of extremities - a fantastic athlete in his prime, a hopeless plodder when he had no inspiration for training.
1500m 3.43,1, 3000m 7.32,1, 5000m 13.06.20, 10 000m 27.22,5, 3000m steeplechase 8.05,4.

"I had prepared myself to bring everything for my country"

I think I was about 18 years old at the time when I started serious training. Before that, I had been a soccer player. Soccer was my first big love, but having met Kip Keino in my district, I realized running would be my sport, and that would get me away from my country. Kip Keino indeed was a hero for me especially after the 1968 Olympic Games. Coming to study in the United States I saw it was a good opportunity for me. A good programme. I came here in 1976 after Montreal Olympics. My biggest motivational problem came in 1980, when - after having broken world records in 1978 - I had to miss the Olympic Games for the second time in my career. I had prepared myself to bring everything for my country in Moscow.

I was still in the United States at the time, but I was travelling a lot. For sure I was going to bring two gold medals for Kenya. So it all was a big setback for me because I was aware of what I could have accomplished. The persons that were big at the time were Miruts Yifter, and Bronislaw Malinowski in the steeplechase, but I had run the best times. I always enjoyed my running. That is my advice to young people as well. You should enjoy running in the way I

PORTS
Nationwide
47

was enjoying it. Running and training were very simple things to me. So the way I advise an athlete is to not take it too seriously. You just have to get up in the morning and run and then another time in the evening...

Another setback of mine was in 1981 when there was the World Cup, and Africa could not allow me to run. They wanted Miruts Yifter instead, and that gave me more frustration. I was enjoying my running more than anybody else, but the setback was a political one. There was a lot of manipulation, and people - especially the federal officials - wanted to get money from the athletes. Other than that, my running was enjoyable, but as I said, the people wanted money from me. I was the only big runner in Kenya at the time. Young African runners should learn from all that I went through.

They should have a good training and racing schedule to get them through. A young runner should train and run with time. When you are not in shape, you cannot get a good time. Then you lose. So the way I used to run was having time targets. Young athletes should time themselves.

One of my biggest disappointments probably was in 1982 when David Moorcroft took my world record in the 5000 metres. It was a big surprise and it frustrated me. Self-confidence always comes to an athlete when he is developing his times. When he is running against time, he gets more self-confidence than racing against one another. Self-confidence comes from hard training and from what kind of nutrition you are eating. Your weight is important as well. When you gain weight, you cannot run very fast.

In later years I started having weight problems, but I well knew that after training 3 months on a diet the weight would come off. As soon as I got my weight off, I started winning big races. An athlete needs to be fit to be able to win. Paul Tergat did not win the World Championship in Athens, but he knew that as soon as he would get his weight down a little bit he would break the world record - and he did. My message for young athletes is that they need to get a good programme, sponsorship are important so that federation can develop young runners to run better. You shouldn't hurry: there must be enough time to develop the programme.

The best thing in running is the independence and the fact that you can do something for yourself. To get up in the morning and train, and go out in the evening and train. When an athlete is able to do that, he can achieve big things. I think an athlete has accomplished something when he gets to the same level as me and Kip Keino. I feel proud of that.

RYFFEL Markus

born 5 Feb 1955 Stäfa, Switzerland.
At 5000m, Ryffel was an Olympic silver medallist in Los Angeles in 1984 and a European silver medallist in Prague in 1978. Indoors, he collected a set of two golds, one silver and one bronze at European Championship 3000 meters.
1500m 3.38.57, one mile 3.58.05, 2000m 4.59.54, 3000m 7.41.00, 5000m 13.07.54, 10 000m 27.54.29, 20 000m 59.55.80, one hour 20 029m, marathon 2.16.40.

"The main thing is to have a long vision and be patient"

I became a serious runner in 1971, encouraged by my older brother who was a national class distance runner. I started training with him even if my parents at first did not like what I was doing. I enjoyed running because it is an individual sport. My career, however, did not start very promisingly due to the fact that I was lacking speed and I was always feeling such terrible nervousness before a race. I was afraid of being beaten. I gradually learned to control my nerves and also realized that you cannot become a winner before being able to handle a defeat. I have some unpleasant memories from my early success due to the fact that there were a number of untrue comments about me in the newspapers. However, I learned that you have to be able to accept many things in sport. There are good days and bad days. If you are not hard enough in your mind to handle difficulties, you will never become a champion. I got my first coach in 1971. In my view, the most important thing for a coach is to understand his athlete as a human person. A coach must be able to communicate and take notice of an athlete´s needs.

Even if I made an international breakthrough in the 1976 Olympic Games, I did not really reach world class until 1978. Today, after so many years of top racing all over the world, travelling is not such an exciting thing any more. Nowadays I feel it more like a business. In the early years it was always exciting to meet other top runners. Some of my idols those days were people like Grete Waitz, Lasse Viren and Thomas Wessinghage. As to my training, I like to plan six months ahead. It is not possible to follow the schedule without some changes every now and then. I am bothered by changes, but not to a great extent.

My advice to young runners is to train in versatile way, developing yourself in many ways in the years when you are growing up. There is no hurry to have an exact training program, but when the time comes, you have to listen to your body very carefully. My experience has taught me that you should never neglect any pain that bothers you longer than a couple of days.

I always have a high respect for my rivals, never getting into the trap of underestimating them. I am able to admire and congratulate them after a race whenever they have been running well. The best way to build one´s self-confidence is to do excellent training sessions. Yes, I have to admit I have had an occasional urge of dropping out of a race, usually due to various injuries. Nevertheless, I usually try to finish the race no matter how badly I have been doing. Dropping out of a race is a very negative thing. As to handling a defeat, the most essential factors are what kind of race it was, in what way did you lose and by whom. Cheating: all athletes doing such things should be closed away from running tracks.

Money: if I hadn´t the financial means, I wouldn´t be able to train twice a day and to race on world class level. However, I want to tell the youth that money is not the key to success. Speaking to young athletes, the main thing is to have long vision and be patient. You don´t become a top athlete overnight. The best thing in running is that it is an individual pursuit, the success in it being dependant on nobody else but you.

SAID-GUERNI Djabir

born 29 Mar 1977 Algers.
A brave and wonderfully confident runner, Said-Guerni made his big breakthrough at the 1999 World Championships in Seville, improving his 800m race after race and finally taking a surprising bronze medal. Another bronze followed in a tactical Olympic final in Sydney.
400m 46.15, 800m 1.43.09, 1000m 2.14.52.

"My only motivation has been to be the best"

In 1996, I did not make it to the semi-finals in the World Junior Championships in Sydney. After the race I said to myself, "can I do better in the future?" It was there and then that I decided to become serious about the sport. I had already been racing in Europe in 1994, at the international Schools Championships, when I was still a child. Ever since deciding to test my limits, my only motivation has been to be the best. The best 800 metres runner in the world. I enjoy challenges. A running race is like a big fight, in which everyone wants to win. Before my first very big competition in the Seville World Championships I had been running times around 1.47. There I improved my personal best in every race and finally took the bronze medal. I have been told that experts in TV and other media did not know where this man came from. Well, I come from Algeria (laughs). Seville was a breakthrough for me. I think I made it as if I were an artist. It was a natural thing for me. In earlier years I had idols like Kipketer, Sebastian Coe, Johnny Gray... I always liked Gray because of his brave attitude. He used to take the first lap around very fast. Then there was Morceli... He is a bright light for us in Algeria. It is something more and bigger than being just an idol, really.

Yes, I enjoy most of my training even if I am not the type of person who likes running slowly for more than perhaps 20 minutes. I don´t like running long and slow. As to the training systems, you have to believe in what you are doing. If you don´t, it is unlikely that you will progress. Before Seville, I had a problem with my hamstring. I probably got it when I was dancing. There was just one month to go, and I was quite worried. Luckily I got over it in time. What I learned from this was "never go to a night club again" (laughs)!

Athletes sometimes do stupid things because they want to get away from all the pressure, to feel free. As to financial incentives, I don´t come from poor background. My family wasn´t rich, but we weren´t poor either. So, unlike with many other athletes, money hasn´t been a motivating factor. Whenever you are beaten in a race, my advice is "don´t worry". Being defeated should not be a problem. Winning sometimes is! You may not learn much from winning a race, but it is good to be beaten every now and then.

Self-confidence? I don´t need any, because I got all of it when I was born (laughs)! Self-confidence means that you have it in your body and in all areas in your life, and you don´t even think about it. It is something automatic. I have always been like this, being in peace with myself. Self-confidence certainly is something that you need. Even if I lose, I don´t lose my confidence. Well, maybe for a few minutes or so, but when tomorrow comes I have forgotten all about it. You have to remember this is just sport. It is most important for a young runner to believe in himself. You have also to believe in your coach. Also, try to avoid doing stupid things (smiles). You have to forget all small problems.

I was given some good advice by my uncle when I was a child. "However well you succeed in life, never forget those people behind you." What he meant were the poor people, sick people in hospitals, the old people. You have to have a balanced view of life. There are people who cannot run, which is why you must be thankful for what you are able to do. I am a very happy person. Maybe the happiest man in the world (laughs)! As to the 800 metres run, I´m not yet the fastest man in the world, but perhaps someday I will be. The best thing in running is the challenge. Every day there is a challenge in track and field. That is what makes sport such a great thing for me.

SALAZAR Alberto

born 7 Aug 1958 Havana, Cuba. Came to Florida, U.S.A. in 1960.
One of the hardest ever trainers, Salazar started his brief but sensational marathon career by winning four times in a row - always in sub 2.10 times - at New York in 1980 and 1981, and Boston and New York in 1982. He also finished 2nd in World Cross Country Championships in 1982 and 4th in 1983. After finishing 15th in the 1984 Olympic Marathon he gradually left the limelights, but surprised once more - after long period of injuries and illnesses - by winning the prestigious Comrades ultra marathon in South Africa in 1994.
1500m 3.44.56, 3000m 7.43.79, 5000m 13.11.93, 10 000m 27.25.61, marathon 2.08.51 (2.08.13 short course).

"My problem was that I was training too hard"

I began serious training at the age of 14 as I was entering High School. My oldest brother Ricardo - four years older than me - was the best distance runner at our high school before me. He went on to run a 4.07 mile in college. I never had any motivational problems. My problem usually was that I trained too hard and didn´t take adequate time off when injured or sick. I enjoyed my training very much. Running was my only hobby or activity outside of school. I was rather shy and didn´t socialize much with other kids, so running was my life. The most important thing in training is to emphasize quality over quantity. Young athletes should run primarily at a distance under what they think will eventually be their best one. For example, an athlete

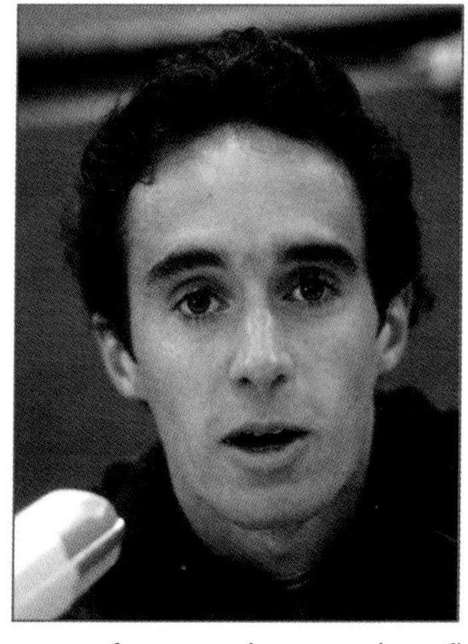

that wants to specialize at 1500m eventually, should concentrate on the 800m until he is 18 years old. An eventual 5000m runner should concentrate on the 1500m until age 18. They should get the speed first then add the strength later. It is very hard to do the other way round, i.e. getting the speed later. Yes, I´ve had several setbacks, primarily due to injuries. This is very common for any runner who pushes himself or herself to their maximum. What I have learned from these setbacks is to make them as positive as possible by: 1) Keeping your conditioning up as much as possible through cross-training, 2) Working on weak areas of your makeup, such as flexibility, muscular strength etc., 3) Planning for the future on how to avoid that setback again, 4) Realizing the human body always needs a rest, so treat that setback as an unplanned rest that will allow you to come back stronger eventually, 5) Remembering that what distinguishes champions from others is the ability to come back from setbacks.

As to a defeat in a race, it really shouldn´t matter. The main thing is concentrating on your own performance, i.e. how you ran compared to your potential, not whether there were one or five people ahead of you. If you focus on your own improvement, you will ultimately go further. Self-confidence to me means believing in one´s ability despite nervousness to achieve what one´s training indicates he or she should accomplish.

It is possible to acquire self-confidence by progressing one step at the time. Don´t shoot for too much improvement at one time. Realize that your workouts need to indicate probable race improvement. You must not have false hopes based on unrealistic training results. My advice to young generation of runners is to be patient. You have to realize that running requires long term development and that everyone develops at different rates. You have to concentrate on your own improvement no matter how little it may be at times. As long as you keep improving, you are on the right track. The best thing about running is that it can help teach you how to deal with much greater adversities in life.

SANG Patrick

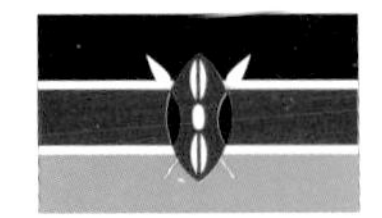

born 11 Apr 1964 Kapsisiywa, Kenya. Member of Nandi tribe.
An eternal second in championship meetings, Sang was a 3000m steeplechase silver medallist at the 1991 World Championships, 1992 Olympic Games and 1993 World Championships. In 1997, aged 33, he improved his eight-year-old steeplechase personal best to 8.03.41. In the early 2000s, he lives in Switzerland and does mostly road-racing.
1500m 3.44.17, 2000m 5.03.46, 3000m 7.44.13, 5000m 13.32.86, 3000m steeplechase 8.03.41, half marathon 1.01.02, marathon 2.14.03 (debut in 1999).

"By running, you will learn to understand mankind in a more mature way"

As a young boy I was racing in schools meetings in Kenya, but did not start serious training until I was 19 years old in 1983. Later, I went to study in the United States. There was a sports stipend available for top athletes in our university. Encouraged by this incentive I started training, thanks to which I was improving as a runner year after year.

I gradually learned to understand that running was good not only for my performances, but for my health as well. Moreover, I noticed that running was making me mentally stronger. As soon as I started regular training, my studies also improved at the same rate. When you know something is good for you in so many respects, you don´t have motivational problems. Running became a part of my life, and I was enjoying my daily training very much. However, I have to admit I have made some errors in my training. The most serious one of those has been overtraining. That has happened when I have been trying to do too much too soon. Because of this mistake, I have been suffering from various injuries. It is important to realize that the human body can take only a certain amount of training in a certain time. The most important thing in training, especially for a young athlete, is patience. A young athlete should not compare himself or herself with the best athletes in the world. You have to realize that it takes many years of gradual improvement to reach the top of the ladder in our sport.

Whenever I am convinced that the training I have been doing should have brought better performances, I know something has gone wrong. It may be due to illness or some other reason. If I cannot do 8.10 in the steeplechase, I am disappointed. Anything slower than that doesn´t make me happy. On the other hand, if I know I have given everything and I am happy with my performance, I feel strong motivation to go on with my training. If I have run fast, it really doesn´t matter if I have been beaten by better athletes on the day.

Self-confidence means that you know yourself. An athlete generally cannot prepare himself for losing. You always have to prepare in a positive way. Even if you don´t feel everything is fine before a race, you should have a positive attitude, For some time, African distance runners have been the best in the world in their sport. One of the reasons for this may be that whenever top African runners come back home, they have so many interesting things to show. Young people have realized that running can change their lives. Consequently, every talented runner is trying flat out to reach higher and higher. When their day comes and they succeed in big international meetings, it is their turn to encourage the following generation of runners. The economical side of running is a motivating factor which makes the young crop of runners work very hard, up to their limits.

It is typical for any Kenyan athlete to give everything in a competitive situation. If he wins, it is time to celebrate. If he is beaten, he tries again in the next race. I have noticed that athletes of some other countries sometimes bring some strange attitudes to the sport. When they win they become so arrogant that they don´t want to speak with other athletes any more. Every athlete should realize that running is a way of getting to know other people, to understand and to get along with them. As soon as hostility is brought into sport, it is not sport any more.

SCHUMANN Nils

born 20 May 1978 Bad Frankenhausen.
A tall youngster with a fearsome finishing sprint, Schumann enjoys surprise victories. After winning the European indoor 800m title in 1998 (aged 19), he won the European Championship outdoors as well a few months later. In spite of these merits, Schumann´s Olympic gold medal in Sydney 2000 was something that even the best experts couldn´t have predicted.
400m 46.62, 800m 1.44.22, 1000m 2.17.44, 1500m 3.40.36.

"Winner never doubts, and doubter never wins"

I have been a sports fan all my life. My father - a high school sports teacher - has always backed me whatever I have been trying. By age 6, I was playing football, training about twice a week and having a match at weekends. At 8 years of age, I also started going to athletics training sessions, with my father, about three times a week. At first I was doing many events - hurdles, long jump, ball throwing - until I realised I was unbeatable in my age group in track and cross country running. That was when I became a middle distance runner at about 11 years of age.

I was growing up in the late GDR, and those were the days when sportsmen and sportswomen were our heroes. Much more than nowadays in Germany. I knew I also would have a future as a competent runner. The main reason for my running always has been the enjoyment. I have liked to run as long as I can remember. I was looking forward to the solitude and the natural beauty in the big forests in the neighbourhood of which I was living. I couldn´t understand why so many of my school mates hated running.

They did everything to avoid these jogs in the woods. For me, they were the highlight of the day. Of course I was also enjoying the fact that I was doing so well in this sport. Every child likes to show what he or she can do. Nevertheless, it was not always easy for me to win in spite of the fact that I had the ability to reach my limits whenever it was needed. I still have this fighting spirit.

As a young boy, running around was more like a play for me, and that is what it should be. Gradually, it became more serious and I had to work harder to beat my rivals. Whenever I was defeated, that was a moment for learning and drawing conclusions. By the time I was running in the junior class, it was getting more difficult for me. I liked going to discos and partys so much that it sometimes took great effort to skip them and going to training track instead. Gradually I was learning the fact that there is the time for concentrating for the sport, but you can also relax every now and then. It is not unusual for me to feel uninspired before a very hard training session. You don´t always want to punish yourself on the track. In winter, most of all, when it is cold, or windy, or slippery footing, you think there would be many more enjoyable things to do than toiling around in the snow.

Nevertheless, these are the very moments which decide if you have the ambition to reach the top. No talent in the world is enough if you haven´t got the will. My coach once said to me: "In every one of us, there is a lazy loiterer. You have to fight against him every day. It is a kind of inner conflict. Whenever you succumb to laziness, it is more and more difficult to start again. So, what you have to do, is to keep the discipline." As to young athletes, my advice is to try and find a good coach, with whom you can talk on all things in the world. Also, you shouldn´t dwell too much on your feelings. When injured or badly beaten in a race, you should learn from these not so likeable things. Some day it will be your turn to do well.

In my view, it is dangerous to expect too much from yourself, because you may be so full of euphoria that you will train too hard and destroy your long-term plans. Training is a job of continuity and methodology. That is the most important thing.

Yes, I have some very difficult times during my career, but I have learned from them

In 1997, after winning the European Junior 800m title, it was found out I had a stress fracture in the tibia. At first I was told I should stop all running for six weeks. No problem for me and my coach. We decided to do some sort of daily training anyway, even twice a day. I was swimming every day, as much as three kilometers at a time, I was bicycling - even doing tempo sessions on a bike - and doing lots of muscle training with various machines. Also, I was running in water with an aquavest two or three times a week.

After six weeks I got the bad news that my tibia still hadn´t healed and that I had to wait another six weeks. Altogether, it took 15 weeks without running a step before my leg was in order again. As difficult as it was, I still think that the versatile background training I was doing helped me in many respects. My general condition had improved so much that after starting running again, it didn´t take me long to be very fit again. Soon after, I won the European 800m title in Budapest.

By no means these months were easy to me, but thanks to the wisdom of my coach, I didn´t become depressed. In spite of all the doubts I made it, and it was a wonderful feeling to be able to run again. As to defeat in a race, my worst moment so far was in 1999 at the World Championships in Seville. First, I almost didn´t make it to the final, making the semifinals only by time, and just-and-just, by six hundreds of a second.

Then, in the final, I had no chance and ended up well beaten eighth and last

It was easy for me to see that the only person I could accuse of this poor showing was myself. I had not been training enough, and I had been thinking too much of myself. Nevertheless, it was a good lesson, because a year later I became an Olympic Champion. My bad performance in Seville made me think about my laziness and gave me the necessary motivation to come back.

There cannot be success in running if you don´t have the self-confidence, the mental strength. In every Olympic or World Championships final there are eight athletes standing on the starting line. Every one of them is full of talent, and they have been preparing well for this race. But where the difference is, is in their heads.

In my view, you can win only if you believe you can do it. Whenever you don´t have the faith in yourself, you don´t have the slightest chance. Or, as my coach said: "Winner never doubts, and doubter never wins."

You certainly have it easier when you have the self-confidence from early age on. It is good to know you strengths. But generally, where you get most of your self-confidence, is your training. With good training sessions you will build your self-confidence, and that is something that your rivals will sense in you as well.

As to young athletes, I am still only 22, a young man myself. What I can say is that you should enjoy your training and racing. Maybe you always don´t manage to do that, but those are the days when you can dream of your goals. It is a wonderful feeling to stay on the top of an Olympic podium and listen to your national anthem. Have a goal and give everything to achieve it.

For a young runner, it is essential to have smaller goals to make you enjoy your sport. Gradually you will want to aim higher.

The best thing in running, for me, is the feeling of moving freely in the nature. I come from the countryside and love the forests. There is nothing better than work hard in the natural surroundings. My body enjoys this kind of challenge. What better than being able to do it every day, even if you are a professional athlete and doing this as a job. As much pressure as I sometimes have in my sport, I still love all kinds of running.

SCOTT Steve

born 5 May 1956 Upland, California.
World Championship silver medallist in the 1500 metres in 1983. 2000m World indoor record holder in 1981 (4:58,6). Very long career (still racing in Masters competition in 1998 after successfully recovering from cancer). Ran a sub-4 minute mile almost 150 times, more often than any other athlete.
800m 1:45.05, 1000m 2:16.40, 1500m 3:31.76, mile 3:47.69, 2000m 4:54.71, 3000m 7:36.69, 5000m 13:30.39.

I started running when I was recruited to run in junior high school at the age of 13 in a cross country race of a mile and half against another school. I placed among the top 15 and the local high school coach recruited me to come up to the cross country team. It was like a football coach came to ask if you wanted to come to that sport or a water polo coach asked if you wanted to come to that sport. In my case somebody wanted me to come and run. That is the only reason why I went out for running.

The coach felt that I had some ability and I can win some trophies and medals. That was my motivation for going out for cross country. As to my present training, usually I work in three different cycles. First cycle is a strength building cycle - the base work - and the longer that cycle goes the better. I may be on that cycle for 12 weeks or 20 weeks. For me the strength and base cycle has been the biggest and most important. The next cycle is more interval training, and it lasts 4-6 weeks. After that I have a speed training cycle which takes me into the racing season four weeks before a major competition which for us would be our national championships in June. After that it is mostly maintenance work. I don´t think about training during the competition season. I just want to make sure that I am well-rested when I step to the starting line. Sometimes I am able to follow my plans, sometimes not. If you have a minor injury or if you become sick, your plans have to change a little bit. When I set my training goals for myself they are not written in stone.

I train to race, I don´t train to train

I know that things happen and you have to change your plans. It doesn´t bother me if I have to change them. If you stick to your program and if you don´t deviate from it even though things in your life create diversions, then you are going to be in trouble. I am very flexible even on a daily basis. If my training schedule says that I have an interval or a hard workout on Wednesday and I do not feel very good, or even if I get to the track and the first couple of intervals are very poor, I stop the workout. I take an easy day and try the hard workout a couple of days later. I am not forcing myself to run hard if I am not ready to do it.

When the competition season comes closer, I want to test myself against other people or against my stopwatch. I do other races before the big ones. I do 10K or 5K races to break up the monotony of just day to day training. I measure myself against the performances of the past. I keep a training log. I am always aware of what a specific training session will do for me and why I am doing a particular training. In the past if I wasn´t aware of the purpose of the training, I would ask an explanation from my coach. If you miss a training day you just let it go and don´t add training to catch up with what you have missed. Do as I say, not as I do. I have made some extremely bad errors in previous years.

Some errors have cost me championships, some errors have cost me entire seasons. I have done the error of overtraining, a way too much strength training. I had to rest four weeks in the middle of the season to recover from overtraining. For example in the Olympic year 1984 I thought I had to do more interval training instead of keeping my training at the same level as in the previous years.

"Young runners should not worry too much about their mileage"

The most important thing in training is the idea that more is not always better especially with young athletes. Many young runners are thinking that they have to reach a certain amount of mileage per week. There are some 16-17 year old juniors who are running 70-80 miles a week. They believe that more running is better in that particular time in their life. When you are younger, it is more important to do shorter, quicker work. Don´t worry so much about the quantity or the number of miles you are running.

I think that young athletes should develop their speed as much as possible, do repeats, shorter and quicker intervals, and they should not worry so much about the overdistance training. I haven´t had any major injuries to set me back, but I have had some illnesses, which in a way are even worse than injuries. If I got a stress fracture, I would be out for six weeks, but I could do alternate training - ride a bike or run in a pool. After the six weeks I won´t be that much behind when I just got the injury. If you get a flu or a cold and you have fever and cough, I think every day you have fever takes a week to recover. You may have been sick for just a couple of days, but two weeks later you are still not feeling good. If I feel tired, I listen to my body and try not to overtrain. I am capable of handling a great amount of work, but if I do feel tired I will take a day off and I am not concerned about it. If I have a minor ache or pain, I interrupt my training and check if that is something worse. If I feel some pain in my knee, hip or hamstring, for example, I will stop training, have some therapy on it and not continue training until it is healed. Some athletes are afraid of taking days off and keep training until something very serious has happened.

"I try to dissect the race"

If I am beaten in my race by some runner who was better than me, it is OK. But if it was a tactical mistake on my part, then I am upset. When I am defeated I try to dissect the race and understand why it happened, to improve it by the next time. If I am beaten by a guy who blows past me in the last 100 metres, next time I race him I´ll use a different tactic. I am not going to wait until the last 100 metres. I try to move out with 300-400 or even 600 metres to go to try to burn his kick out of him. If you race the same person three times and are beaten three times, you´ve got to change something to try find his weak spots. When I am defeated I´ll look for tactics or ways to make myself better. I don´t dwell in the fact that I was beaten.

I come up with an honest analysis of my performances but it is not always easy because sometimes you have a bad performance and there is absolutely no reason for it. There are times you´ve had brilliant performances and shouldn´t have run as well as you did. The meaning of the training is to be at a prime shape at the right time. Losing is part of life, and you have to learn how to cope with it. Losing is not something you have to enjoy. If you enjoy losing you have got a problem. But you have to learn how to cope with it. You have to be supportive to the people who beat you, congratulate them, tell them that it was a good race. But at the same time you don´t have to like it. We are all going to lose sometimes in sport or in life. You may not get a job you want, that´s losing. You may break up a relationship, that´s losing but when you learn to go on you have learned a valuable lesson. Major losses are great motivators for me. It is an inpiration for me to work harder or to race harder or to be more dedicated. The better runner you are, the harder losing is. At the very top, losing is very hard.

"Self-confidence can be lost overnight"

I am friends with my rivals, but when we are on the track we are rivals, we are enemies, we are trying to beat each other. You try to do the best you can, and if that puts you on the first place, great. If it puts you on the eighth place and you did the best you could on that day, then OK. The people I am racing against are people that I have the most in common with. We all know what each other goes through to get where we are. We are stepping on the line together against each other. We have a real strong bond in common with each other. Some of my best friends are my competitors.

After the race there is friendship. It is easier after the race than before it. Afterwards we need each other. Self-confidence is not something that happens overnight. It is something that takes a long time to build, but it is also something that can be lost overnight. Self-confidence is something you build upon successful training, successful races or it is just an overall feeling about yourself. It is a slow steady progression. At times I have been extremely confident with my abilities, and there have been times when I have questioned my abilities. All in the same season. You can´t have supreme confidence without seeing something on the training track. Again you have excellent training but you can´t have supreme confidence until you see it in a race.

In an Olympic final, physically very little separates the runners. Everybody is physically very fit. The thing that separates who is going to be the first and who the last is the mental attitude. The one that is the most supremely confident in his abilities or the most relaxed is going to win. The key in a major competition is relaxation. If you are in a major competition, that doesn´t mean that you have to be more up for the race. You don´t have to be more excited than would be normal in a normal competition. I think you would need to be less excited because the bigger the race, the more adrenaline is going to be flowing. So what you have got to do is to calm yourself down, not psyche yourself up. My biggest problem when I reached the Olympic final has been to be relaxed.

"African runners don´t know the pressure"

If I keep thinking the race over and over again, I use a tremendous amount of energy that I should be using in the race itself. The bigger the race the harder it has been for me to be mentally relaxed and confident in my abilities. If you look at the 1988 Olympic Games, no one even knew who Peter Rono was. He knew how good he was. He was confident and extremely relaxed. You have to admire the African runners. They don´t know what the pressure is. All the athletes I know hate to lose because athletes are very competitive. In some cases an athlete has been born with a competitive nature. It is something that was born within him, but it may also be a learned attitude.

I don´t drop out. I have felt like giving up but I have never done that. I have had some frustrations along those lines. Things don´t go that well. Sometimes I have worked hard all year, but have never seen the fruits of my labor. However, I still have that motivation and desire. If you still have these qualities, there is no reason to quit. I can still go out on a daily basis and train hard and have these great expectations on myself. If you have those qualities, then you can remain in the sport as long as you feel competitive.

"I have to make a living"

Publicity was a lot of fun in the beginning. Then it has become a bit of a problem because there are so many demands on you and your time. It pleases your sponsors to go to publicity whenever you take an advantage of it. Publicity is definitely positive. You cannot be giving interviews all the time if you are a top athlete. You try to give the interviews that give most exposure to the sport. I think there is more to the publicity than just yourself. As athletes we have an obligation to the sport in general to try publicize it, try to make it more popular.

In the United States you would be a fool if you didn´t take an advantage of the interviews because track & field just doesn´t rank very high among the sports in the US. In television giving comments is a lot easier because they are quoting you word for word on a video tape.

If you say something it is right there. You can watch yourself saying something. The newspapers and magazines can change it around a little bit to make it sound a lot worse than what it is, but I have never really let that bother me. I am married and have two children and a mortgage, so the money matters for me a lot compared to runners who are single and still go to school.

Part of the reason why I am competing is to make a living. I still have the basic goals of running like doing my best in the championships but the financial factor is definitely in there. Money can also hurt you more than it can help you. If you run only for money, eventually you will have a fall.

"In running you can develop, and it takes longer"

My message for young runners: Everybody matures at a different rate. I know that some runners mature at the age of 16-18, but for some runners it takes much longer to develop. If you are not the best of your school or club at the age of 16, it doesn´t mean that there is no hope. In swimming if you are not at your best when you are 16 or 14 is different. In running you can develop, and it takes longer. Have patience, don´t have tremendous expectations very early. The longer you stick with running, the greater your chances of success. In most of the sports the opposite is true. If you don´t have success very early, your chances in those sports are less.

There are different ways of training. Don´t be afraid of a switch. Try to do something different. As many athletes as there are in the world, as many ways there are to train. The best thing in running is the competition. It is getting the best out of yourself physically, mentally and emotionally. That is what the training is designed for. Challenging yourself and being the best you can possibly be. That is the ultimate challenge in anything you do. For me that is most exciting. There is no feeling like the one after winning a race. The bigger the race the better the feeling

SEKO Toshihiko

born 15 Jul 1956 Yokkaiichi City, Japan.

A legendary marathon runner, Seko was at his best in big city races, winning at Fukuoka in 1978, 1979, 1980 and 1983, Boston in 1981 and 1987, Tokyo in 1983, and London and Chicago in 1986. One of the favourites before the Los Angeles Olympic marathon in 1984, but he had a bad day and finished 14th.

800m 1.51,7, 1500m 3.50,9, 5000m 13.24.29, 10 000m 27.42.17, 20 000m 57.48,7, 25 000m 1.13.55,8 (World Record in 1981), 30 000m 1.29.18,8 (World Record in 1981), 30K road 1.28.52, one hour 20 280m, marathon 2.08.27.

"What matters is your preparation for the race"

A student at a junior high school, I was a pitcher in our baseball team. Unfortunately, even if we came close, we failed to advance to the prefectural championships tournament. Realizing that our failure was due to an error committed by a team mate, I decided to give up baseball and run track instead. Part of the reason also was that I had always been the best at our school at distance races. Even if I was not a member of the junior high school track team, I was recruited to run some ekiden relay races. Also, I thought individual sports suited me better than team sports.

Finally, entering high school at age 15, I joined the track team. In 1972, my freshman year, the Olympic Games were held in Munich, and marathon champion Frank Shorter naturally was my hero. When young and competing well, I just wanted to run. I could hardly hold myself from my desire to go out and train. Later, however, as my training load increased over the years, permanent fatigue set in from time to time, making it painful to run. When not overly tired, I mostly liked all kinds of training. "Enjoyment" perhaps is not the right word, because sometimes the training sessions were so very hard. What kept me in training was the anticipation that I was going to do well in the upcoming race. With the competition approaching, I could hardly wait. One of my most memorable races was the World Games in Helsinki as a college senior. Since I could sense that my training had gone well, I was looking forward to going to Europe and racing the best athletes in the world.

Toeing the starting line of 10 000m in Helsinki, you can imagine my veneration when finding out that Finnish super stars Lasse Viren and Martti Vainio were in the race! I could feel myself shaking with excitement. Incredibly, I managed to win the race ahead of these great runners. "Did I really win?" It was quite a strange feeling. This victory gave me the confidence to become a world class runner. "If I try, I can do it."

"The winner has done more than you have"

You asked about the most important thing in training. Nowadays, there are many training methods available for distance runners. There are many ways to choose from. In my time, my coach Kiyoshi Nakamura and I were constantly searching for the best possible methods. Although the details of training may differ from one athlete to another, the training volumes of all top runners are similar. The difference is mainly mental. It is important to maintain a competitive spirit, strong desire and love for track and field. It is also important to work towards the goal you have set yourself. Never give up your goal! These things cannot be taught to athletes. Each athlete must learn to deal with them on their own. The coach´s job is to motivate an athlete, to help him or her to think about the essential things I mentioned before. Ideally, a coach must know how to restrain his athletes from overtraining. I had lots of injury problems during my career, the most serious of them being the knee injury after the 1981 Boston marathon. It was bad enough to stop me competing for one year and 10 months. What I realized at the time was the fact that I cannot accomplish my goals just by myself. Moreover, I cannot rely only on my coach. There are other people capable of helping me as well: an athletics trainer who takes care of my body; an acupuncturist fighting against my injuries; and the cook/nutritionist (who happened to be my coach´s wife) preparing excellent meals for me.

During the time of injury, I learned to appreciate those who support me. I also learned to maintain a sense of stability even when things were not going well. As to handling a defeat in a race, the race obviously is a competition, but who am I competing against? I think it is a competition with myself. A win or a defeat is not what matters the most, for sometimes they depend on luck. What matters is your preparation for the race. In the marathon, it is said that the outcome of the competition is often already determined the moment the runners line up for the start.

Whether you have prepared yourself or not to do your best in the race, that is the vital question. If you are defeated after having done everything in your power, then you must accept the loss. The winner has done more to prepare for the race. Then, you have to think what you changes you should make so that you can do better next time. What you must do is overcome your weakness. Self-confidence: I repeat again, it is important to train consistently. The preparation is all-important. In my view, the ability to do one´s best is something that can be acquired. As you train consistently every day, which is very time-consuming, you realize you are in better shape than you ever could imagine. It is very important to win races, however small. Athletes who have more experience in winning races are more likely to prevail when it counts. I think publicity has a positive aspect, whereas over exposure, could become detrimental. In my view, the publicity surrounding Naoko Takahashi and Yuko Arimori is a very positive thing. As to myself, I did not like the media focusing on non-athletic aspects of my life.

When you ask about cheating, I see it as a most radical method to improve one´s performance. Performance-enhancing drugs may be the most effective way to prepare for a race, but even if you win, with the help of a drug, can such a victory fulfill your life as a runner? If you are using drugs, I think it is not fair to those athletes who train and race following moral guidelines. Money: it is an objective measure of one´s performance. When I was competing, there was much criticism about the monetary aspect, especially prize money in Japan. At the present time prize money is better understood, and current athletes are fortunate to be able to concentrate on their running.

My personal message for the young generation of runners: there are things in life you must do while you are still young. As a distance runner, while you are at your athletic peak at age 25 to 26, it is time to invest for the future. When young, you must use all your strength to increase your capacity to train. Later in an athletic career, what influences the length of a career is knowing how to maintain one´s strength and how to avoid the onset of permament fatigue. In other words, how you have trained in your youth will influence your athletic career during your maturity. The time passes quickly. It is important to start today, not tomorrow. Each day is important. The best thing in running? In my case, I just loved it, therefore I simply think that running is a wonderful thing. Personally, I had many happy moments when having a beer after a good training run!

SEPENG Hezekiel

born 30 Jun 1974 Potchefstroom, South Africa.
Started as a fun runner in road races, then ran 800m in 2.05 in 1991 and improved to 1.47.51 the following year. A wonderfully versatile runner with an excellent fighting spirit and finishing kick, Sepeng was 5th in the 1993 Worlds, 2nd in the 1994 Commonwealth, 2nd in the 1996 Olympic final behind Vebjörn Rodal, 2nd in the 1998 Commonwealth and 2nd in the 1999 Worlds, almost beating Wilson Kipketer. He is the first black South African athlete to win an Olympic medal (Josiah Thugwane won the marathon gold a few days later).
- In Sydney 2000, Sepeng missed a medal in a tactical race, finishing 4th.
100m 10,7, 200m 21.67, 400m 46.75, 800m 1.42.69, 1000m 2.19.46, 1500m 3.38.24, one mile 3.57.33, 3000m 8.14.88.

"Meeting Peter Snell would be a great honour for me"

I am 22 now. I don´t feel old! I played soccer at first. In South Africa it is very difficult to be a professional soccer player, so I went into individual sports... athletics. I was enjoying it so much I soon realized this is the sport for me. During the isolation I was running half marathons, cross country, just for fun. I did not know what was happening outside South Africa. Then I realized I could get Springbok colours like so many other athletes had done. Planning my training with my coach, we usually look ahead to the end of the next racing season.

We have a season of our own in S.A., starting in February. Because of the European circuit, you sometimes have to peak twice. Last year (1996) my plans went very well. The previous year I was racing too much at home - every week sub-1.46 times. In 1996 I was training better. I was able to run 1.45 without peaking, even 1.44. If something distracts my plans, I don´t feel happy. I don´t like to be too flexible about my training. I am trying to follow the plan as well as I can. I always motivate myself. I always believe I can run faster. It was not enough for me to run a South African record. My focus was to do well in Atlanta. I don´t think 1.42 is my limit. I know I can run faster. I am enjoying my training when I am able to do it exactly as my coach wants.

It feels great when I am able to run well in training, but there are days when I don´t feel that good. It was a surprise for me to win the silver medal in Atlanta. I was aiming to reach the final. I had been training very hard. I had been in a training camp for many months, away from my parents and friends.

In Atlanta my attitude was wrong. I did not believe I could win. "Let us see what happens." Vebjorn Rodal went into to race to win. Afterwards I thought, "Gosh, I should have won this." However, I was happy with the silver. It was close. You are thinking about so many things after a race. 1996 was a turning point in my training. Everything started to come together. I realized I don´t need more 400m speed. I needed more endurance. An English friend of mine bought me Peter Snell´s book. He was doing long runs in the 1960´s. I started training along these lines, and in my first race ran a sub 4-minute mile. I would like to meet Peter Snell sometime. That would be a great honour for me.

The most important thing in training is to listen to your coach. You have to have the guts to make your program through. You must go through the hard sessions, not blaming your coach that they are too tough. You must trust the person who is helping you. You must be friends with each other. A coach is someone who is motivating you, telling you that you can do it when you think you can´t. Whenever I am surprisingly beaten, I feel bad. Sometimes I hate myself for that! I am ashamed of letting people down. When that happened, I went immediately back to the changing rooms!

I don´t like watching a bad race of mine, but if I have to, I sincerely want to learn something about it. What went wrong? Whatever it was, I don´t want to do it again. My advice for young runners is to think positively. Think about a good race you had. You have to stay positive, forgetting the bad stuff.

I am friendly with my rivals whenever I meet them, but things change when we arrive at the warm-up area. That is the time when I start having full focus for my race. Afterwards, we are friends again. Self-confidence means that you believe you can do it. You can feel it inside. Don´t sit back. You have to believe you are able to run the first lap in 50 seconds. I think my self-confidence comes from the fact that I can run 1.45 by myself, with no one else in the race. I can go hard all the way. That comes from training hard and well. Self-confidence comes from training, not so much from winning. South Africans call training "practicing" for a race. We "practice" for training situations, which is a good word.

Kipketer was not unbeatable back in 1994. He was vulnerable then, but he was practicing! What he did in the World Indoors was the result of practice. You have to practice a lot to be able to win. When you lose, you also lose your self-confidence, and you have to go back to hard training. Doping is not fair. It is simply cheating. It is not right that some are running clean, with their talent, and some people are not. When I go to a race, I don´t think whether someone is using drugs. I know I am O.K. when I have been training well. Even Kipketer had to train hard for many years to be the best. I think I can do the same.

Publicity in sports certainly is a good thing for South Africa. When I ran the Olympic silver, people started noticing who I am and where I come from. I have noticed some people being envious of what I have achieved. You can see it in their faces. They have to greet you, but you can see they are only pretending. They are not happy about what you have done.

What I can say about money is that I can survive with what I am making at the moment. I am not in this sport for money. I like athletics. I have always believed in long-term goals. I want to win the big championships and break world records. My advice to a young athlete: have goals in your life, both short-term and long-term. Don´t make goals that you cannot reach. I know that myself. I am not dreaming of 1.40 yet. I want to run sub-1.42 first. I have goals for every year in my career.

For me, the travelling is the best thing in running. Seeing the world. Being a South African that hasn´t been very easy for me. When you travel, you can make friends all over the world. You can have great races with them. My goal is Sydney.

SHORTER Frank

born 31 Oct 1947 Munich, Germany.
Shorter ran himself into history at the Munich Olympic Games in 1972, speeding away from his rivals in the early stage of the race and winning the marathon gold medal in the streets of a city in which he had been born 25 years earlier. That run, together with his silver medal in the 1976 Olympics and four consecutive victories in the Fukuoka marathon in Japan in 1971-74 made Shorter an icon of his sport. Thanks to him and Bill Rodgers, millions of Americans became road runners and the astonishing "Running Boom" was launched.
3000m 7.1,4, 3 miles 12.52,0, 5000m 13.29,6, 10 000m 27.45,9, marathon 2.10.30.

"Yes, I wanted to drop out in my every marathon race"

My aim was to peak three times in a year. Basically, I was training on a weekly cycle. I usually had no problems with following my plans thanks to the fact that I was flexible, especially with regard to modifying interval workouts. I never had any motivational problems. I enjoyed my training and did not find it difficult heading out of the door. I was not worried about the long months of strenuous training waiting ahead. As to a single very hard training session, I felt an excitement similar to that which I felt before a big race. I don´t think I ever made any big mistakes in my training. I never added extra into my log, in fact I always rounded down. I always knew why I was doing a specific kind of workout. If I missed a workout for a reason or another, I was not worried because I knew that an anaerobic session can always be done another day. My advice to young distance runners is to be consistent in your training, setting realistic, attainable, incremental goals. Yes, I certainly had many setbacks during my career. What I learned from them is that healing takes time and all the therapy in the world does not speed up the process very much. I have never really considered losing a race to be a surprise. For me it has been just a fact. If I have had a bad performance, I used the emotion to motivate myself to train to win the next time. My attitude towards my rivals was the same before and after a race - that of respect! However, I always felt that if I´m ready physically and mentally, I can beat them. I think it is possible to build one´s self-confidence by having a realistic training schedule and watching one´s improvement. In my view, however, the will to win is a born thing. To win big races you have to concentrate on maximizing your own performances. It is essential to be able to be the initiator of the big moment in the race.

When I am asked if I ever had such a bad moment during a race that I wanted to drop out, my answer is - yes, in every marathon race! To improve yourself as a runner, you have to know how to handle losing. View it as a part of your improvement. Be willing to admit that you could have done no better that day. Being defeated naturally feels bad, but I ask myself, "I tried my hardest, so what can I do to do better?" Cheating in sports is totally unacceptable. I believe in permanent retroactive penalties for drug use and blood doping. Everyone likes publicity. I do not try to avoid it. I try to use it to help accomplish my goals. I see publicity mainly as a positive thing until one´s ego gets too big. I don´t find it easy to watch a bad race of mine on videotape. I don´t see many tapes of myself anyway. If there is an untrue comment about myself in media, yes, it hits me hard, but there is really nothing you can do about it. Also, time seems to dilute such things. People seldom remember those things long. Yes, I have noticed people being envious about me, and I don´t find it nice. There have been some problems in my life because of these things. I have never run primarily for money. I could not train as hard as I do if making money was my primary goal.

My personal message for the young: find out if you truly like running. Then realistically evaluate your talent and then set your goals realistically as well. Running is a very personal activity that appeals to the individualistic personality. It can be corporated into just about any lifestyle, and the reward is most often equal to the effort expended. That, for me, is the best thing in running.

SKAH Khalid

born 29 Jan 1967 Midelt, Atlas Mountains, Morocco.
One of the most feared finishers on running tracks, Skah was the 10 000 m Olympic Champion in Barcelona 1992, World Championship bronze medallist 1991 and 1995, World Cross Country Champion 1990 and 1991 and Half Marathon World Champion 1994. He briefly held a two mile world best of 8.12.17 in 1993. Originally, Skah was disqualified after the Olympic 10 000 m final in 1992 due to being helped by a lapped teammate during the race; he was however reinstated after a counter protest by Moroccan team. Has been living for many years in Norway. Skah in Arabic means "Runaway".
1500m 3.38.10, 2000m 5.03,9, 3000m 7.36.76, 2 miles 8.12.17, 3000m steeplechase 8.19.30, 5000m 13.00.54, 10 000m 27.14.53, half marathon 1.00.27.

"Running is the mother of all sports"

My parents have nine children, which is not unusual by any means in Morocco. As a boy, I was playing ball games at school and doing some running from age 11 or 12. Even today, it is not customary in my country to force young runners to train too hard. The main attention is paid to well-proportioned physical maturing and correct way of running. I have always admired Lasse Viren and his fluent running action. I know a lot about his training as well. When I started my career in the 1980´s, people thought I was crazy because hardly no one was running in Morocco those days. Now you can see runners and joggers in all the bigger towns, and running has become a most popular sport.

At 16 years of age I was training six or seven times a week with older runners, including fartlek and some track sessions. At 19, I was running twice a day, also visiting Atlas mountains for altitude training. Nowadays I train 12 months a year. I plan my programmes with a long view. If I occasionally miss a training session, it bothers me because I am trying to do everything as well as possible. I am using cross country races as a preparation for the track season. Yes, I enjoy my training in spite of the fact that I am doing it practically every day. Of course it is sometimes hard to follow the schedule for month after month, but at the same time it makes me feel good. Sometimes I train with a group, some other time I am running alone. After reaching the top it is easier to stay there by following the training schedules that have proven to be good. Nevertheless, I change my training to some extent every year.

In the beginning of a new training period I am avoiding running tracks. Instead, I go to the forest, where I run for 45-50 minutes, accompanied by stretching and circuit training. After about a month of this I move over to hillwork, track training and fartlek. This period may involve running as much as 250 km a week. Sometimes it may be less, and I am always trying to take care of speed as well. I also sleep 10-11 hours a night and do lots of stretching to recover faster from my training.

"Junk food is out of question for a hard-training runner"

My diet consists of lots of vegetables, salads, pasta, rice, meat and fish. I am avoiding junk foods at all costs. I find it essential to back up my diet with vitamins in order to stay away from possible deficiencies. As to my training, I try to be flexible to a certain extent. Some days I may run 12 kilometres of intervals. During the track season the amount of intervals comes down, whereas speed training becomes more important. With major races approaching I am running my intervals with shorter recovery in order to get accustomed to racing rhythm. As a distance runner, I don´t need lots of muscular power; hill training is enough for that.

I train at altitude maybe four or five times a year. Before major races, I go to the mountains to improve my blood count and to take use of other advantages of altitude training. For me, two weeks in the mountains usually is the minimum, three weeks the maximum period. No matter if you go up for three weeks or one year, the effect is the same. You will get the best advantage by alternating altitude and lowland training. I find myself acclimatizing so well to the altitude that I am able to train hard the very first day. I think I am reasonably honest when writing my training diary. I usually write everything down very carefully. I always know why I am doing various types of training sessions. Whenever I miss something, I try to compensate for it by training on a planned rest day, or by doing an extra session.Yes, I have made errors every now and then, for example by not training as much as I should have. The most important thing in training is to know what you are doing and being able to follow your plans.

I haven´t had many adversities so far, but there have been times when I have been injured or ill (mostly with fever). Whenever that happens, I have stopped training, but not for a very long time. I have learned some things during the years - for example the importance of proper warm-up before every track session. When I have been surprisingly beaten, I take it hard, but at the

same time I am trying to get my self-confidence back as soon as possible. I always try to analyze my defeats in a most honest way and start then looking forward to my next race, aiming to win. Sooner or later, every runner will be beaten. A defeat is a good lesson. It makes you train harder and have a deep look in your training schedule in a constructive way. It is very important to get to know the good and bad sides of your rivals (endurance, finishing speed etc.), and also their personal bests at various distances. You should know as much as possible about your opponents in race. Afterwards, it is all peace with everyone; then it is the time to learn about them as human beings as well.

Self-confidence is an essential part of an athlete´s armour. You generally acquire it by winning races, but there are other means as well - for example by running very hard races, in which you improve your self-confidence by running fast lap after lap and by improving your personal bests. In my view, it is not possible to win big races without proper physical preparation, high morals (which means positive attitude) and a successful execution of the race. Mental strength is a born thing, which nevertheless needs to be cultivated year after year. It is not my way to drop out of a race, no matter what. You have to prepare mentally before every race, keeping in mind that every competitor is planning to win but that there is just one that will eventually do it. Cheating is the worst thing in sport. I find it immoral, and such things have to be torn up by the roots from the sport.

Publicity is a positive thing, to a certain extent. In my case, publicity has been mostly positive. I do read most stories written about myself, and preserve them. Of course I am offended by any negative things written about me that have no truth in them. Whether I like watching bad races of mine on video, depends on my frame of mind. Yes, I have met envious people, but I am not bothered by them. I find envy to be a human thing. Money is an essential part of one´s life. In my view, there is no need for an athlete to be a rich person, but he should have all the basic things one needs in life.

My message to the youth? I always tell young people to look forward, to have firm belief in themselves, so that one day they will reach their potential. The best thing in running? For me, running is the mother of everything in sports. To succeed in running is very hard, but it has some great things such as the feeling of challenge and naturalness. I really enjoy running in faraway places, all by myself.

SNELL Peter

born 17 December 1938 Opunake, Taranaki, New Zealand.
Three times Olympic champion: 800 m in Rome 1960, 800 and 1500 m in Tokyo 1964. Five world records: one at 800 m, one at 880 y, one at 1000 m, two at the mile. Snell also ran a 1000 yards indoor world best of 2:06,0 in his first ever indoor race. His 800 m world record remained unbroken for 11 years until 1973. Last male runner in history to win 800 and 1500 m in the same Olympics. Retired from racing at the early age of 26. A pupil of legendary coach Arthur Lydiard, Snell was one of the first middle distance runners to thrive on big mileage, logging routinely a long run of 30-35K each week. With his massive thighs and calves, Snell (183 cm, 80 kg) looked like a weightlifter.
440y 47,9 (relay), 800m 1:44,3, 880y 1:45,1, 1000m 2:16,6, 1500m 3:37,6, mile 3:54,1, 2000m 5:12,6, 3000m steeplechase 9:38,8, marathon 2:41:11.

I started serious training at the age of 19. Prior to this time my interests were in a wide variety of sports, particularly tennis. At high school I participated in the annual track and field championships and, in the winter, the annual cross-country race. My best time at the age of 18 was 1:59,6 for 880 yards. During my final summer vacation before commencing work on a full time basis, I entered an all-comers meet in my home town on New Years Day, 1958. It was a handicap 880 yards race, in which I was given a 15 yards start on the top runner in the race, Bill Baillie, a former New Zealand champion at this distance. I won the race in 1:57 and was very happy that Bill was not able to catch me. It was much later that I learned that Bill was tired from hard training and was not racing seriously on this occasion.

This success encouraged me to take a serious training program, and in 3 weeks I lowered my best 880 yards time to 1:54, a time that in 1958 in New Zealand was only 2 seconds away from national class. I was now very excited about the prospect of competing in the national championships in March and decided to focus all my sports interest into athletics. About this time I renewed acquaintance with Arthur Lydiard, who agreed to coach me.

"I thought my defeats were due to lack of talent"

I finally chose running as my event because it was apparent that I could achieve the most success in running. This fact was not recognizable in high school because of the competition from well-trained athletes who were much superior (a fact that I mistakenly attributed to talent rather than training). I have enjoyed a number of sports as a teenager - tennis, golf, rugby and cricket. When I retired from athletics in 1965, I resumed participation in tennis and golf for pleasure. By then athletics had satisfied my achievement need. At 19 years of age I read Emil Zatopek´s book "Marathon Victor" which impressed me greatly. Locally I admired Murray Halberg who played an important role in helping me believe that even though New Zealand was a small country, we could be successful in athletics.

My goal at the beginning was to represent my province at the national championships and get 1st, 2nd or 3rd in the 880 yards. (I was 3rd in 1:52,8). The next goal was to make the provincial cross-country team the next winter. After that it was to win the New Zealand 880 yards championship and so on... Arthur Lydiard assigned me to run with club members who would help introduce me to his system of marathon type training. In general I would attempt to run with training partners particularly for the long distance work. During the track season I generally preferred to do interval training alone, but not in secrecy. Those days, I was not living with my family but as a paying guest in a private home. This family adopted me like a son and gave me every encouragement. Also, I developed a new set of friends who were runners.

During my first training year Arthur Lydiard suggested that I could become New Zealand´s best miler and represent my country at the Olympic Games, but he also emphasized that it would be a long process - maybe 4 years. I never really considered giving up running even though there were times when injuries (stress fractures) were discouraging. Probably the reason for this is that I worked towards achievable objectives and was constantly improving my performance.

"Training became easier and pleasurable"

I often thought training was difficult and boring. However, as one developed fitness, training became easier and pleasurable. The attainment of training goals (eg 100 miles per week) gave me a feeling of achievement in its own right independent of the realization that there would be a performance "payoff". In my early races I was rarely over-excited as the public expectation of me was fairly low. This was parrticularly true in the 800 final at the Rome Olympics where, if I had finished last I was still a "success".

Once my reputation and athletic credentials were established I was often motivated in a race by fear of losing particularly to bragging rivals. These days (as always) I consider success and winning to reflect the quality and quantity of preparation or training for the event. When these have been lacking, performance reflects this fact. My earliest success came at the age of 13 at the annual school track and cross-country championships. No one trained for these races. The community I lived in was small (pop. 3500). For some reason I could always win long distance races. I participated in sprints, too, without succeeding.

There was usually a small mention of our races in the local newspaper, and I preserved the clippings. Later, I believe these reports and in some cases optimistic speculation about my potential was a distinct motivating factor for me. This early success was important, but as there were a few opportunities for racing I sought success in other sports. I cannot recall anything negative associated with my early success, but in many ways I believe I sought this success at the expense of proper application to academic pursuits.

"I realised the meaning of training"

My high school experience was a bit unusual because at 15 I was sent to a big boarding school, where I competed against well-trained athletes. After being used to winning, I found myself 40 yards behind in the 880 yards and 120 yards back in the mile. I interpreted this as a talent differential rather than a reflection of training. Naturally once I recognised that training paid off, I aimed higher but always towards goal within reasonable reach. As soon as I decided to "go for it", my life outside my job (8:30 a.m. to 5 p.m. Monday to Friday) was almost exclusively devoted to running, and recovering from workouts. The main adversity I had to deal with was a stress fracture of the tibia in a road race in Sept. 1959. The initial prescription of the orthopedic surgeon was 3 months of rest. I sought advice from a British expert and learned that certain activities would facilitate recovery. Even so there was not a great deal of time to get into peak form for the Championships in February and March on which selections for the Rome Olympic Games would be made. One of my biggest disappointments was finishing 55th in the New Zealand cross-country championships when I was 19. I resolved to work harder for the next year´s event in which I finished in 4th place.

"Arthur Lydiard did a great deal to improve on my long-term goals"

My first and only coach was Arthur Lydiard. I was introduced to him by a high school colleague who was coached by him. Arthur at this time was the coach of some of the best runners in New Zealand, including Murray Halberg, our best Olympic runner. Thus I was very gratified when Arthur agreed to guide my training. The work of the coach changes with the maturity of the athlete. In the beginning (in my case) it was to provide the necessary nurturing to help me accept a radically different program for a middle-distance runner: marathon training. The coach´s role was to provide a convincing rationale for the training regimen, encouragement and support when there was no apparent progress. As the athlete becomes more experienced, the coach´s role is more involved in fine tuning the program. To sum up, the most essential thing a coach can do is to motivate the athlete so that he will believe success will ensue. On the other hand, the most difficult thing for a coach is to provide the fatherly support that many athletes seem to demand. In my case, coach Lydiard was very good at rationalizing defeats, especially if they were not major championships.

The reason that I did not concentrate on running exclusively until the age of 19 was due to my lack of perception that I could become a good runner. Arthur Lydiard did a great deal to improve my long-term goals; however I did doubt that I would reach the level of performance that he predicted. Later, after setting world records in 1962, I subconsciously felt that my goals had been achieved and I lost the edge that one has when striving to be the best. (P.S.: Two years later Snell won two more Olympic gold medals!) I first competed in an international race for New Zealand in Australia in March 1960 and won an 880 yards race which included the great Herb Elliott. New Zealanders often crumble in international competition, but I proved that I could win against runners that Australia would be sending to the Olympics, and I believe this race was the single most important factor in my selection on the New Zealand Olympic team. Six months later I won the Olympic gold medal at 800 metres. Prior to the Olympics my best time for 800 metres was 1:48,5; in Rome I ran 1:46,3, so the success happened quickly.

New Zealanders in particular are always impressed by trips to other countries and I was no exception. "There is always the danger of overtraining becoming a major problem." As to the training, in the beginning I planned 9 months ahead from the end of one track season to the next, although the specifics of the actual track work were not considered at this time. In general I preferred to follow plans; I did not like deciding what to do at the last minute. But I was flexible in my training plans usually when it was rather obvious that my body was tired and the workout would prove unduly arduous. In retrospect I feel that this was very important as "overtraining" can be a problem if lighter training is not adopted when symptoms occur.

There was usually no problem with daily training as it was part of a regular routine. At the end of 1962 I changed my employment and was required to travel away from home at least once a month. The disruption of the "routine" did cause some motivational problems. In general I enjoyed my training, the major problem being that it caused me to be tired in the evenings so that I needed to get to bed early at 9-9:30 p.m. The months of strenuous training were regarded as part of a necessary process to become better than the opposition. Experience indicated that the quality of results of a track season were in direct proportion to the quantity and quality of the endurance phase in the preceding months. Once this fact was understood, the training ahead was no problem.

Another help was the use of sub-goals during winter training, for example in cross-country races. In terms of a very hard training session, these were often very satisfying when they were accomplished, and sometimes provided a mental "breakthrough" in accepting the training load. I was honest about my training. There are gaps in my diaries which were periods when I missed training or was running poorly. When I was running well, my diaries were well documented. I never consciously falsified training times. In fact when I was doing a speed session that was wind-assisted, I would note this advantage. If anything, I would prefer to err in the other direction and later be "surprised" when competing in my first track race of the season. In case I missed a training session, I did not try to compensate for it but rather rationalized that I needed the day off. In some situations however, when I was shooting for a certain weekly mileage, I would try to fit in extra running to ensure that I hit my target. My schedules were always made out by or under the supervision of coach Lydiard. If I could start again I would probably do training that would closely resemble that which I did in the 1960´s.

The one change would be to maintain a session of interval running once per week during the winter, rather than doing long slow runs only. My advice for young athletes: The single most important thing I learned in training is that a sound endurance base allows a middle-distance runner to do a greater volume of race-related running without becoming overtrained. Many athletes have not been able to understand why they should run slowly if race pace is considerably faster. It is to condition their muscles to survive the demands of intense running.

During my top years as an athlete, there were several adversities to note. The first was a stress fracture of the tibia in September 1959, which caused me to lose 6 weeks of training. A stress fracture of the tarsal bone in the winter of 1962 interfered with my preparation for the British Commonwealth Games in Perth. In January and February 1964 I was being beaten in New Zealand by John Davies and decided to spend a month racing in South Africa where the competition was easier.

"Many of the injuries could have been prevented"

Many of the injury problems could have been prevented by being more careful and patient in the transition from one type of training to the other and being aware of the symptoms of overtraining, i.e. elevation of morning heart rate, sleeplessness, loss of weight etc. If I was surprisingly beaten in a race - and this happened several times, the best known example being by Jim Ruyn at San Diego in 1965 -, it was usually accountable for by some external factor, particularly the inadequacy of training in the months preceding the race. If I felt I performed up to my best, I had no problem in running 2nd and would resolve to try even harder for the next race. I do not consider factors such as motivation on the day as contributing, but rather the quantity and quality of the previous 6 months of training. In my experience, when this was well done, racing success automatically followed almost effortlessly.

I feel that the emphasis on external factors tends to make losing much more acceptable. Performance is largely dependent upon inherited and developed physical abilities, motivation and tactics. For most top-line athletes the state of motivation may be considered maximal, therefore the only factors left are tactical considerations and training. Running is not like a skill sport such as golf or tennis when some days all your shots are near perfect, although much practice will increase the probability of this happening.

"A defeat or two can be good for the soul"

My advice to youngsters who are beaten stem from my high school experience when I was easily defeated by others. At the time I felt that performance was a reflection of ability, and did not appreciate how training can transform an ordinary runner into a great one. Defeats must also be put into perspective: was I at my absolute peak of form? If not, "no big deal", bide your time until you are ready. A defeat or two can be good for the soul. My attitude towards my rivals before a big race was somewhat detached. I concentrated on trying to run my best rather than entertaining aggressive thoughts about my rivals. Later as a world record holder, a primary motivation was fear of losing, at least in big-time races. The meaning of self-confidence is knowing that you will be able to perform up to a level indicated by your training and previous races. In this context, winning is irrelevant.

The main requirement of a great victory is that the performance is not expected, as illustrated by Billy Mills in Tokyo 1964. There are two extreme types of athletes: the one who extravagantly predicts his success, and the one who plays his chances down. The first one increases his chances of disappointment, while the other is always being successful. I believe that the mental power for winning is apparent from the sacrifices that an athlete makes in preparing himself for the competition. The important personality characteristic may be a strong desire for recognition and achievement, and while this is present in many people, some talented runners do not have it. I do not believe in the so-called "killer instinct". In 1965 I raced a mile in Vancouver while suffering from diarrhoea. The last lap was a nightmare and my time was 4.15 while the winner did 3.56. This was a case of pressure from the promoter against my better judgement. (This also in the days of no appearance fees.)

On the preparation for winning: As a winner you need to keep in mind that others are going to train harder to try and beat you. This I believe is the mechanism of the progress in world records. A runner does what is necessary and only necessary to be the best. The only bad thing about being beaten in a race is that spectators and writers attach so much significance to winning per se. I suppose, as an achiever personality, this is exactly what we want rather than the rationalization we apply to our own performances. I mentioned above that I travelled to South Africa in order to get into races that I knew I could win and not subject myself to the speculation that I was "finished" when getting beaten at home. Cheating in sports is a natural outcome of the importance placed on success and winning. I do not condone it. As to publicity, I worked in public relation for 10 years and so hated the need for publicity that I educated myself into a profession (scientific research) which is somewhat independent of publicity.

Yes, people have been envious. It has caused some problems in work situations where co-workers feel that I´ve already received enough attention and now it is their turn. In New Zealand, when I attempted to have something to say about fitness, the leader of our physical education community stated that I was not qualified, rather than attempting to utilize my public credibility in achieving a common goal. The fact that I now choose to live in U.S.A. may relate to this question.

"After it was all over there were only memories"

I had a full-time job when I was training and occasionally had to have time off for overseas competition. Therefore when I felt I had satisfied my achievement need I retired from competition. My feeling about professionalism was that it made no difference during the competitive years. The amateur adopted a professional approach in his dedication, but after it was all over had only memories, while his non-athletic colleagues had spent their excess energy advancing their careers.

My personal message: Athletics is much more than simply deciding a winner. It is a means by which you can discover a tremendous power within yourself to reach heights that are far out of reach of ordinary people. Finally, the best thing in running is that it feels great to be able to run hard at speed and to enjoy the feeling of fatigue that accompanies a high level of fitness. Best of all, it can be retained well into an age of life when unconditioned people are stricken with heart disease and many other ailments arising from a sedentary and opulent lifestyle.

SZABO Gabriela

born 14 Nov 1975 Bistrita, Romania.
Of Hungarian descent, Szabo is a diminutive (158 cm) runner with a quick metronome-like stride and a fearsome finishing sprint. Won her first international title, 3000m at European Juniors, in 1991 aged 15, then collected several more junior medals and moved up to senior ranks with full flight. Winner of 1997 and 1999 World titles and 2000 Olympic gold at the 5000 meters. Olympic 1500m silver in 1996 and bronze in 2000. In 1999, Szabo won World Indoor 1500 and 3000m titles as well as the overall IAAF Grand Prix championship, collecting a massive amount of more than one million dollars for her running during that memorable season.
1500m 3.56.97, one mile 4.19.30, 2000m 5.30.53, 3000m 8.24.31, 5000m 14.31.48 (European record in 1998).

"I like to train because it is my life"

In April 1988, when I was 12, I was asked by my sports teacher to take part in a 600 metres school race. She had seen me running several times and thought I might be a very good addition for the school team. Szolt Gyongyossy, nowadays my coach and husband, saw this competition and asked me if I would like to start some training. In his opinion, I had some talent for running. In my first period of training, everything went well. I liked running and it was great fun. In my junior days there were no problems regarding motivation. Today, after many years and many competitions I perform at a high level of running, and it is not only pleasure, rather it is hard work. Even if I get paid for it, money is not everything. Without motivation I cannot perform at the highest level.

Generally speaking, I like to train because it is my life. During training, I have nothing else to worry about besides running. Of course I do have a difficult day once in a while, but that is normal. Whenever I have a difficult time, I try to motivate myself by thinking about my rivals and future competitions. One of the most important things in training is variety. Speed, endurance, coordination, everything is important for a good performance. When in training, I always have the upcoming competitions in my mind. No matter what race it is - a small meeting or an Olympic final, I want to get the

best out of myself and win the race. Training is very important because I can check all the necessary parts from speed to endurance. No training, no good competition. So far I haven´t had many injuries or problems with health. That may be because after every training or competition I am taking good care of myself with a bath, a sauna or have a massage. Having pain after a tough training session is normal - it means you are getting stronger. The only injury I have had was in 1996 when I slipped when running in the snow.

My most important advice for the young generation is to have fun in your running

The most difficult years are when you are changing from junior class to the seniors. It will take two or three years to make it, and you will have to train very hard to run at the top of the field. At that time you get easily injured, so you have to try and recover well after every training session. It is a fact that you cannot always be number one. Sometimes you will finish second, third or maybe even tenth. But that is what life is about. In every race you will learn more about tactics, concentration and so on. You can make use of this experience in future competitions. Self-confidence is essential for a good performance. I believe in myself. I trust in my body and in my mind because I want to keep this high level of running.

Of course it was my mother who gave me this self-confidence, but the real power and strength is given by God. To succeed, you have to be self-confident both in training and competition. I work very hard and believe that I can always improve as a runner. My message to all juniors in the world is not to give up in difficult times. When you are a junior, it is so much easier to get into local or national teams and to various championships. Don´t lose everything you have learned when you are a senior. You have to work hard to win. Attention: take your time to grow up! Support from your family, coach and federation also is very important in motivating you not to give up. For me, running is great, it is my life. Sometimes I hate to run when 40 minutes feels like two hours, but if I didn´t like this job, I wouldn´t be here!

TANIGUCHI Hiromi

born 4 Apr 1960 Nango Town, Japan.
A very economically striding runner, Taniguchi won the marathon gold medal at the 1991 World Championships in Tokyo, bringing the only victory for the host country. At the Barcelona Olympic Games in 1992, Taniguchi finished 8th in spite of falling and losing a shoe in the crucial moment of the race when the pace was picking up.
During a world class career of more than a decade,Taniguchi ran his fastest marathon of 2.07.40 in Beijing in 1988, finishing 2nd. Some of his big victories were in Tokyo 1987 and 1989, London 1987 and Rotterdam 1990. 5000m 13.49.17, 10 000m 28.34.18.

"Every training session is a part of a big picture"

In the junior high school I was primarily a sprinter although I also participated in other events. My bests those days were 12,5 for the 100m, 25,5 for the 200m and 1.70 for the high jump. I finally got interested in distance running in high school when I was 16 years old.

The conventional wisdom those days was not to drink water (during exercise), "because it causes side stitches and stomach cramps". It was unthinkable to consume liquids during a run. One day, seeing runners take a drink during a marathon race on a TV broadcast, I was mystified. That was when I got the idea of trying to run a marathon some day, even only once. Also because I imagined the runners were taking fruit juice. I thought, "how wonderful to a have a fruit juice during the race".

I didn´t look up to anybody in particular as an idol when I was young. This was partially due to lack of information about sport at the time, in the late 1960´s. I was living in a small town. In fact I don´t even have any memory of the Olympic Games. Early in my running career, before developing the discipline to train on my own, I did have motivational problems from time to time. It probably was because I did not have definite goals to motivate myself. But once I started running the marathons, these motivational problems were gone.

I did not always enjoy my training. However, when I fulfilled my goal in the race after enduring hard and painful training, it was very satisfying. Thinking about the satisfaction which the successful race brings, made me enjoy training more. I never did like speed training, nor was I very good at it. The important thing is to have the purpose in each training session on a daily basis. In addition, it is important to understand the meaning of each individual session as a part of the entire training sequence, as a part of the big picture.

Unlike in baseball and soccer, in track and field the main task of a coach is to assist "Kantoku". The coach needs to relay messages from the athletes to "Kantoku" and from "Kantoku" to the athletes. (According to Ken Nakamura, an expert of Japanese distance running, Kantoku is at the top of team hierarchy, although sometimes an Assistant Kantoku position exists. Although most teams have a Team Director, they are essentially administrative positions. The team director never sets up training menus for the athletes. Several coaches, including the head coach who is at the top of hierarchy among the coaches, work under Kantoku. The coaches´ directory guides the athletes. All this is a part of the Japanese cultural system.)

When injured, I learned to appreciate the time when I was able to run. It reminded me about the joy of exercise as I pushed my body. I think it is an opportunity for you to look into your inner self closely. It is a time to examine your training as well as your attitude towards training, and see yourself objectively and ask yourself a question: "Was I really serious about my training?" When injured, think about the time when you will be able to start running again. Whenever you need to rest, it is time to study and learn about various subjects even those not directly related to running. Even at the time of setbacks it is important to set yourself goals.

My firm belief is that a victory in a competition might come as a fluke, but a defeat always has a reason. When searching for the reason of the loss, I find what I need to improve. By repeating this process, success eventually comes. As a consequence, I find joy as well as many other possibilities opening up for me. It is hard to win all time, but that is the very thing which I find so challenging.

As to self-confidence, it is necessary to believe in whatever you are doing. I am sure of the fact that many athletes have a feeling of insecurity. Even if you train hard, it rarely brings instant success, whereas with careful planning of training frequency and intensity one will improve fitness gradually but surely. Thus it is important to attain consistent goals as a result of training. Confidence comes with the fact that your training system results in a good racing performance.

I think publicity is a positive thing, but only when you do not lose yourself in the hoopla

"Easy to say, but hard to turn into action." It takes time to attain top condition, but you are always one step away from losing it all. However, since I was training not only for my own contentment, but also for the praise by others, I liked to be at the center of attention. Such a good experience again motivates you to train even harder to run better in the next race.

It is not easy for me to watch a videotape of a bad race of mine. In my case, for all competitions, I analyze my mental attitude, starting with my training phase. The analysis of my mental state from the start to the finish is written down with the help of a videotape. This is how I find what I need to correct for the next competition.

As to drugs, basically, since they are detrimental to an athlete´s health, they should not be used. Recently, even if this doesn´t apply to myself, due to the big monetary rewards in the sports, I suspect that some athletes are using drugs for a brief period. I also suspect that some athletes have the mentality "as long as nobody knows" or "I will retire as soon as I have made good money". Will there be games where performance-enhanced drugs are legal? Can a human person become a robot? I wonder...

Money: I think it is a good thing to evaluate, and a reward for those who put in a good effort. The time to concentrate on hard physical training is in one´s twenties. However, at that time one should also make one´s contribution to society and build up one´s professional career. Being a runner means one must forego many things to be able to concentrate on training. I consider that prize money and/or appearance money are the rewards for making such sacrifices.

The proper time to train one´s body, in one´s twenties, also coincides with the period in our lives when we want to have fun. Since temptations are part of the life for young people, it is hard to concentrate on training. However, it is the best time in your life to train your body, so what you must do is train hard and try to find out if you have the potential. In my opinion - and this is important as well -, distance running is a highly technical event.

The best thing about running is that good and bad results are obvious to everyone. Being mediocre or average, which is perfectly acceptable in Japan, is not acceptable in distance running. Being superficial is not accepted in this sport. In distance running, we can challenge ourselves to be the best and change ourselves for the better.

TANUI William

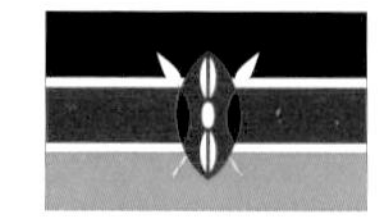

born 22 Feb 1964 Kobujoi, Kenya. Member of Nandi tribe.
The highlight of Tanui´s long career was winning the 800m Olympic gold medal in Barcelona in 1992. A very consistent and reliable competitor, he has been posting times of 1.43 and 1.44 through the 1990´s. Recently he has been leaning more towards the 1500m and was moving as well as ever indoors in 1999 aged 35.
800m 1.43.30, 1000m 2.15.83, 1500m 3.30.58, one mile 3.50.57, 2000m 4.57.31.

"There is no such thing as a born will to win"

Kenyan runners usually come from the countryside where there is a long way to go to schools and shopping centers. Consequently, young milers improve their endurance in a natural way. I train quite hard which means that not so seldom I have to force myself to do the important sessions. I keep a training diary, in which I write down every morning and evening session, including the time spent and the number of kilometers. If I miss a training session, I may do it later on another day. I do a lot of cross country running for several months from the beginning of the year together with the Kenyan cross country team. This is because I want to build up my endurance in the best possible way. No athlete can avoid setbacks. When you train hard, you will inevitably get injuries. I, for instance, had to miss the 1991 Kenyan World Championship trials due to leg injury. I want to emphasize to young runners that you should not neglect taking care

of even the smallest injuries. You don´t get rid of them if you continue training. A small injury eventually may result in a very serious and time consuming problem. Whenever I have a bad race, I seriously think about what went wrong. Maybe I have underestimated my opponents or made a tactical error. I find it easy to accept the facts. You cannot win every race. Defeats are part and parcel of the sport. In a way, they make you resolve training harder. Of course you may be annoyed by being beaten, especially when you think you are in good shape and then are shoved off the track in a physically hard race. It is wrong to have a hostile attitude towards your rivals. You have to remember that without competitors there would be no race. Everyone tries to win, but afterwards we all are friends with each other. Self-confidence means that you believe you are capable to a certain performance. You build up your self-confidence with more experience during the years. For instance, an athlete can say, "if others can do that, so can I". You don´t achieve exceptional things without mental balance. With the race approaching, you should avoid any social or family problems, so that you can fully concentrate to the task ahead.

I don´t believe there is such a thing as a born will to win. I think you will build your winner´s instinct when you train and race hard for many years. I was very disappointed, almost to the point of retiring from racing, when I was disqualified - wrongly in my view - due to stepping out of my lane in the World Indoor Championships in Seville in 1991. It was a hard decision to take after winning a race. Afterwards, however, I decided to show I would be a big champion some other time. I have never heard any Kenyan athlete having used doping substances. We don´t even think about such things. It is very bad to be a cheater. It is better to finish last cleanly than win by illegal means. My advice to young athletes is that it is vitally important to have full concentration on sport.

Publicity is not always a positive thing. There are sportswriters who write in a negative way, and others who have a positive attitude. I always read the papers carefully and preserve everything written about myself, even in foreign languages. At home in Nairobi, my name is known but people don´t recognize me in the street. Naturally, I find it annoying if I notice people being envious of what I have achieved in sports. They don´t realize how hard I have been working for many years. Money doesn´t make me run. Love for the sport does. Money is just something that comes with the achievements. The best thing in running is the great feeling of winning a race. Every runner enjoys winning. That is when you get the reward for your efforts.

TERGAT Paul

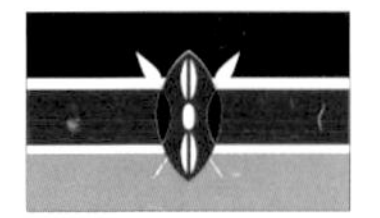

born 17 Jun 1969 Baringo, Kenya. Member of Tugen tribe.
In 1991, without much training, Tergat ran his first-ever 10 000m race at the altitude in Nairobi in 29.46,8. A decade later at the Millennium, he was the winner of five consecutive World cross country titles in 1995-99 and five-time 10 000m championships medallist: World bronze in 1995, Olympic silver in 1996, World silver in 1997 and 1999, Olympic silver in 2000 after a monumental last-straight fight with his ever-present rival Haile Gebrselassie. Tergat also held the 10 000m World Record from 1997 to 1998, and was planning a much-awaited marathon debut in 2001. Without doubt, he already is the best half-marathon runner who ever lived.
1500m 3.40,3, one mile 3.58,4, 2000m 4.57,4, 3000m 7.28.70, 5000m 12.49.87, 10 000m 26.27.85, half marathon 59.06 (World best in 2000).

"Self-confidence comes from your inside"

It was not until 1992 - in the Army, after finishing my school - that I started serious training. At the time I had no idea of my talent. At school, my only sports had been volleyball, basketball and soccer. Personally, I have never had any motivational problems. I usually have very, very good planning of my whole season, from winter to summer. Choosing or selecting the races has always been one of the priorities. As a top athlete, I always have a meeting to enter as long as I am in good shape.

In my opinion, the most essential thing for a young runner is discipline. You don´t achieve anything in life without sticking to regular preparation. Becoming good in any field requires hard training. However, training has never been an easy endeavour, especially if one is training for a major championship or a world record attempt. But if you know exactly what you are after in life, you definitely find very exciting everything you do - no matter if it is hard work or just jogging in the woods.

For the ten years I have been at the top, I have enjoyed both the training and the success. Success is the only real motivation since it is the pay or result of the hard commitment. This total commitment plus determination are the key to everything, knowing or bearing in mind that there is nothing good coming easily in the world. There is no small or big talent. We are all gifted in a way. The more you try hard to exploit your talent, the more you develop it. Partners: training with a group is one way which is very important, especially when you are training for a long distance race.

"I was not sure if I could ever run again"

I certainly have had my setbacks. In 1992, I was in great shape for the World cross country championships in Boston. At the last moment I was injured and could not run. I was very disappointed about that. I was not sure if I could ever run properly again. It was such a bad injury that it took me six months to come back. After injury, the only thing you can do is to look forward. As long as it may take, some day you are feeling well again and are able to ease back into training. Being depressed doesn´t help. Even if everyone of your rivals is running well and you aren´t, you just have to keep your focus into the future.

I know what I am talking about because of the fact that after getting back from injury I have become better and better. I was overjoyed at getting back into my 1992 condition. I still remember many people telling me that my career was over. It is normal to think that way, but unfortunately it may have a negative effect on an athlete´s mind. What do I think of being beaten in a race? Every athlete must be able to cope with defeats. Fair play is part and parcel of the game. Nowadays, distance running is almost like playing darts. Someone wins today, perhaps someone else tomorrow. You have to accept being beaten. You will have your turn in some other race. For any athlete, self-confidence is of utmost importance.

With big self-confidence, almost anything is possible for you. Whatever one does in life - either in sport or in other professional career - confidence is paramount. You have been training well, you are ready - that is what I call self-confidence. It is impossible to succeed in big races if you are thinking "I am a nobody". On the other hand, when you have confidence on yourself, you can beat anyone in the race. For me, self-confidence comes both from training and from inside. Sometimes you may think "I am not feeling good today, in fact I am dog tired", but in fact it is just in your brain. When you understand this and sure about yourself, you will go out and train like any other day.

Determination: when one is determined to achieve the best, it is the mental will which will drive you to any height, especially when the going gets tough. Tolerance: without the heart to tolerate, persevere and fight, we are not going anywhere. I don´t believe that the winning power is something we are born with; it is a gradually built thing. Whenever I am beaten, I have a look at myself and my training. Have I been lazy? If so, I have to do something about it. You should never let defeats ruin yourself. You have to accept the fact that you did not win, but at the same time you have to make up your mind to do better next time. That is something that I call the spirit of the sport.

"Doping: most unfair"

It is absolutely ridiculous for any athlete to use doping substances. I find it most unfair that some people are training hard and some others take advantage of forbidden methods. In my view, anyone caught from doping should be penalized severely. He or she should never be allowed to compete again. Athletes like this should stay away from racing tracks. John Ngugi´s case? What I know, Ngugi never has used doping substances. It just happened that when someone unfamiliar with Kenyan culture knocks on your door and asks you to submit a test in front of your children, parents and other family, it just isn´t the thing to do. We don´t go about it in that way. As far as I can remember, a few days later he submitted a test which was negative. I still think it all was a misunderstanding. Nowadays we in Kenya are better advised how to proceed in such situations. I find publicity a positive thing. It is good to be a well-known person. I read most stories written about me. I find it interesting. Also, I don´t mind watching a videotape of a race in which I did not run well. You always learn something no matter if you win or lose. I am a professional runner today. Running nowadays is almost the same as professional soccer or boxing. You may make lots of money in all of them.

I find it solely a positive thing to be a well-to-do person. For the last five years (1995-1999) in the distance running world, training has been intensified. Athletics has become a full-time career for many. That is why most athletes spend most of their time in training camps all over the world. Most facilities available have been maximized or utilized, i.e. gym, new technologies introduced, i.e. light spikes manufactured by various companies.

Pace setting, too: pace makers have been fully accepted, they really do a great job when fast times have to be realized in races in which world records are being attempted. The future of distance running? Personally, no comment! It´s interesting to see what will come up after this. Most records have already been pushed too far, like 3000m 7.20, 5000m 12.39, 10 000m 26.22 etc. All these are great times by any standard. The best thing in running? It promotes unity between different nations. Also, great friendship between the sportsmen. Running has helped a lot of athletes to make a living out of it.

Running has made many good things, it has helped both joggers and top athletes to be in sound health. I like meeting different people from different cultures. It is great to be part of a very competitive race. I get a deep enjoyment from my sport. Maybe there are people who do this just for the money, but in my case, running is in my blood.

THUGWANE Josiah

born 15 Apr 1971 Bethal, South Africa.
After running promising marathons for six years, Thugwane won the South African Olympic trial in Cape Town in 1996 and, two months later, surprised the running world with his gold medal in Atlanta, becoming the first black South African Olympic champion and also the smallest (158 cm) Olympic winner in marathon history.
In 1997, Thugwane ran 3rd in London in 2.08.06 and won the Fukuoka marathon in his personal best of 2.07.28. More recently, he has been plagued with various injuries. - Half marathon: 1.02.08 (1995).

"You can win even without the best equipment"

I started running at age 17 in 1988. Before that, I was playing soccer. There was no future for me in farm areas in that sport, and I soon realized running would have more money to offer. I have to say money was the major reason for me becoming a runner, but of course there was also the enjoyment of running. I have no motivational problems, but naturally I am resting when I feel tired. The essential thing in running is to listen to your body and enjoy as much of your training as you can. I certainly have had many setbacks during my career. In 1992 I had a bad knee injury, in spite of which I ran Berlin Marathon and was out of action for three months afterwards without running a step! Injuries are part of running however much you take care of yourself. If you haven´t got any, you probably don´t train hard enough. When injured, the wise thing is to rest when this happens and get proper treatment, starting over again when healthy and able to train. Competition is so hard that you just cannot win all the time. Sometimes you win, sometimes you lose, but the important thing is to keep trying.

Training gives you self-confidence and helps you realize that the best shoes and/or money cannot make you good! You can be the best even if you don´t have all the equipment that many other runners have. The way to cultivate self-confidence is to do what you are good at, and the confidence will come through training. Don´t always look at others to measure yourself. Measure yourself against yourself and you will improve.

The best thing in running is when you can test yourself against competition, and see how the training has improved your fitness!

TULU Derartu

born 21 Mar 1972 Bejoki, Ethiopia.
During a great 1992 season, Tulu won African and World Cup 3000 and 10 000m titles and took the Olympic 10 000m gold medal, aged 20. After injury-ridden years she came back to win the 1995 and 1997 World Cross Country titles and a silver medal in the 1995 World Championships 10 000m. In another great come-back in 2000, she won the World Cross Country title again and took the 10 000m Olympic gold in Sydney eight years after the Barcelona games, improving her personal best time by almost a minute. A small but feather-striding runner, Tulu´s weapon is a fearsome finishing kick.
1500m 4.12.08, 3000m 8.52.90, 5000m 14.44.57, 10 000m 30.17.49, half marathon 1.08.04, marathon 2.26.09.

"I was told about Abebe Bikila"

I started training in 1989 at age 17, joining the national team. I can´t remember any specific reason why I got into running, but I had my first races at school. I also remember listening to the radio and being told about the great achievements by such athletes as Abebe Bikila, Mamo Wolde and Miruts Yifter.

I was a good runner in high school, and we have many good runners in Arsi. It was something that was quite natural to all of us.

I never have problems with motivation. I enjoy my running very much. There were some small problems coming back of the birth of Scion because of the injuries I had. It all started to come together again in the beginning of 2000.

Also one thing that I experienced – not really a setback – was the birth of my daughter after the Atlanta Olympics. It kept me out for about two years, But I really wanted to have a family. This was no sacrifice at all. I knew I could make it back to high level training again.

The most important things in training are inspiration, hard work and following your schedule as closely as possible. You have to train so hard that racing feels easy.

A defeat should make you determined to go and train harder so it does not happen again. This has been my philosophy in the marathon. The best kind of self-confidence comes from excellent physical and mental preparation for a race. You have to train hard enough so you know you can win the race.

Yes, self-confidence can be acquired, but it can only be done through training. Without training, talent means nothing. In my view, young running talents should train together with the leading runners of their countries.

The best thing in running for me is the effect my success has had on the people of Ethiopia. I dont 't only run for myself or my family, I run for my country as well.

VÄÄTÄINEN Juha

born 12 Jul 1941 Oulu.
In his home country, Väätäinen -- "Juha the Cruel" -- will forever be remembered as the double European champion at 5000 and 10 000 meters in Helsinki in 1971. That was the culmination of a long and dramatic career -- including Finnish junior title at 400m hurdles in 1960 and Nordic 800m championship in 1965 -- which did not find its true magic until after moving up to longer distances. Väätäinen still is the only Finn to have placed among top six at all distances from 400 to 10 000m in the national championships. In the 1971 European 10 000, he ran the last lap in 53,9 seconds, winning in front of home crowd and thus starting the great era of Finnish distance running during the 1970´s.
100m 11,1 (1961), 200m 22,1 (1967), 400m 48,9 (1967), 800m 1.48,4 (1967), 1500m 3.43,7 (1968), 3000m 7.53,4 (1972), 2 miles 8.33,0 (1971), 5000m 13.28,4 (1972), 10 000m 27.52.78 (1971), 25 000m track 1.19.42,0 (1971), 400m hurdles 56,2 (1960).

"I got an immense enjoyment from hard training sessions"

At age 15, I won my school races so easily that I made the decision to find out what I could accomplish as a runner. Later, in the army, I still was considering a career as a cross country skier even if I already was the national 400m hurdles champion. Living in the countryside in Northern Finland in the 1950´s, I used to listen to sports broadcasts in my uncle´s radio. I was closely following the careers of top Finnish runners like Eero Tuomaala and Urho Julin. Later, I was fascinated by great sprinter Voitto Hellsten and his magic deeds. I was dreaming of winning a race in the match against Sweden at Helsinki Olympic Stadium some day.

My parents gave me lots of encouragement for my sport, my father having been a local decathlete and my mother having competed in cross country skiing. My friends also were quite sportsminded. We used to have our own Olympics every weekend, summer after summer. That was a big thing in our home village.

Strange as it may be, I always got an immense enjoyment from hard training sessions and never thought of packing it in. The harder I trained, the faster I ran. That was a simple fact that gave me enormous motivation. I have to admit running became more important to me than my school work. It was fantastic to go to a training camp because all I needed to do there was go out and run. For me, the effect from training hard, and thus improving, was a kind of a miracle. I never felt I was lacking inspiration. I never purposely missed a training session even if it may sometimes have taken 15 or 20 minutes to get myself into the right mood. I have run on airports, big cities, savannahs of Kenya - everywhere. A runner should do a run every day.

I got great satisfaction from the fact that I was capable of training sessions that were impossible for most athletes in the world. Whenever I compare my training at age 30 to that of 10 years earlier, there is huge difference - two very different worlds. And yet training hard is not enough. I always knew exactly why there was this or that kind of workout in my daily schedule.

You have to be able to do that to become a great runner. Even all the coaches don´t know why they are asking a runner to do this or that kind of session. It is a fact of life that no one can avoid making mistakes. In 1972 I made the mistake of not racing enough. Had I done otherwise, running history

might be different now. At the time I thought I was injured, but in hindsight the problem may have been in my mind. In the early races of my career I always was extremely nervous due to the fact that I had such an overwhelming desire to impress everyone. I remember having been defeated in a cross country race. Afterwards I was explaining seriously how "it was impossible to pass the leaders because of all those trees!" During my top years nerves usually weren´t a problem. Even if no runner can avoid certain anxiety, it never was the reason for my running badly. I was not afraid of defeats, but I certainly hated them! From the very start of my career, defeats always were a most motivating factor for me. In the small home village of mine, my races were closely followed. With some success coming I gradually became some kind of King of the village. As much as I was enjoying my improvement, it rankled me that there always were a couple of runners in the area that were better than me. When I finally managed to beat them, it was a start for another era. I never was beaten by them again.

In the early years I never seemed to get rid of all kinds of injuries. I very seldom had a completely healthy season. For example, when once making hay, I fell from the top of a tractor, fracturing my ankle. I learned to analyze my defeats at a very young age. I gradually was able to admit to myself that I hadn´t really been beaten because of the trees. No, I was beaten because there were some things that I had to correct as to my preparation. I did not have a coach until 1962 when Paavo Meskus started making regular schedules for me.

I was a hurdler at the time, but my idea was to train with the milers. In some of the first training sessions I was badly humiliated by them, but I did not give up. I had a deep faith in legendary coach Meskus. He had already realized how, for me, sprint training was just waste of time.

"Coaching for me means a fruitful contact between two people"

It is extremely difficult for a coach to make his athlete work with maximal capacity. You can never know another person well enough, which means there will always be errors. The main thing is not the schedules, the technical side of the sport. The main thing is the fruitful contact between two people. I at first had some doubts as to my capabilities because of the fact that I came from a small village in Northern Finland, whereas my main rivals were from Helsinki.

I finally made the mental breakthrough in 1965, when I won the Finnish and Nordic titles at 800m, in the latter race beating young Swede Anders Gärderud, who became a steeplechase Olympic champion 11 years later. In 1970, after having run 10 000m in 28.19, I realized I could become as good as anyone in the world. With that performance, I completely lost my inspiration for 800 and 1500 meters. In a way it is a pity that I did not see what I could at those distances. I still think I could have run 1.45 and 3.35. My advice to young runners is that you should set yourself a goal, you should love your running, and you should train hard. Whenever you are injured, you have to stay calm. It is foolish to hurry before you are healthy again. Better start a week too late than a week too early.

"In fact I had already lost the race before it started"

Whenever you are surprisingly beaten, it makes you think about the reasons. With the bell clanging for the last lap in the European Cup 5000m in Helsinki in 1970, I was one of the six men in the leading group. I finished sixth. I was grimacing badly, massaging my stomach in pain. Well, as painful as my stomach was, I had already lost the race before it started. I had no proper tactics. I had a deep faith in my finishing kick, and yet I was spending all my energy by leading much of the race. After six more weeks of training I was in invincible shape.

I always had a deep respect for my rivals. The day before the European 5000m final I told Jean Wadoux of France -- a good friend of mine, "I think I will win, but if not, then I hope you will." I had been training with Jean several times. I don´t understand athletes who consider their rivals as enemies. "Hatred" is such a negative word it is impossible to succeed through it. To win a race requires self-confidence, but you don´t necessarily get it by winning. First you have to conquer yourself. The first thing is to be honest to yourself when planning your training schedule. You have to believe in what you are doing. You get self-confidence by training hard. I remember having a look at my training diary: 245 km a week, 970 km a month... I closed the book; my self-confidence had no boundaries.

"It is always possible to grow up mentally"

The will to win is something that everyone can learn. It is always possible to grow up mentally in the same way as bodybuilders develop their bodies. For two years I was preparing myself for the European 10 000m final on August 10, 1971. "Victory ceremony at 9.10 p.m." I had written that down in my training diary as well. I was thinking about the race every day for two years. Well, I admit it may border madness, but only in a positive way.

Home crowd always lifts one´s spirits. That was something I took full advantage of in 1971. Yet I had enormous problems in those championships as well. I was not myself after the victorious 10 000 meters, and I wasn´t feeling good in my 5000m heat. I also was fretting the decision of my Federation of not letting me run the marathon, for which I had been selected. Even today I am sure that I would have won the marathon as well.

I find it very hard to watch the Munich 5000m Olympic final in video. (Väätäinen finished last.) I had all the tools for winning the race, but I had made serious mistakes as to my preparation. I would have needed a coach at the time, but I had none, Paavo Meskus having died already in 1968.

The best thing in running is the fact that by it you can express yourself. You can run just for the pure joy of running. Running is the most natural way of moving about.

VASALA Pekka

born 17 Apr 1948 Riihimäki, Finland.
Vasala´s great 1972 season was crowned by an Olympic 1500m title in Munich ahead of Kipchoge Keino. A few weeks earlier he had missed the 800m world record by just two tenths of a second in the dual match against Sweden in Helsinki.
400m 49,6, 800m 1.44,5, 1500m 3.36.33, one mile 3.57.13, 2000m 5.07,6, 3000m 7.50,8, 5000m 13.35,8, 10 000m 29.09,6. - By 1998, Pekka Vasala´s son Antti was an 800m runner in the Finnish national team and nephew Samuli Vasala one of the most promising 5000m runners in Europe.

"Is there anything better than running in the life of a young man?"

I did not start real training before I was 17 years old, but of course there had been many other sports before that. I liked most of all basketball and ice hockey, thanks to some early success in school competition. At home, we had "Backyard Olympics" of our own, including most events from shot put to long distance running in which I seemed to be doing best. The athlete whom I was admiring most in my childhood was legendary Finnish sprinter and quarter-miler Voitto Hellsten. Even if I was following the 1960 Rome Olympic Games very closely via radio and newspapers, I don´t remember having had any foreign idols those days.

I got my first training advice from a sports teacher who was organising a couple of weekly running sessions at a local fire station. My parents had a kind of neutral view on what I was doing. They were not pushing me, but neither were they lacking interest. Later, I remember my mother´s worry about my not-so-good school reports and my tiredness after strenuous training sessions. I had two kinds of friends those days - runners and non-runners. I gradually drifted away from the company of the latter ones. For many years I did not have a clear picture of the mental and physical requirements needed to reach the top in my sport. It was not until the disappointing years 1969-71 that I realised how hard I would have to train. In fact I was so fed up with running after the 1971 European Championships - where I again finished 9th just as two years earlier - that I was ready to hang up my spikes at age 23. Luckily my coach Kari Sinkkonen made me realise that in the view of my training so far I had been doing pretty well. Earlier, I used to be quite nervous before races.

Most of the runners probably are. My rivals were some kind of enemies to me. I was so afraid of losing that I have to admit being beaten was a nightmare for me. At the end of 1971 my attitude changed completely. From then on, I was able to concentrate on the races in an ideal way. It did not matter any more if I won or if I was second. The main thing was that I had been doing everything as well as I could. I had no obsession of winning in Munich, because winning wasn´t a matter of life and death to me any more. I very seldom read anything written about me before I was 20. The common view those days was that people would be spoiled by success. This may have been the reason for the fact that I was keeping such a low profile. I knew my father was collecting press cuttings which he then presented to me as a beautiful volume in 1975, when I had retired from racing.

Even if I was enjoying my success at the national level, sports generally weren´t in high regard in Finland in the 1960´s. To most people, things like art, science and literature had much bigger value than sports. Many of my friends could not understand why I preferred such a simple life - early to bed, early up for a morning run, not even going to dance at the weekends.

In the early part of my career I had major problems with my fragile legs. There just weren´t good enough running shoes available those days. My first running shoes were a pair of basketball boots. Even after getting my first running shoes at age 19 I still did not get rid of leg problems. I certainly had many things to correct in my training as well. Due to my temperament, I had periods of very hard training followed by several weeks of lazying around before attacking the roads and tracks again. Everyone knows this kind of attitude is not good for an athlete. That is why I was in continuous pain. As to the 1968 Mexico City Olympic Games, I was not really disappointed of finishing among the last in my heat in a very slow time. I was disappointed because I had got an attack of "Montezuma´s Revenge" (diarrhea) in the days before the most important race of my life. After having run 3.41 a few weeks earlier I was expecting something much better.

"I lost all my motivation"

The most important thing a coach can do is to be able to explain how and why various types of training are done. It is a kind of schooling process. A coach is supporting and educating his athlete until his protégé is mature enough to make his own decisions. By that point, a coach has become more of a psychological mentor. The goal of every coach should be to teach an athlete to take care of himself or herself. The most difficult task for a coach is to make an athlete train on a long view and prevent him making any stupid mistakes. If an athlete is lacking motivation towards the end of his career, he needs a coach to help him find new inspiration.

I lost all my motivation for racing after becoming an Olympic Champion in 1972. I had achieved the goal of my dreams and did not see any reason to go on. If I had not succeeded in Munich, I would certainly have tried for the next Olympics. The truth, however, was that I was feeling completely empty. I always had lots of self-confidence from almost the beginning of my career. It was more important for me to search for my limits in sport than in the professional world. Luckily I managed to combine running and studying quite well. Yet I think it was a sign of self-confidence that I wasn´t afraid of making big sacrifices for the sport. I think self-confidence is something that can be cultivated, whereas the will to win is more of a born thing.

My international breakthrough came in 1971 when I beat Kip Keino in Helsinki, breaking the 3.40 barrier and being the first Finn to do so. Beside Keino, I had been admiring runners like Michel Jazy and Ron Clarke, whom I had seen racing at World Games in Helsinki in 1965. It was an unforgettable evening, one of the best ever up to that time.

"Sometimes I was downright lazy"

Even if we always had a long-shot plan for the next 12 months with my coach, I never wanted to look more than one week ahead. It might have been depressing to see all the strenuous training sessions for several months on the

same piece of paper. Nowadays, looking back, I have a different attitude. Is there anything better in the life of a young man than being able to run an hour in the morning and two hours in the evening without any other worries! It is much more fun than working eight hours a day for your living. I have to admit I did not always follow the schedules of my coach very closely. When he told me to run 60K a week, I sometimes ran 100K, or it might have been other way round. My training was quite impulsive by nature. Sometimes I was downright lazy, which made me feel ashamed of myself and then compensate for it later.

It was sometimes difficult to find inspiration for a training session, but as soon as I had been out for 10 or 15 minutes on the road, I was feeling great. I find it impossible to describe the magnificent feeling after a good run. Every one of us has to experience it by himself or herself. In spite of the fact that I always knew why I was doing this or that session I certainly made all the possible mistakes in the early years of my career. In a way we were guinea pigs - the first generation of runners who were doing great amounts of training.

The most decisive thing in training is regularity, and that is why my most important piece of advice for a young runner is to have patience. If a doctor tells you to rest for two weeks due to an injury, you have to do exactly as he says. Don´t make the mistake of trying to "test" your injury after a few days hoping that there would be some kind of miraculous cure.

Before Munich, I went through the list of all the favourites in the 1500m with my coach, considering all the possible tactical variations against Kip Keino and Jim Ryun. We even were wise enough to realise the role of Rod Dixon as a possible Dark Horse - which he was. We knew all the German and Italian runners. For the final, we had three tactical plans, none of which was needed. The first two laps were much slower than we had been expecting. I never thought about my rivals immediately before a race, instead concentrating for my own task. I tried to forget where I was. I was living by myself in a world of my own.

Did I ever want to give up? Well, 800 and 1500 metres as such short races that you really don´t have time to drop out. But yes, sometimes when I was not in such a good shape, I gave up and jogged in. I did not give a hoot whether I finished 8th or 10th. As to cheating in sports, the ideal thing of course is that everyone on the starting line would have the same chance. In practice, it is a difficult thing. I guess we shall never get rid of the things we have seen gaining a hold in sport.

The best thing in running, for me, is the clear, fresh and sunny runs in autumn and in winter, when you are feeling good and enjoying the beautiful countryside from all your heart. What I would like to tell young runners is that it is essential to be honest with yourself. You have to be realistic in what you are doing and what you are aiming at. I like to quote Herb Elliott: "If you are aiming at something else than Olympic victory, you will probably achieve something else."

VIRÉN Lasse

born 22 July 1949 Myrskylä, Finland.
The only distance runner in history to have won Olympic gold in the 5000 and 10000m twice. Viren did this feat in Munich in 1972 and in Montreal in 1976. In the Munich 10 000, he broke Ron Clarke´s seven year-old world record in spite of falling before halfway. World records also at 2 miles and 5000m in 1972. In Montreal, Viren finished 5th in his first marathon just one day after winning the 5000. European Championship bronze 5000m 1974, 5th place Olympic 10000m 1980. Viren´s weapon was his long, gradual acceleration during the last few laps, which ate away the finishing kick of rivals much faster than him.
800m 1:54,3, 1500m 3:41,8, 3000m 7:43,2, 2 miles 8:14,0, 3 miles 12:51,6, 5000m 13:16,3, 10 000m 27:38,4, one hour 19 500m, 20 000m 1:01:25,0, marathon 2:13:11.

I started serious training at around 16 or 17 years of age. Having some success gave me more inspiration to continue. In my youth there were no indoor facilities whatsoever, so the only alternative for running was cross country skiing, which I did in wintertime for several years. However, I never intended to concentrate on this branch of sport. I never had an idol of the type "I want to be like him". At first I really had no definite goals either. The first couple of years, I was running without any training programmes. In 1965, I was listening to the radio broadcast of the annual match between Sweden and Finland, which that year was held in Stockholm. Finnish distance runners did not do very well during those days. For some reason I started to think: "It would be nice to run for Finland some day and do better than those guys." That was about the only dream of the future I can remember from my youth.

My early running was occasionally done with a couple of friends, but after finding it more and more difficult to find company I started training by myself. In my family there were four brothers, all of whom were into some kind of sports. Our parents kept on eye on what we were doing and gave us all the encouragement we needed. "Distance running is not painful or difficult at all. On the contrary, it is a most enjoyable activity." Training hard never was a problem for me. I never thought I was making any sacrifices for the fact that I

was running. I remember Jouko Kuha (3000m steeplechase world record holder in 1968) wondering in the Finnish running monthly JUOKSIJA why everybody thought running was such a strenuous thing. I can only agree with what he said. In fact, running is not painful or difficult at all. In the contrary, it is a most enjoyable acitivity, suitable for everyone.

As a youngster, I of course sometimes had to drag myself out for a run, but with training gradually becoming a habit I found it a normal and invigorating thing to do. I never thought about retiring from the sport until 1977, when I had some big dificulties with my legs. I think it is completely normal to feel nervous before a race. Every competitive runner knows those last-minute flutters. No matter if it is a village meeting or Olympic Games, there always is some anxiety before a race. My breakthrough race was at the Finnish junior championships in 1967. I won my first national title and found my name mentioned in the sports pages. It was much more than winning district titles.

With more success my appetite grew, of course, but everything happened gradually. There were no dramatic changes in my training. I didn´t have any big disappointments in a long time, either. Everything was proceeding smoothly. The only negative thing I can remember was being left to a 4th place in the junior match against Estonia in 1967. I had earlier beaten the same rivals, so understandably I was angry about my bad performance for some time.

"I always enjoyed running even without winning"

I really cannot say defeats have troubled me very much. I have been beaten by better runners on the day, and that´s it. I never have let defeats depress me. I always have enjoyed running even without winning. I was coached by former international runner Rolf Haikkola for almost the whole of my career. I never had any other coach. In the early years I was getting some advice from my brother Nisse and my clubmate Pertti Sariomaa (10 000m 29.25,2 in 1965). It was Pertti who took me to meet "Rolle" Haikkola for the first time. The most important thing in the relationship between an athlete and a coach is to have complete faith. An athlete has to believe in what the coach says. On the other hand, a coach must make an athlete believe that that these are the correct systems to do.

"Somehow I sensed I had the tools to run much faster"

The moment when I realised I could reach international level probably was in September 1969, when - immediately after the European Championships in Athens, which I attended as a tourist - I ran a Finnish junior 3000 metres record in Berlin. My time was about 8.05, and somehow I sensed I had the tools to run much faster. It was a big thing to travel abroad those days. The time I spent in the USA in the winter of 1970 was an important period for me, helping me mentally in many ways. I was a country boy, living a quiet life, so going to foreign countries was really different to me. I always liked to see the world. From the training point of view, of course it was useful to be able to train in warm climate, as opposed to the cold Finnish winter. I guess my international breakthrough took place in in Rome, in May 1971 when I ran 5000 metres in 13.35, a Finnish record. But by no means did I feel I was a complete runner even then. Therefore I didn´t consider my performances in the European Championships later in the year (5th in 5000m, 17th in 10000m) as big disappointments. I felt I had done well to get into the team. We had so many good runners those days. Maybe the 10K could have gone better, but I stupidly did a wrong type of training session before it - it was not my coach´s fault, because I was listening to someone else - and I didn´t recover in time. I was feeling very tired during the 10 000m race.

"Rest days were not planned, but they never were a problem"

In general, my coach made a full one-year plan for me. Everything aimed at big meets, Olympic Games etc. Again, that plan was divided into months, weeks... When I went to train abroad, I had the programme for one month or so in my bag. It was a year-by-year system; we were not thinking several years ahead. It might have become too heavy to handle. Long plans like that are not needed. I was generally able to follow the plans. No rest days were ever planned, but if they came - like during long flights - they came, and there was no need to worry. We made it clear that if I missed a day or two, I never tried to catch them back, to compensate them. What was gone, was gone.

I usually never tried to skip training, but after the Munich games there was so much of hullabaloo and celebrating that I was not able to train as much as I needed for several months. However, it is wrong to say that the Olympics were the only thing to me. It was not meant to be so. In 1973 I just couldn´t get in enough preparation, in 1974 I was injured etc... Nevertheless, I have to admit that in later years I gradually lost interest for ordinary everyday races, which did not mean much to me. They became just training runs. Thinking back, the couple of easier seasons after Munich may have been a blessing for me when preparing for Montreal. I needed the recovery after the 1972 Olympic Games. Thus I was saved from a lot of needless pressure, and was able to give everything when it really mattered again.

"Training hard was a source of immense satisfaction for me"

As a young athlete full of enthusiasm, I just didn´t give much thought to things like weather. You have a quick peek outside and decide what kind of gear you will be wearing. That´s it. But when you get older, you start to succumb to temptations: it is raining, so who cares if I don´t run today? I enjoyed training hard. It was a source for immense satisfaction, and sometimes you couldn´t wait going out and run. However, some conditions must be filled. It is no good going out for a run in a hurry. I always ran when I felt I liked it. Morning runs at 6 a.m. were another thing - I was so punctual that my neighbour was able to check his watch by my runs - but in the evening I waited until I felt good. Also, I tried to avoid all kinds of fuss after the run so that I was able to concentrate fully on it. Sometimes I was feeling tension before an unusually heavy training session.

The previous day I was thinking "oh boy, tomorrow I will suffer, I hope I will make it". But fortunately my coach usually was there to help me mentally to go through it. When training alone, it is easy to skip the hard ones, but when someone is there watching and encouraging you, you just have to do it. Afterwards you feel absolutely great. Gradually I was learning to know myself and the purpose of particular training sessions. And if I didn´t, I could always ask my coach! I don´t think I ever made many big mistakes in my training. The only thing may have been the depletion and carbo-loading thing that I tried for the 1971 Europeans and - as I already told - which went wrong. I fully approve that method, but it was a wrong time for an experiment. It has been said that I was training too much like a marathon runner before the 1980 Moscow Olympic Games. Perhaps... I got injured at a critical time. If I had been able to do the speedwork along the plans, I think I would have run much better.

There were some other bad injuries, too. In 1974 a thigh problem ruined my plans for the European Championships. In 1977 I was injured on a hunting trip. Then, in 1978 I could not run in the European Championships in Prague because of a very bad knee. The most annoying injuries were the ones that remained a kind of mystery; at first no one seemed to know what it was all about. It is much easier when you know immediately what the trouble is. Speaking to young runners, I would say that you always have to take an injury as a very serious thing. You have to start very slowly again to get over the trouble. It is essential to be patient.

"It is a big mistake to do the warm-up with someone else"

Being defeated is a part of the game, and you have to accept it. But you also have to try and learn something from it. On the other hand, sometimes it is a good thing to fall from the clouds back to reality. After a surprising defeat - and there were quite a many of them - I first had a good drink (laughs), then had a deep talk with my coach about what happened. An honest analysis was needed in situations like that, even if it may be human to try and escape the real reason - that you were really bad, or you did something wrong.

For my money, the race starts when you start warming up. I think it is a big mistake to do the warm-up with someone else. This is an individual sport, and you have to be able to prepare for it by yourself, in your own peace. When on the starting line, I tried to be aggressive. My wife Päivi says I always got introverted a few days before a big race. I was not in the mood to talk. In Montreal I really had nothing to lose - I already had two Olympic golds - and I could take some risks. Before the 5000 final, in the warm-up area I had an uneasy feeling like "everything is not right", but my coach "Rolle" just slapped me on the buttocks, saying "don´t talk rubbish, those guys have no chance whatsoever against you", and that made me feel much better. Suddenly I was feeling relaxed, brimming with confidence. I never really was consciously acting like "a hard guy", even if I always thought I had a mental grip on my rivals after the Munich games. Well, perhaps I tried to look as if I was not taking it too seriously (smiles). Outwardly I may have been looking kind of happy-go-lucky, which of course I wasn´t. After the race I always was friendly with everyone, whatever the outcome of the race. You just have to be ruthless when it matters. I never was ruthless outside the competition; I think friendship is one of the greatest things in sport.

"Self-confidence is developed step by step, by succeeding"

As to self-confidence, I suppose it equals being sure of what you are doing. A big race is a very hard thing mentally, and if you have problems with self-confidence, at the last moment you may lose all of it. It is like being a building contractor. If you are planning to build a 10-floor house, you have to be sure of being able to do it. Self-confidence is developed only by hard work, step by step, by succeeding in what you are doing. I have met 14 year-old boys who tell me they are going to be Olympic champions. That is fine, but they have to realise what it takes and that only very few people are able to make it. I very seldom had thoughts of dropping out of a race. Sometimes you are feeling real bad, but you have to remember that so is everybody else in the race. It was a very unusual thing for me to not finish a race. It may become a habit of which it is very difficult to get rid of. I have seen runners who have spoiled their chances by having the completely wrong mental attitude towards a race. I tried to think as little as possible of the upcoming competition. If you let yourself sail with your thoughts - what it will be like to win in the Olympic final etc. - it all takes away from your energy which will be needed in the actual

race. Generally it was not difficult for me to accept having been beaten in a race, but if I had prepared really well, it was another matter. The older I became, the easier it was for me to accept a defeat. I did not find anything negative in publicity.

When you have success, publicity is a natural thing. You have to be able to manage with it. In the early years I used to read everything written about me, but later only if I was told there was something unusual in the paper. In Finland, I had good feelings with almost everybody in the press. Abroad, some bad things were written, but I did not care, or perhaps did not even hear As to videotapes, I have been asked if it is a burden for me to watch the 10 000m final in the Moscow Olympic Games. I can say that nowadays - when the years have passed - it is no problem for me to watch it. Perhaps it was not always so, but in fact, in spite of finishing fifth, I consider it one of my best races ever.

In my time, money was a minor factor in track and field. Nowadays it may be another thing. Anyway, the money I earned by running was not really worth mentioning compared with what the runners are getting today. For me it was impossible to get rich by running. The best thing in running was having goals, and the gradual process of reaching them. On the other hand, I enjoyed the actual motion of running as well, the sheer enjoyment of it. For me, the biggest enjoyment was the great feeling after having a good, nice run. But you have to be in a fairly decent shape to be able to feel it. If not, then it is more of a burden, or even a bore. For young runners, I would give the advice of keeping a training diary from the very beginning. That is one of the key things. Through your diary you will learn many things later. Also, in my case I have been regretting about not preserving the press cuttings, meet programmes etc. from the early years. I would enjoy going through them now. These may look like minor things at the time, but much later, with years passing and when you have retired from a long career, you appreciate the memories in a very different way.

WAITZ Grete

born 1 Oct 1953 Oslo (née Andersen).
A true pioneer of women´s long distance running, Waitz won the inaugural World Championship marathon in Helsinki in 1983. A year later in Los Angeles, she was 2nd in women´s first Olympic marathon. Uniquely, she won the New York marathon nine times between 1978 and 1988, the first of them in her debut marathon with a then-world-best 2.32.30, which indeed opened a new era in women´s distance running. From 1970 to 1982 Waitz was unbeaten in cross country, including a set of five world titles (1978-1981, 1983). Originally a track runner, Waitz won the 3000m at the 1977 World Cup and ran world records at this distance in 1975 and 1976.
400m 57,6, 800m 2.03,1, 1500m 4.00.55, one mile 4.26.90, 3000m 8.31.75, 5000m 15.08.80, 10K road 31.00, marathon 2.24.54 (1986), high jump 161 (1971).

"You have to grow up with your fame"

I noticed very early I had more talent as a runner than as a jumper. Ever since starting training regularly at age 15 or 16, I have been able to follow my plans to about 95%. It wasn´t until I got older and started having injury problems that I had to change my schedules every now and then. Yes, I have been feeling angry and frustrated whenever I have had to miss training sessions. All I could do was to think about something else. Luckily, I was relieved to notice that by doing some other type of workouts I was still able to stay quite fit.

I never have had motivational problems. I have always enjoyed training and racing. Now, at the time of this interview, I am still running every day in spite of the fact that I retired from competition two years ago. I always felt extremely inspired and motivated to train hard for an important race. I wanted to run well, which meant there was a lot of very strenuous work to do. As soon as I started having success, it encouraged me to go on.

As a young girl I did not know much about training. All I could do was to obey my coach blindly. Later, I became interested in the theoretical side of

running. I gradually learned why I was doing interval training or why it was important to run just easily every now and then. I don´t think I ever erred very much in my training. I must have done most of the things right to be able to succeed so well. Nevertheless, I am ready to admit that I might have done even better by resting a little more in the midst of hard training.

"It takes lots of patience to become a good runner"

My main advice for young runners is that the number one thing for becoming a good runner is patience. You have to have patience to wait for many years, slowly developing yourself. It is no good to run too much too soon. No matter if you are a boy or a girl, it is better for you to take part in many sports to build your general fitness first. You have to do many kinds of sport up to the time when you grow out of your teens. My advice is to not concentrate on running before you are 16 or 17 years old. I have seen boys and girls running hard at age 12 or 13, and that has always been a mistake. I find it extremely important to tell young athletes about the mental and physical process taking place in the body at a young age. That helps them to understand why it is wiser to wait. You have to learn how to lose in order to win. It is part and parcel of the sport to have bad races as well. Too many runners are so afraid of being beaten that they have no courage to go to the starting line. They always have excuses for why they are staying away.

Winning, of course, is good for your self-confidence, but self-confidence most of all means that you believe in what you are doing and are able to see yourself as a successful runner. Your mind dictates what you can do. It is not possible to become a great runner without having an iron will. The only way to become a successful runner is through experience and positive thinking. An athlete really cannot prepare for losing, because thinking like that means a most negative attitude. You always have to see yourself as a winner, as a better athlete than the others. This is what the experts call mental training. You continuallly have to think in a positive way, telling yourself that you will make it. As soon as you lose this trust in yourself, it will affect your performances. Dishonesty in sports, in my view, means using drugs. I want to see the sport free of bad things like this.

I have learned to live with publicity. At first it was very difficult due to the fact that I prefer being by myself. I am just an ordinary person who doesn´t enjoy being in the limelight. Nevertheless, the years in which I have been racing around the United States have taught me to accept publicity as an essential part of the sport. You have to understand the wishes of sponsors and race organizers. You have to grow up with your fame.

"As a youngster you think and read about running"

In the early part of my career I always read everything written about me. Later, I became more choosy. I realized I was the only person to read all these stories in the way I did. As a youngster all you think and read about is running. It is the focus of your life, which makes you think all the others are thinking the same. But of course it isn´t so. With more experience you start seeing the world around you. The little world of your own isn´ t the real world after all. In later years, I didn´t care much what was written about me. I thought it was only today´s paper, which tomorrow would have other purposes -- wrapped around fish or flowers. An athlete has to be able to relax when reading these stories. The main aim for a writer, after all, is to have a good story, be it black or white. It is

part of a journalist´s job. I don´t care any more what they write about me in the papers.

I have never met a person who has been envious about me. I know not everyone likes me, and there are many people who don´t like to see me succeeding. Envy is part of the Scandinavian culture. There is nothing I can do about it. I have my friends and my family. No one can live in a way to please everyone. You shouldn´t let money dictate your doings. If you do, I don´t think you will have the best possible success. Love for sport comes from inside a person. If you don´t like training, there is no hope of doing well. You have to give 100% of yourself to be able to succeed. If you give too much of your time to other things, it is very difficult to live an athlete´s life very long.

A young athlete has to understand that sometimes even a 100% attitude isn´t enough. It is not necessarily the hardest trainer who wins but the one who trains in the most clever way. We all are individuals. What is good for someone, may not be good for someone else. There are so many ways to become a world champion, and each of us has to find his or her own way. The best thing in running is the feeling of freedom. Running also brings you lots of vitality. It is good for body and soul. I love running in the forest and on country paths. Running has nothing but positive sides for me. I hope to be able to run all my life, no matter if I some day will be very slow.

WAKIIHURI Douglas

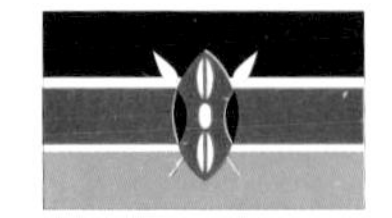

born 26 Mar 1963 Mombasa, Kenya. Member of Kikuyu tribe.
A forerunner of the great Kenyan marathon generation, Wakiihuri won the World Championship gold medal in 1987, Olympic silver in 1988 and Commonwealth Games gold in 1990. He also won London marathon in 1989 and New York marathon in 1990. After a long spell of injuries, he made a fine come back in 1995, winning the World Cup race in the original marathon course in Athens. For the most part of his career Wakiihuri has been living in Japan.
1500m 3.50.22, 3000m 7.56.69, 5000m 13.24.01, 10 000m 27.59.60, marathon 2.09.03.

"I am ready for training only when my body is ready"

We had no buses or bicycles where I lived as a child. I had three kilometers to go to school. On the way, we often had playful races on who would be the first back home in the afternoon. We ran to school at 8 o´clock in the morning, then back home for lunch at 12, then back to school and back home again. In spite of so much running I never knew I would become a top runner. As a boy, I was just one among dozens of good runners in my area.

Before the London marathon, I stayed nine weeks in New Zealand with my coach. We lived together, we made our food together, we ate together. We had been working for our goals for six years. We have excellent communication. We understand each other very well. He knows everything about running. We always have a talk before a very hard training session. If we both think it is a good idea to do, then we take the risk. I always have a certain basic schedule. I am always ready for changes according to the feelings in my body. I am willing to train hard only when my body is ready. On the other hand, if there is a 10K run in my programme, but I am feeling great, then I may do a much harder training session. All that an athlete needs is a basic schedule. Whenever I am unable to follow my plan, I am not worried as long as there is nothing wrong with my fitness. Flexibility certainly is a most important factor in my training.

I have no motivational problems. I always enjoy training. If I don´t, then it is impossible to run well. Hard training sessions make me realise that at last I am ready to race and win. One great victory is enough to make a man happy for the rest of his life. Three months or one year of strenuous training is well rewarded by the fact that it can bring you contentment for the rest of your life. Hard training never bothers me, but injuries certainly do. Whenever you are not honest in writing down your training, you are just deceiving yourself. I never do anything like that. If I have run slowly, that is what I write down in my diary. What is the use of lying?

If you have no idea why you are doing this or that kind of training session, you might as well quit the sport. I always know the purpose of every run. With a big race approaching, it is vitally important to concentrate on things like endurance and speed. Yes, I sometimes may miss a training session due to various reasons. I may have needed a rest, or I may have been travelling or ill. Whenever I miss a session I always think twice about trying to compensate for it. If I have been ill, I have to get healthy again. If I am feeling very tired, then it is no use training as much as I would like to.

Everyone makes mistakes, but fortunately you can learn from. Once it happened that I was supposed to run 5000 meters in 15 minutes, but I did 13.57. Also, when preparing for a race, I made a mistake of running on an uneven surface, where I twisted my foot. A young runner has to be able to cultivate his or her talent. The vital things in training are concentration and self-discipline. I have had some serious setbacks. A couple of times I have been badly injured. It is essential to listen to one´s body for the fact that you usually sense there is something wrong there. When training hard, you have to take care of sleeping well, eating well and generally feeling well. Whenever I am defeated in a race, I just laugh about it. You have to be able to relax and start planning for the next race. I tell myself, "You won´t lose again. You will do great next time." An athlete must have self-confidence, but there are two kinds of competitors. Some, after being beaten, become psychologically ill. Others just think, "Okay, so what?" I have been training as well as I could, and this was the result I have to accept. What you have to do is to ease back into training and make sure of not repeating the same mistakes next time.

"Don´t worry about your rivals. That just makes you nervous."

Before a big race, I never think about my rivals. The starting line is full of fine competitors, but you shouldn´t think about them. It just makes you nervous. All you have to do is ask yourself if you are ready to race. If so, you just go and do your best. I am friends with my rivals. Whoever wins the race may not necessarily be a better or more talented runner than the others. I may have made a mistake, thus losing my chance. The winner had a more positive attitude, which made him the winner on the day.

If some other runner with two legs can win, then why can´t you? You mustn´t admit anyone else is a better runner than you are. You can do what the others can. A young athlete, running with an older and more experienced runner, may think that he cannot be beaten because he is the World Champion. But one day you realise he is not unbeatable after all. Besides winning, you get self-confidence by training and by strengthening your mind. Life in Kenya is so hard we grow to be mentally strong people. We have to fight for our living. We don´t let life defeat ourselves. In the Western countries, you have everything you need -- you have the best possible opportunities for training, and yet you don´t run very well. In Kenya we have none of these things, and yet we run very fast. It is very difficult for an athlete to become a top runner without being mentally tough. No matter if he or she comes from Africa or from Finland, attitude and mental strength always are the main things.

You have to realise that when you are in great shape and mentally strong, you can beat anyone in the race. A coach may think he has to take care of all possible things with his athlete, but it really isn´t so. A coach is the one to make a training plan, but an athlete is the only one to know his or her own body. It is a coach´s duty to know what an athlete is eating, what is worrying an athlete and so on. A coach always must be near his athlete.

Practice is the best way to educate yourself as an athlete - not the books. Everyday training teaches an athlete new things and how to make changes in training plans. Dreams are made true by mental strength. I have always been dreaming of becoming an Olympic or World champion. You should never drop out of a race. Dropping out may become a habit. I have always finished every race I have started. Even if you are unable to win, you should try and do as well as you can. The main thing is to finish. If you don´t, it has been a worthless race. After six months of training, dropping out of a race after couple of minutes of running certainly would make me feel guilty.

As a youngster, I had no one to ask advice from. Young runners are capable of thinking by themselves. All they need is common sense. What they got from mother was their life; from then on they have to learn to rely on themselves. Nowadays it is very difficult to keep away from publicity. It pays an athlete to be co-operative with the media. I sometimes preserve press cuttings and mail them to my mother and father. Money: you need it to be able to train and race, to be able to succeed as a runner. The best thing in running is the freedom.

WALKER John

born 12 Jan 1952 Papakura, New Zealand.
In spite of winning the 1500m gold medal in the 1976 Montreal Olympic Games and breaking the 3.50-barrier in the mile in 1975, John Walker probably is best remembered for his astonishingly long career at world class level. He ran his first sub 4-minute mile in 1973 and his last one - after more than 150 others - in 1990 aged 38. Walker also broke the 2000m world record in 1976 and finished 4th in the World Cross Country Championships in 1975. At 800m, Walker won his first New Zealand title in 1972 and last one (eighth) in 1990!
400m 48,9, 800m 1.44.94, 1000m 2.16.57, 1500m 3.32,4, one mile 3.49.08, 2000m 4.51.52, 3000m 7.37.49, 2 miles 8.20.57, 5000m 13.20.89, 10K road 28.34, half marathon 1.04.45.

"Talent, training, ambition, tactical skill"

My first race was at a school cross country meeting around a football pitch. It was about 800 metres, and I finished last. Next day I went to see my teacher and told him I was capable of running much better. He told me to start more aggressively in my next race. I did so and won. I was 7 years old. I have been working with my coach Arch Jelley since the day I started training with a schedule in 1971.

We always plan with long view - for 4 or 5 months ahead when we are preparing for Olympic Games or World Championships. Having done this, we cut the schedule down into smaller chunks. We try to follow the plan as closely as possible except for the competitive season, when you have to be more flexible. Injuries, of course, also make you to change your plans every now and then. I never want to miss speed sessions. Whenever I have to miss them, I try to do them later as soon as I can.

Flexibility means that when you want to run a time trial, and it is wet and windy, it is impossible to do it on that day. Along with time trials, the long run of 1.5 to 2 hours once a week also is very important for me. I have lots of motivational problems. I am not the type of an athlete that enjoys his training. I have to force myself to do it. On the other hand, I enjoy racing. I have always been a great competitor. Yet, even if training is boring for me, I also know you cannot do shortcuts. I am trying to do my training sessions early in the day so that I can relax for the rest of the day. I always feel more motivated when training with others. In my opinion, runners always should train in groups. It is better to train with someone else than by yourself. It is very hard to run fast when you are trying to do it alone.

"14 years in Europe"

I start with a base period of three months or 100 days. I don´t do many speed sessions at that time, but I am gathering lots of mileage. I used to keep a training diary when younger, with very exact details written down, but I don´t bother any more. I don´t believe it is useful for any athlete to train seven days a week. It just isn´t possible. You need rest days for mental and physical reasons.

I don´t think I have ever made big mistakes in my training. Everything has been progressing smoothly. I have been racing for 14 years in Europe, which is why I have always been well focused. I owe my coach a lot for the fact that I have always been in top shape during my European tour as well as at Olympic and Commonwealth Games. Young athletes should avoid training too hard too soon. I know many cases in which young people have become too competitive, burning themselves off with excessive racing. Their motivation has gone at about the time it should really start to blossom. The main thing for young athletes is to enjoy the sport.

Yes, there have been some setbacks for me due to injuries. I had a very bad leg problem in the months before the 1976 Olympic Games. That may have been a blessing in disguise because I managed to win. I also had two leg operations in 1978. I got over the problem even if my leg never fully recovered

again. In younger days, it would have been impossible for me even to contemplate a surprising defeat. I was so good those days that I simply didn´t lose that often. Even now, at age 37, forgetting how old I am, I feel bad about losing. I still feel I am able to compete well with anyone in the world. Nevertheless, I now am able to accept a defeat whenever I think I have had a good race. An honest analysis with my coach is no problem for me.

For young athletes, defeats are part of the game. It is not worth crying when you have lost to a better runner. From the point of view of an Olympic Champion - and after a very long career at the top - I can truthfully say that running isn´t the most important thing in the world after all. As a young boy I was seeing running as a matter of life and death. With more maturity it has been worthwhile to realise that there are other meaningful things in life: marriage, family, friends...

Top competitors of the world travel together, and are friends with each other. As soon as the gun goes off, everyone is there to win. After the race we have a chat: what went O.K., what went wrong. There is the dinner and maybe a beer, after which we just forget about the race because there will be another one very soon.

"Even Aouita was beatable"

No athlete can succeed without self-confidence. It is 30% of the race. If other competitors have more self-confidence than you have, it helps them to run better. In 1976 I knew I was the best miler in the world. I was nervous before the Olympics, but I still believed in myself and knew other competitors would look me up. Thanks to self-confidence I won by two metres. Self-confidence comes with success and wins. The more you win, the more self-confident you become as compared with the others. As soon as Said Aouita is beaten, other runners realise he is beatable. It used to be the same with Steve Ovett and myself. Today most runners think Kenyans are unbeatable due to the fact that they have recently won almost everything. You need wins to become self-confident.

It is a coach´s job to build up an athlete´s self-confidence as well. My coach has lots of mental strength and self-confidence. He believes in my capacity to run well. An athlete must have born talent, but he also must have a sound training program to become a more secure competitor. When you ask about the factors of a big win, my answer is: talent, training, ambition and tactical skill. Victories certainly are a great motivator. If you don´t win, you don´t develop your will to win. Belief in yourself is the key thing. If you believe you are going to win, then you have a big chance to win. If you don´t, then you don´t win either. There is no room for cheating in sports. Cheating means greed. Greed means money.

I don´t look for publicity. I am doing everything I can to avoid it. Publicity may be a positive thing as well, but all of it certainly isn´t. Yes, people have been very envious of me. I am not. If someone wins 5 million in a lottery, I am ready to congratulate. If someone does well in sports and gets lots of money, I am happy for him. Most of all, envy is a problem in little countries. Irish people have this same problem as do New Zealanders. It is very difficult not to notice what there has been in the New Zealand newspapers about me. It makes me very angry to read something written about myself that is not based on facts. I sometimes have the urge of hitting the writer, but generally it is better to forget about it as soon as possible.

Money is the cause of all evil in sports, but it is also a reward for the job well done. Money can make you happier, but it can also bring about greed and dishonesty. In the early years of my career there was no other incentive for runners than improving one´s performances. Money was not a big issue those days. Today, runners are more interested in money than improving their times. In my opinion, it should be the other way round.

I want to remind young runners that success doesn´t come overnight. To have a chance to reach the top you have to have the talent, to do enough training and to have a realistic view on yourself. Dishonesty eventually always leads to a failure, and all crooks sooner or later have to pay for their doings. The sporting world certainly has room for hard-working individuals with high morals even today.

Friendship is the best thing in running. I was thrilled to meet the famous athletes I had been reading about as a youngster. I realised they were ordinary human beings like anyone of us. Sports should be fun. As soon as it stops to be fun, it starts to be joyless toil.

A coach should know what he is doing. Many coaches can have success for a while, but it is the injuries and setbacks that finally measure the caliber of a coach. It is easy to be a coach when everything is going fine, but as soon as difficulties arise, bright brain and knowledge are the decisive things.

WAMI Gete

born 11 Dec 1974 Debre Dirhan, Ethiopia.
Small in stature (153 cm), but one of the most fluently striding runners in the world, Wami made her breakthrough when winning the World Cross Country title in 1996. At 10 000m, she is an Olympic Champion 1996, World Champion 1999 and began the new Millennium with two Olympic medals in Sydney - bronze at 5000 and silver at 10 000m. In cross country, she won her second World title in 1999 and third in 2001.
1500m 4.01.47, 3000m 8.29.48, 5000m 14.30.88, 10 000m 30.22.48.

"Cross country... joy and satisfaction"

Like so many East African runners, I started competing at school races. At 15 years of age, I gradually began training in a more serious way. It is impossible for me to say exactly when it happened. In fact I really did not notice. In Ethiopia, it is a most natural thing to run. Year by year, I was progressing from district level to national level, and before long I found myself competing internationally in the 1995 World Championships in Gothenburg and the 1996 Olympic Games in Atlanta.

At this very moment - at the time of this interview - I am very happy here in Belfast because I have managed to repeat my World cross country championships title. All went fine in the race, and with some two kilometers to go I knew I would win. I was leading the race, feeling very good. From the very start of my career I have wanted to become as good a runner as I possibly can. That is why I never have had any problems with getting myself out to train. As tired as I may sometimes feel, it is not my habit to skip training sessions. You have to be ruthlessly ambitious to succeed in this sport.

It really is not possible to become a great runner in a short space of time. You need lots of patience. You have to get over setbacks, training day after day even if you initially don´t do as well as you would like. Most runners, sooner or later, have to face problems with injuries. My longest pause because of an injury has been seven months. I was very afraid of not being able to run ever again. However, I had the patience to come back and finally made it back to the top. You should never hurry getting rid of an injury. Doctors usually know what they are doing, but it is equally important to progress in small steps after being injured. When you cannot run, you have to take it easy and accept it.

Winning and losing are part of the running game. Whenever I am defeated, I usually know the reason for it. If I don´t, I will do what I can to find out and then make the necessary corrections in my training and preparation for the next race. Defeats can make you a better runner. Self-confidence is an essential part of every runner´s training. Whenever I am perfectly healthy and training well, it does great things for my self-confidence. But you don´t have self-confidence without having respect for yourself and for the work you are doing.

Of course, winning a big race also does wonders for one´s self-confidence. I know it from my own experience. It is a great feeling to become a World champion like I have managed to do today. My message to young athletes? Perhaps you saw me win the race today. It is possible for you as well, but only through many years of methodical training. I enjoy sports, and most of all running. Regular exercise makes me feel very good. I will continue running even after my competitive days are over, because I want to feel good and healthy even later. Through sports, I have been able to meet people all over the world. I am very happy for the fact that I have seen so much in my life. Without running, I would have nothing of this, really. I enjoy racing in many kinds of conditions and surfaces. For various reasons, cross country running is the sport that gives me most joy and satisfaction.

WOLDE Million

born 17 Mar 1979 Ethiopia.

Wolde´s kick proved be the best in the tactical 5000m Olympic final in Sydney, thus bringing him one of the most surprising victories of the games. During the Olympic year, almost 20 men in the world ran this distance faster than Wolde! Earlier, his main merits had been the World Junior Cross Country and 5000m titles in 1998 and 8th place in the Seville World Championships 5000m final.

1500m 3.39.15, one mile 3.58.21, 3000m 7.32.36, 2 miles 8.17.68, 5000m 12.59.39, 3000m SC 8.29.21.

"Happy mind and good spirits"

If I remember right, I started some serious running at age 16, after finishing school. I was encouraged by the news of Ethiopian distance runners´ great achievements in foreign countries. I thought I might become a good runner myself. Now that I am racing myself in far away countries, it is a wonderful feeling. I have accomplished much more than I ever thought would be possible. I appreciate being friends with foreign runners and receiving moral support from them.

I always train with happy mind and good spirits. I enjoy all types of training except running at high altitudes. Also, I very seldom go to the track in Addis Abeba due to its worn and uneven surface.To become a good runner, one has to understand the requirements of hard and regular training. It is no use training every now and then. You have to go out and run every day.

I haven´t had many setbacks except for a race in which I was knocked down to the track. What I learned from the incident was that you have to keep your eyes open in a racing situation and not let others push you around. I have never had long layoffs in training, but there have been times when I haven´t been able to race due to being ill.

Winning and losing are part of the sport. It is a fact that every athlete has to understand. Even if you happen to win, there is no reason to celebrate wildly. When you lose, you need not dwell too much on it. You should forget bad races as soon as you can. Victory and defeat are like sisters or brothers, going hand by hand. Self-confidence means that whenever I am toeing a starting line, I am able to give everything that I have. There is no need to worry before a race, no need to carry all the pressures of the world. Self-confidence is mainly cultivated by training wisely, but also by winning races. You should always have a positive attitude in your sport.

The best thing in running is being happy after a great race, when you have achieved a big victory or a world record. Yes, I do have some idols. I always have admired the great distance runners of the world. By grace of God, some day I hope to be an idol for young athletes myself.

YIFTER Miruts

born 15 May 1944 in Ethiopia (possibly 28 Jun 1944 or 8 Jun 1947).
One of the great phenomenoms and mysteries of distance running history, Miruts Yifter - just 162 cm tall and father of six children - won the 10 000 and 5000 metres Olympic gold medals with his amazing finishing sprint at Moscow Games in 1980. Eight years earlier, he had been a 10 000 metres bronze medallist behind Lasse Viren and Emiel Puttemans in Munich. In fantastic form in 1976, he missed the Montreal Olympics due to the African boycott, then collected double victories at World Cup 5000 and 10 000 metres in Düsseldorf in 1977 and in Montreal in 1979 before kicking away from the rest of the world on Moscow Olympic track. Unbeaten at 10 000 metres from September 1972 to September 1981.
400m 48,0 (unverified time trial), 800m 1.48,8 (time trial), 1500m 3.48,3, 5000m 13.13.82, 10 000m 27.40.96, half marathon 1.02.56.

"I was chasing apes with other boys"

I got interested in serious running at about age 20, when I moved from my home village Sirasso to Asmara (capital of Eritrea). From then on, I was able to run with school children. Otherwise, there was no special reason - I just liked to run. My idol from the very beginning was captain Abebe Bikila, whose great achievements I wished to emulate some day. I never seriously thought about trying any other sport. As soon as I started regular training - almost always with the rest of my team -, I was aiming as high as possible.

As a child, in my home area at Tigrai, I was chasing apes with other boys, running so fast that my parents were afraid I would have a heart attack. Later, with success coming in running races, they had a positive and encouraging view on my sport. Many of my first running mates soon left the sport. Nevertheless, they still followed my progress with interest. Yes, I have to admit I also seriously thought about quitting running at times because of the poorness of my family. I seldom had proper food to eat. The turning point in my career came when famous coach Nigusse Roba - later one of the leading officials of Ethiopian Athletics Federation - visited Asmara in 1968, just before Mexico City Olympic Games. He gave notice to my talent, encouraging me to move to Addis Abeba, where I joined the Ethiopian Air Force. Without this big change in my life I would certainly not have become an international runner. At first I had problems with getting a coach and proper equipment, which made training difficult. I even didn´t have a pair of running shoes, but, thanks to Ethiopian toughness, I finally made my way over the difficulties.

Even if I at first lost many races to runners better than me, I never had any inferiority complex. I knew I would get better with hard training. I always wanted to win. Later, progressing steadily, I was elated when I was hoisted by my friends and tossed into air after winning a race. According to Ethiopian calendar (which is about seven years and nine months behind the European calendar), that was on February 1, 1961. I was proud of what I had done, feeling absolutely brilliant. Later on, I seldom experienced that kind of boyish delight. I was afraid of losing, but I usually was able to stay in control before and during a race. I always went into a race with fighting spirits, knowing I would be able to win.

Two years later I started to win more and more races. It is impossible for me to remember all those competitions. Perhaps the people in the Ethiopian Federation can help in that respect. My first international victories were well reviewed in foreign newspapers. I had a collection of press clippings until everything went astray when I moved into a new house.

"I was like a flower...."

My early success? I was like a flower which is hiding through the winter and then blossoms in the spring. I was very happy about the fact that I was improving steadily year after year. My friends were curious to see how I was doing... and so were my enemies as well. Nevertheless, I did not have any

negative experiences except for the fact that some people were asking why I was running, and for who. I did not like that kind of questions. Striving at running faster and faster, I did not want to make any changes in my training, because I was afraid any unwise alterations would slow me down.

Having achieved some early success it is usual for any athlete to be sought after by press people. There are some dangers in such situation. I know myself. For instance, there were untrue rumours being spread behind my back. Even if I am married, there were lies that I was having an affair with another woman. Gradually I learned to live with such false stories. They never depressed my inspiration for training. Like always, I still have high morals and am behaving well. Among my early defeats, there was an international race in which I counted the laps wrong. Sometimes I lost because of just being too tired. I always learned something from defeats and vowed to do better next time.

"He told me I would not make it in my job"

At first, I was coached by colonel Godana Kotu of the Ethiopian Air Force. He was a superior of mine. At the time of joining the Air Force, a Bulgarian doctor told me there was something wrong with my lungs, and I would not make it in my job. My coach did not believe the doctor and took me into the

Air Force on his own responsibility. To me, he was like a father, and an idol as well. After him, I was coached by Nigusse Roba. In my view, the relationship between an athlete and a coach should be like that of a boy and a father. However, they may come across the problem of not getting along with each other, quarrelling about various things.

Whenever I was beaten in a race, I did my best to find out the reasons for running badly. My self-confidence was improving during the years. I gradually started to believe I would be a fantastic runner some day. I finally reached international top class level in a couple of races in the United States and in the African Championships. It always was a pleasure for me to run abroad and meet great runners from other countries. My favourite runner those days was Lasse Viren from Finland. As to my training, it was depending on the races I was aiming at. Nevertheless, I always tried to prepare very carefully. Most times, I started the final preparations about a month before the race. I did my best to follow the planned schedule, but if I had to adjust it for various reasons, I was not worried at all.

I never had any motivational problems. I enjoyed my training. Generally I was well aware why I was doing a particular training session. I don´t remember having made any bad errors, but there are two races I have no good memories of. Due to a techical fault, I was not able to start in the Olympic 5000m final in Munich in 1972. Another time, in a race in the United States there was a pistol shot with a lap to go. Not knowing the local custom, I thought the race was over and was defeated because of my mistake. In my earlier races abroad, I had been accustomed to a bell being rung with a lap to go.

"I don´t like to go overboard praising my rivals"

Any young distance runner wishing to succeed has to remember the following things. (1) You must follow the training programme made by your coach. (2) You have to avoid all things harmful to an athlete. (3) You must eat enough, and proper nourishment, after every training session. Every athlete has to be ready for confronting unpleasant surprises every now and then. While in Toronto, Canada, I got an attack of very bad diarrhoea the day before the race. I immediately went to hospital for first aid and then managed to win the race. In the United States I was involved in a car crash, which prevented my taking part in the competition. There have also been some pushing and hitting incidents among the countless races during my career. It is the nature of the sport that sometimes you win and sometimes you lose. I always have held my rivals in high respect and, if I have been defeated, made sure I have congratulated him in a sportsmanlike manner. I don´t like losing, but whenever it happens, you have to take care of shaking hands with your better. However, I don´t like to go overboard with praising my rivals, because that could be understood as accepting my own weakness.

I think every defeat has a positive side in the way that it teaches an athlete to correct his or her mistakes for the next time. When you learn things, it paves the way for your success. Of course, I always enter a race with a thought of winning, but whatever may happen is not something to worry about. Self-confidence is a must for an athlete. In my view, it comes from high morals and goal-oriented training.

When you are competing at world class level, the only aim you may have is to succeed in big competitions, thus bringing fame and reputation for your country. The will to win is a born thing, but it is also something that can be cultivated during a sports career. I never had an urge of quitting in a race. Whenever I stepped to the starting line, I tried as much as I could up to the very end. I see publicity as a positive thing. Thanks to publicity, I have achieved everything that I have today. I always try to keep a track on anything written about me, and collect as many press clippings as possible. I also enjoy watching my races on video, even the bad ones. I don´t mind seeing the mistakes I may have done.

Of course there are envious people everywhere, but I have never let them bother me. Money: I never competed because of financial gain. I was racing for the love of running and for the love of my country. My advice to young runners is to stay in touch with new training methods which may help you run faster.

ZÁTOPEK Emil

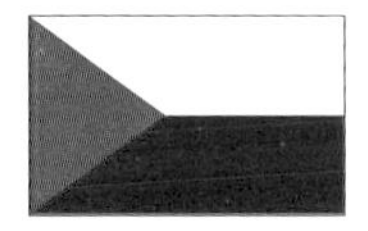

born 19 Sep 1922 Koprivnice, Czechoslovakia, d. 21 Nov 2000 Prague. Emil Zátopek will always be remembered for his unique triple of winning the 5000m, 10 000m and marathon gold medals at the Helsinki Olympic Games in 1952. At the 1948 Olympics in London he had won the 10 000m gold and 5000m silver. At 10 000m, in which distance he remained unbeaten in 38 consecutive races in 1948-54, he also won European Championship gold medals in 1950 and 1954. At 5000m, he also won the European gold in 1950 and bronze in 1954. A pioneer of extremely strenuous interval training, Zátopek set 18 world records: one at 5000m, two at 6 miles, five at 10 000m, one at 10 miles, two in the one hour race, two at 20 000m, two at 15 miles, two at 25 000m and one at 30 000m. He was the first man to run 10 000m faster than 29 minutes and 20 000m faster than one hour. There are experts who don´t hesitate in naming Emil Zátopek the Number One distance runner - or even the Number One athlete - of all time. In a storybook fashion his wife Dana (née Ingrova), also born on 19 Sep 1922, won the Helsinki Olympic javelin gold medal on 24 Jul 1952 - the very same day on which her husband won the 5000m gold medal.
1500m 3.52,8, 3000m 8.07,8, 5000m 13.57,0, 10 000m 28.54,2, 20 000m 59.51,8, one hour 20 052m, 25 000m 1.16.36,4, 30 000m 1.35.23,8, marathon 2.23.03,2.

"I had a strong urge to reach my limits whatever they would be"

I started training at age 19 in 1942 when I became a member of Zlin (now Gottwaldov) Athletics Club. Working at Zlin shoe factory and also going to an industrial evening school at the same time, I was ordered to take part in a cross country race organized by town officials. I finished 2nd. That was the start of my athletics career. In other words, I did not choose running as my sport. I took part in a race because I had to. To be honest, I did not really have any other sports to choose from. The only sports idol I ever had was Paavo Nurmi. At first, my targets were not very high. My parents did not like my running, but that was no problem since I was living by myself in a student rooming

house in Zlin. Older athletes did not approve of me because they thought athletics should be just a secondary thing in life and not goal-oriented hard toil which I was doing. I had no idea whatsoever what it would take to reach the highest success in sport. I just was curious to see whether I was able to break the records for my club, my country and finally for the world. I never felt like retiring from sport and never considered training as difficult. I just had a very strong urge to try and reach my limits whatever they would be.

In my first races I was feeling very nervous, being afraid of the other competitors. Later, even if I always detested losing, I never had any problems with controlling my nerves. I went on running even after my competitive career to stay fit and healthy.

After three years of training I was a Czechoslovakian record holder. After another three years, in 1947, I went to race in Helsinki and managed to beat the best distance runner in the world, Viljo Heino. The year after that I was an Olympic 10000m Champion in London. Even if my victories were reported in all the newspapers, I never preserved the clippings. I was always very happy about my achievements, without any negative thoughts whatsoever. It was very encouraging to be able to set ever higher and higher goals.

I don´t remember having had any difficulties or disappointments as to training or racing. Some of my early defeats may have felt depressing for a while, but on the other hand they made me try even harder. I never had a coach. The only advice I ever got from others was in regard to warm-up and such things in the first year of my career. Nowadays I see it as a must for an athlete and other supporting people to have a coach. My motivation always stayed excellent due to the fact that I was setting myself higher targets. The only times when I felt sub-par were when I was ill, injured or otherwise incapable of running.

I felt inspired by my first trips abroad, because I was able to meet much better runners than in my home country. I was very impressed by the leading athletes of the world. I still enjoy travelling thanks to the fact that I am able to meet and talk with old friends. I used to do a hard training session every day. With a race approaching, I used to cut back to maybe half the usual amount or even less. I always tried to plan my training as exactly as possible. I was enjoying the hard work so much because I knew that would be the only road to success. The best advice for young runners is to train with patience and to race with determination. Never give up. Whenever I was too busy to go out and run, I tried to do a set of various gymnastic exercises at home. I was happy with what I was doing even if it was not as scientific as they are doing nowadays.

My biggest setback was in April 1952 when I took part in a race when I was ill with a throat infection. Afterwards, it took me two months to recover from the illness and tiredness. Being defeated in a race always is a bitter thing. On the other hand, a defeat requires analysing so that you can do better next time. This way, a defeat is a blessing in disguise, something that in fact helps you to develop as an athlete. No matter if it was before or after a race, I always had a friendly and cordial attitude towards my rivals.

You need self-confidence to be good in any field in life. It is vitally important to find out your optimal level of training. That is why you most need a coach to help you. Also, you need talent, patience, extreme fitness and good luck to become a great winner. I sometimes had weak moments during a race, but I never gave up. The will to win is a born thing that can be cultivated by means of training and racing. An athlete can prepare himself or herself for winning by correct mental attitude which takes use of all the resources of body and mind in the decisive moment.

Publicity is very important for sport and, in my view, certainly a positive thing. I still read sports magazines with interest, but skip over anything written about myself. I really don´t have any interest in watching old films on my past races. I never ran for money, because there just wasn´t any money in the sport those days. The best thing in running is that it is an excellent sport for all young people.

Epilogue

It has taken me 14 years to gather all the material for this book. I can certainly say it was an immense task both mentally and physically, interspersed by two heart attacks and a by-pass operation. I don´t think anyone would have been surprised if I had thrown the towel into the ring. Strangely, however, it turned out that it became impossible for me to stop.

I am not hiding the fact that there were many difficulties. Most of all, many times I felt betrayed and neglected by the very people to whom I had put so much hope and belief. At times, I was so disappointed that any kind of comment - however unpleasant or disparaging - was better than nothing.

Nevertheless, there was a strong array of friends who were giving all the imaginable help with this project. One of them - and one of the very first - was great runner and great human being Emil Zatopek, who, to my wonderful joy, immediately saw the idea behind this book. Without support from so many of the leading athletes of the world, we would never have fulfilled our dream. What I learned during these years was how deeply all these runners were feeling for their sport.

So many people gave me this advice: "Never give up, no matter how difficult time you may have. Without setbacks, you don´t achieve anything important in life. Difficulties, and conquering them, brings you the strength to climb to the highest tops." It took me quite a long time to understand that these wise words are not helpful only in sport.

My sincerest and warmest thanks to every runner mentioned in this book!

I am thanking you because of your understanding, your realizing the goal we were striving to achieve. It was you that made all this toil worthwhile. Over and over again you told me "we want this project to succeed, because it means so much to us". Together, we have built a bridge of friendship and understanding between great runners and international youth.

Acknowledgements

I want to convey my sincere thanks for all the various people I was lucky to meet in the distance running fraternity: coaches, managers, masseurs, physiotherapists, pacemakers, rabbits, reporters and other experts, who had the eye to notice my needs and were willing to help. I would very much like to mention every one of you separately, telling about the many joyful moments in the midst of my magic new sphere of friends in the sport. Thanks for your help and kindness.

This book was originally published in Finnish, in honour of Paavo Nurmi´s Centenary celebration in 1997. At that time, I had an opportunity to thank the many supporters of my task. Without the Finnish version there wouldn´t have been this English edition either, which is why I want to thank Markku Weyner, Kim McDonald, Miguel A. Mostaza and Jos Hermens for their notable assistance. I was encouraged by many people in Finland. Jukka Uunila made use of his many tools as an experienced sports leader with remarkable results. Tapani Ilkka, Antti Pihlakoski, Seppo Nuuttila, Heikki Kantola, Rolf Haikkola, Martti Koski, Mike Kosgei, Jukka Härkönen and Jaakko Tuominen also helped in many ways. Support received at a crucial moment is more valuable than a bar of gold. In this friendly spirit I also wish to thank Jane Howarth, Jimmy Beauttah, Enrico Dionisi, Joe Douglas, Ray Flynn, Abdelkader Kada, Ken Nakamura, Duncan Gaskell and Andreas Janssen as well.

It is with immense gratitude that I have so often been thinking of the editorial team at Juoksija running magazine. I have been repeatedly impressed by their professional skill and down-to-earth willingness to take care of any surprising problems. They are always thinking about the best for the sport. My warmest thanks to them for their ever trustworthy helping hand. The pictures for this book were provided by a top man in his field, internationally respected sports photographer Mark Shearman. Matti Hannus has diligently waded through all the interviews, translating and editing whenever necessary and giving insightful comments. The finishing touches into English language have been expertly made by Chris Turner. This duo of sportswriting professionals were always ready to make my life easier at difficult parts of the journey. Thanks for your endurance. Shimelles Tenaw took the task of translating the Ethiopian interviews into the language of another distance running people,

Finnish. Thank you, Shimelles, for making it all so easy. Thanks also to Yilma Berta and Getaneh Tessema. Times were getting harder towards the end. I was given magnificent help by two far away friends. Running professor Tim Noakes immersed himself with the project, in my eyes becoming the godfather of this unusual book. Thank you for the great moments, Tim - there are no words to describe your immense mental support.Patrick Magyar, first of all, deserves all the possible praise for giving me a helping hand at the time when I hardly knew the greatest distance runners of the world. Thanks to him, I soon felt I was at home. Then, with the finish line nearing, his voluntary help came like a gift from the heavens. Many thanks, Patrick! Thanks to these two friends, my waning self confidence was restored at a critical moment, making the last steps of this long run feel such a relief. The idea of this book has its roots deep in pure will to show the young athletes the innermost of our wonderful sport by the great athletes themselves. It is important to try to see it clearly nowadays, when the financial side of the sports too often seems to rise the only important value especially in the minds of our youngsters. However we don´t want to hide the fact that finally the financial support only with will to assist could help us to complete our idealistic dream. I am very happy to have this opportunity, also on behalf of Lasse Viren Foundation to give our warmest thanks to:

IAF - International Athletic Foundation
I.O.C. OLYMPIC SOLIDARITY,
ASICS Corporation,
KALEVA, Mutual Insurance Company.

Finally, the resolution of all this common venture – a piece of advice for young athletes by Sebastian Coe:
"My message for the youth is that every athlete has a responsibility, whether they like it or not, to nurture the well-being of the sport. If they see something that is wrong or morally unacceptable, it is their obligation to make it public and make their views heard... Not to sit back and say, well O.K., I am not going to do that, it doesn´t affect me, therefore I want to forget about it. This is a sport that we all have a part in, whether we are fun runners or competitive Olympians. As athletes, it is our responsibility to ensure that the sport is as or more popular when we leave the sport than when we got involved with it."
Sports should be fun, which is not to say it shouldn´t have its serious side as well.

Helsinki, 15 April 2001
Seppo Luhtala

Photo & Illustration Credits

Photos:	Mark Shearman Reijo Pietilä Juoksija-Lihti (running magazine) Photo archives Suomen Urheilumuseo Sports Museum of Finland Photo archives Polar Electro GmbH
Drawing:	Paavo Nurmi by Matti Pulkkinen
Cover Design:	Birgit Engelen
Paper Collage:	Seppo Luhtala

Be a Serious Runner...

Carl-Jürgen Diem
Tips for Success – Running for Beginners

This book gives the running beginner helpful hints for all questions related to running. It offers information about the form and volume of training as well as clothing and nutrition, and is also a good source of advice for the more experienced runner. It gives practical advice for all those who want to start running as well as for coaches and instructors.

104 pages
Two-colour print
Illustrations
Paperback, 11,5 x 18 cm
ISBN 1-84126-072-X
£ 6.95 UK/
$ 9.95 US/$ 12.95 CDN

Bozo Petracic/
Franz-Joachim Röttgermann/
Kurt-Christian Traenckner
Successful Running

„Successful Running" advises on how to improve performance while avoiding physical injury and trauma.
This book provides runners with general knowledge to aid self-assessment of individual biological and biomechanical problems and overcome common overuse injuries. Hence, athletes are in a position to responsibly and consistently counteract problems in good time, facilitating successful and speedy further pursuit of their sport.

144 pages
11 tables, 179 diagrams
Paperback, 14.8 x 21 cm
ISBN 1-84126-006-1
£ 9.95 UK/
$ 14.95 US/$ 20.95 CDN

MEYER & MEYER Verlag | Von-Coels-Straße 390 | D-52080 Aachen, Germany | Fax +49(0)241-958 10-10

with Running Books...

Arthur Lydiard/Garth Gilmour
Running with Lydiard

Since the outstanding success of his New Zealand athletes Snell, Halberg and Magee at the 1960 Rome Olympics, Arthur Lydiard's name has been synonymous with the best training methods used by the world's top middle and long-distance runners. His schedules precipitated an athletic revolution, stressing as they did physiological conditioning as the means of achieving this. Running with Lydiard contains expanded information on exercise physiology, diet, injury prevention and cure, discussion of Lydiard's methods and revised training schedules.

208 pages
20 photos
Paperback, 14.8 x 21 cm
ISBN 1-84126-026-6
£ 12.95 UK/
$ 17.95 US/$ 25.95 CDN

Arthur Lydiard
Running to the Top

In this book Arthur Lydiard presents an overview of the techniques of middle and long distance running. His description of a systematic, detailed training programme for beginners and top-runners is based on a clear defined conception of fitness. Beneath detailed schedules for training, the book includes tips concerning equipment, kit, nutrition, prevention of injury, therapy and the relationship between the coach and the athlete.

184 pages
Tables
Paperback, 14.8 x 21 cm
ISBN 3-89124-440-1
£ 12.95 UK/
$ 17.95 US/$ 25.95 CDN

MEYER & MEYER Verlag | Von Coels Straße 390 | D-52080 Aachen, Germany | Fax +49 (0)2 41 - 9 58 10-10